Fatal Moments

Fatal Moments

The Tragedy of
the Accidental Killer

by

Gwendolyn Gilliam
and
Barbara Russell Chesser

Lexington Books

D.C. Heath and Company • Lexington, Massachusetts • Toronto

Library of Congress Cataloging-in-Publication Data

Gilliam, Gwen.
Fatal moments: the tragedy of the accidental killer / by Gwendolyn Gilliam
and Barbara Russell Chesser.
p.   cm.
Includes index.
ISBN 0-669-21859-6 (alk. paper)
1. Accidents— United States—Psychological aspects.   2. Homicide—
United States—Psychological aspects.   3. Death by wrongful act—
United States—Psychological aspects.   I. Chesser, Barbara.
II. Title
HV676.A2G55   1991
155.9'37—dc20   90-23279
CIP

Published simultaneously in Canada
Printed in the United States of America
International Standard Book Number: 0–669–21856–6
Library of Congress Catalog Card Number: 90–23279

The paper used in this publication meets the minimum requirements of
American National Standard for Information Sciences—Permanence
of Paper for Printed Library Materials, ANSI Z39.48-1984. ⊚™

Year and number of this printing:

92 93 94 95 8 7 6 5 4 3 2

To those who understand what it means
to take a human life
by accident

Contents

Foreword

Americans have difficulty dealing with death under any circumstances. Coping with accidentally causing a death compounds the difficulty. In fact, accidental killers rate the trauma of their causing a death as excruciating as the death of a family member or close friend, divorce, or a nervous breakdown. When individuals accidentally kill a member of their own family, that experience is consistently considered the most painful crisis ever suffered by the accidental killer.

Approximately 100,000 people in the United States die annually from accidents, making accidents the third leading cause of death. Accidents kill more young children than the five leading deadly diseases combined. Because so many of those killed in accidents are young, more years of life are lost to accidental death than by any other cause. With every accidental death, there is generally at least one person who feels responsible for causing that death—or at least for not preventing it. The emotions suffered by the accidental killer penetrate relationships with family members, friends, and work associates.

Considering the large number of people affected by accidental death and the intensity of the emotions suffered by accidental killers, this book is a milestone. *Fatal Moments: The Tragedy of Accidental Killing* is a platform for a representative number of accidental killers; they share with the reader their feelings and their fears so characteristic of accidental killers. However, *Fatal Moments* goes beyond the tragedy of accidental killing; it shows the triumphs that are possible when accidental killers know how to help themselves and when family members, friends, and professionals know what to do to help accidental killers.

A painstaking researcher and perceptive counselor, Barbara Russell Chesser, Ph.D. conducted this important study while a professor at the University of Nebraska. Gwen Gilliam, at the time associated with Boys Town of Omaha and a freelance writer, became intrigued with the study of accidental killers and assumed a major responsibility for transforming the research findings into a book. Both co-authors brought incredible qualifications to the task of writing *Fatal Moments*. Barbara's experience with accidental killing began early in her life in a painfully personal way. Her own father was killed when she was eight months old by an accidental killer—an innocent twelve-year-old driving farm machinery with no reflectors or lights on a curving road on a moonless night. Gwen's skill in probing the psychology of the human mind and life experiences is reflected in this compelling and poignant book.

I am pleased to recommend to you *Fatal Moments: The Tragedy of Accidental Killing*. I share the wish of the co-authors that it will provide insight, encouragement, and guidance. Sadness is found within its pages, but the essential story is one of hope and one of the human spirit's capacity to heal, to recover, and to transform tragedy into higher levels of maturity and triumphant living.

—Earl Grollman, D.D.

Preface

Twice this book has accidentally died. The first time was in September 1981 in San Francisco's Tenderloin, a year after a short piece I'd written about a pilot study on accidental killers by Barbara Chesser was published in *Psychology Today*. Two hundred people from across the nation had responded with their stories of killing someone without meaning to, and I was organizing them into a book. The manuscript was stolen with my car, which also held the rest of my possessions, as I was moving into town.

The second time was at 6:13 A.M. on January 13, 1983, in a converted office building in Manhattan's Wall Street district. This time it was consumed by a fire that started because of my own casual attitude; I had fallen asleep with some candles burning. Once again all my possessions were lost, including my manuscript, which had been rewritten after many hours of telephone interviews and library research. I was very lucky that my upstairs neighbor was out of town for the weekend, as the fire department was never able to chop open his door. That easily, I could have killed someone.

Accidental killing cuts to the core of what it is to be human. To live in its wake stripped of the slightest measure of control is to go beyond fear. I believe it carries some of the most heavily laden lessons to be learned in life. This book has taught me many things. I hope it can teach you, too.

Thanks to everyone who helped with the book, especially Jeffrey Ladd, who, having known me two weeks at the time of the fire, took all his money out of the bank to buy me a new electric typewriter so I could continue this work.

—Gwendolyn Gilliam

Introduction

Man Drowns During Baptism

Natick, Mass.—A man being baptized in the waist-deep water of Lake Cochituate was swept off balance by a wave and drowned, police said Saturday.

John E. Blue, 37, of Boston was being baptized by the Rev. Harold G. Branch Friday when the two toppled over and Blue fell into deeper water, police said.

Branch said he had performed previous baptisms in the same spot but the waves made them bob slightly, causing them to lose their balance.

—Associated Press

In the midst of a sacred moment, the honoree met his death in a seemingly pointless way. Although details were not available, one wonders what could have prevented the Reverend Branch and the gathered faithful from rescuing Blue. Surely the family was heart-broken, but how did the tragedy alter the lives of those who may have felt responsible? What did they say to themselves?

The focus of any fatal accident is on the person who dies. Outside that focus, however, may be someone who feels in some way responsible for having taken a life, though unintentionally. Although some people may wonder what this person is going through and try to help him or her, generally the *accidental killer* stays hidden from view.

An accidental death is a sudden hush, evidence that Nature's laws make no exception where life is at stake and don't step aside for happy endings. The human condition is exposed in its essence, and people become aware of their own mortality and vulnerability to forces beyond their control. Can it be that life and death hang upon blind luck? The universe, it would seem, does not care if individuals live or die.

Fiction writers often have woven accidental death into their plots.

Kurt Vonnegut, Jr.'s *Dead Eye Dick* features a twelve-year-old who accidentally shoots and kills a pregnant housewife three blocks away. The Alfred Hitchcock film *Vertigo* begins and ends with accidental falling deaths. In John Steinbeck's *Of Mice and Men*, Lenny, a well-meaning mentally retarded man, kills a young girl by hugging her too hard. Even innocent Dorothy in *The Wizard of Oz* accidentally kills twice and is celebrated for doing so.

Greek mythology includes gods in the ranks of accidental killers. Hercules kills several people unintentionally, the first being Linus, his music teacher, who attempts to punish the future Olympian for a mistake. The young Hercules, unaware of his superhuman strength, hits Linus so hard with his lute that the teacher falls dead. The sun god Apollo accidentally kills his lover Hyacinth with a stray discus, naming after the beautiful boy a lily that springs up from his blood.

Accidental death also appears in Eastern works of spirituality. It is one of the manifestations of discord (including wars, disease, mental illness, and injustice) invited to be integrated into the higher mind stream in the Tibetan Buddhist tantric ritual "A Beautiful Ornament."

Volumes have been written on the difficulty the culture of the United States has with facing death. Ernest Becker's *The Denial of Death* states that it is not death per se so much as the fear of dying without having left any trace that is the mainspring of human behavior.[1] But accidental death—in fact, sudden death of any kind—always carries a stigma, according to historian Phillipe Aries. This was true even in medieval Europe, when ordinary death was more accepted than it is today because a shorter life expectancy made it much more a part of everyday living. Aries theorizes that it was not until the Industrial Revolution, with its notion that nature could be controlled by man rather than man by nature, that the fear of death became unspeakable.[2] But in the Middle Ages, sudden death was looked down upon because people expected to know and often did know the exact moment of their deaths days or hours in advance so they could gather the family for a dignified farewell. In theological terms, some said that sudden death robbed the soul of its final ordeal, a harrowing experience in which it could choose once and for all between good and evil.

The stigma assigned to sudden death is illustrated by the medieval order against church funerals for those who died suddenly, ostensibly because their blood might stain the sanctuary floor. It also is illustrated by the tradition of British jurisprudence known as the *deodand,* whereby an inanimate object (such as a tree whose branch falls off) that killed someone could be tried, convicted, and destroyed.

Some deadly accidents are solo events. Falls, fires, drownings, single-car wrecks, and other mishaps claim thousands of lives a year.[3] But most fatal accidents involve at least one other person—one left behind, one forever changed by the experience of having unintentionally snatched the life from a fellow human being. How these accidental killers cope with the rest of their lives is the subject of this book.

Although some fatal accidents result from drunken binges or psychotic episodes, most occur because of one or more slipups, and others involve no error at all. Yet almost all accidental killers suffer tremendous guilt. Depending on the circumstances, questions of innocence and culpability can easily turn into a vale of gradations too fine for anyone to ascertain a person's culpability with any certainty. And yet accidental killers must take responsibility for their actions and for the outcome of those actions. In his essay on moral luck, philosopher Thomas Nagel asserts that the problem has no solution:

> It seems irrational to take or dispense credit or blame for matters over which a person has no control. . . . [T]he truck driver who accidentally runs over a child . . . if he is entirely without fault, will feel terrible about his role in the event, but will not have to reproach himself. . . . However, if the driver was guilty of even a minor degree of negligence—failing to have his brakes checked recently, for example—then if that negligence contributes to the death of the child, he will not merely feel terrible. He will blame himself for the death. And what makes this an example of moral luck is that he would have to blame himself only slightly for the negligence itself if no situation arose which required him to brake suddenly and violently to avoid hitting a child. Yet the *negligence* is the same in both cases, and the driver has no control over whether a child will run into his path. . . . If one negligently leaves the bath running with the baby in it, one will realize, as one bounds up the stairs toward the bathroom, that if the baby has drowned one has done something awful, whereas if it has

not one has merely been careless. . . . The area of genuine agency, and therefore of legitimate moral judgment, seems to shrink under this scrutiny to an extensionless point. Everything seems to result from the combined influence of factors, antecedent and posterior to action, that are not within the agent's control . . . yet . . . one is responsible for what one actually does—even if what one actually does depends in important ways on what is not within one's control. . . . Those acts remain ours and we remain ourselves, despite the persuasiveness of the reasons that seem to argue us out of existence . . . everything we do belongs to a world that we have not created.[4]

Sociological research reflects this dilemma, having become so entangled in a web of factors that efforts toward specific quantification of fatal accidents for epidemiological purposes were abandoned. The search for accident causes was called hopeless because accidents are so often the indirect outcome of a group of circumstances rather than the direct result of a single determinant. There is a problem, for example, with separating the agent of the injury—say, the corner of a desk that cracks someone's skull—from the agent of the accident—the turned-up corner of a rug that the person tripped over. Often, however, these two agents are combined, as when a knife slips in the hand.[5]

In our study of two hundred people[6] across the nation who killed someone accidentally, we found that they share nothing in common except their fatal moment. A few are near sociopaths who feel no guilt despite their reckless choices. Others of more tender conscience blame themselves for what was basically an inability to predict and change the future. Because circumstances and matters of conscience vary so greatly, we accept as accidental killers those who define themselves as such, with certain qualifications.

First, accidental killers are not police officers or soldiers who intentionally kill someone while practicing their professions. Even unintentional killings in this context stretch the point, as people in uniform are poised to kill. Nor are accidental killers drunk drivers or child abusers. Those high-risk situations are entered into by some degree of choice. We have devoted a special appendix to "not quite accidental" killings at the end of chapter 4.

Fatal accidents happen virtually all the time. More than ninety-four thousand people in the United States die annually from them, making them the third leading cause of death after cardiovascular disease and cancer.[7] Because so many of those killed in accidents are young, more years of life are lost accidentally than by any other means.[8] U.S. citizens are nearly five times more likely to die in an accident than by murder, with drownings alone accounting for nearly half the murder rate.[9] Accidents kill more young children than the five leading deadly diseases combined.[10] One researcher has compared the likelihood of modern United States children dying accidentally to the risk of deadly disease before modern sanitation.[11]

High accidental death rates have come with industrialization. While curtailing deaths due to infectious diseases, technology has imperiled survival by surrounding soft human flesh with hard metal and concrete, sharp objects, and things that shatter. In a landscape of motorized giants, the difference between life and death is a matter of fine coordination—for instance, hitting the gas pedal instead of the brakes.[12]

"Accidents will occur in the best regulated families," Charles Dickens notes in *David Copperfield*.[13] And fatalities occur all too easily through carelessness, inexperience, and distraction. They stem from mechanical malfunctions, seizures, and confusion. Small details can override an entire scene if they cast ambiguity on what's happening.[14] Fatal accidents can come from road hypnosis, stress, prescription drugs, nonprescription drugs, fatigue, panic, faulty judgment, and countless other variables. They often occur around holidays, when people's guards are down and their senses drugged.

Most people ignore grave danger, such as beating an oncoming train at a railroad crossing, if they have had success in similar situations.[15] If they do think about it, most rationalize that nothing bad will happen to them. Rarely are lessons internalized from close calls.

The ease with which accidents occur and the weight of their consequences is the central irony of the term *accidental killer*. The impact can be devastating: "It was a horror movie right in front of my eyes. I have to sleep with that for the rest of my life," one accidental killer notes.

Many factors help determine how strong the accidental killer's reaction will be. The effect is most potent on the young, whose egos are still in formation. The age of the victim also matters, as the death of a child is much harder to accept than that of an older person. The level of intimacy between the victim and the perpetrator also makes a difference, as does the accidental killer's level of optimism. Everything about the accident's circumstances enters in, including the overall level of stress in the accidental killer's life at the time. Some accidental killers are constitutionally less able to deflect stress than others.[16]

The accidental killer's proximity to the victim's body greatly affects the accident's emotional impact. If the body is close and exposed, it is much more disturbing than if it is even partially hidden. Sometimes, but not always, accidental killers' own injuries attenuate their guilt. Similarly, lawsuits, though agitating, are seen by some despondent accidental killers as the punishment they deserve. If the accidental killer has accepted the potential savagery of chance, the darker side of the human condition, and the transitory and delicate nature of life before the accident occurs, then the crisis is less traumatic than it is for someone who has not come to those understandings.

The way people close to the accidental killer react is crucial. Many times loved ones are able to comfort and guide the accidental killer through the more dangerous emotional passages. But they also can make things worse by laying blame or failing to recognize the depth of the pain.

Some accidental killers immediately become obsessed with the wish that the victim were still alive. Others become fixated on replaying the accident in their mind. Some accidental killers quickly distance themselves from the accident, while others think and speak of nothing else. Many resolve their accident-related issues by drawing peace from a greater being.

Our study reveals that despite personal variations, most accidental killers experience a similar pattern of responses. This book is organized around explaining each aspect of the recovery process by describing it through the eyes of those who experienced it and by citing research and expert testimony.

Generally, *psychological shock* comes first. During this brief period of mental numbness, the mind hides from the full realization of the victim's death. Next comes *preoccupation* with the accident. In this struggle to make sense of the event, many accidental killers replay it over and over in their mind, trying to wish it away. They also are preoccupied with living with the physical effects of the accident. *Anger* often engulfs the accidental killer. This anger is aimed at every aspect of the accident, including God and the victim. *Guilt* is nearly universal, causing accidental killers to torture themselves for unfounded reasons as well as for error and oversight. *Depression,* also common, may occur in various forms, from a temporary, mild lethargy to attempted suicide.

Most accidental killers in a sense become victims, as they usually experience some form of *social tension,* which may range from getting the cold shoulder to death threats. This tension may result from associates not knowing how to be supportive or from the victim's family wanting to take revenge. *Family stress* also occurs, especially when one member of the family has accidentally killed another.

At some point, virtually all accidental killers begin the process of *healing,* although the *aftermath* of the event continues throughout their lives. Those who are close to an accidental killer can provide help and support. Chapter 10 offers step-by-step suggestions for professionals, friends, and family of the accidental killer, members of the victim's family, and accidental killers themselves.

The stigma of accidental killing encourages isolation. Nearly all accidental killers feel, at least for a while, that they are the only ones ever to have taken a life in that way. In truth, they have much company. Often they are convinced that they have no one in whom to confide. Many of the accidental killers surveyed for this book welcomed the opportunity to unleash the torrent of words and feelings pent up inside.

Speaking out can be freeing, but many people still prefer to run away and hide emotionally. This book attempts to pry open the silence and insert a sliver of hope into the space necessary to mend such a serious loss that can happen, as one accidental killer puts it, "as easily as stubbing your toe."

Fatal Moments

Psychological Shock

I saw headlights, and then it goes black. I don't know where we were going that night, and I lost all memory of the week afterward. In the hospital I was put in the intensive care ward. I had a crushed kneecap, punctured liver, broken hands, a ruptured spleen, chipped teeth, and facial lacerations. Also, I bit off the tip of my tongue.

At that time in intensive care, I wasn't aware of the accident, where I was, or that Dory had been killed. The nurses told my mother I frightened them because at night I would sleepwalk and pull down my traction, trying to crawl over the bed rail.

In the immediate wake of her accident, this accidental killer showed signs of severe psychological shock. When the facts of objective reality are too cruel to acknowledge, the minds of many accidental killers protect them by blanking out. Without this buffer, it would be impossible for them to withstand the strain. According to trauma researcher Peter Levine, "Psychologically speaking, being involved in an accident that harms or kills another person can be potentially even more traumatizing and cause more shock than an injury to the self."[1]

To reel backward into a vale of numbness is the mind's natural reaction to sudden, unthinkable disaster. Only someone psychologically abnormal could remain completely untouched by crisis. This form of self-protection is integral to the human makeup. There is no "hysterical type" of person.[2]

Sometimes psychological shock seems like a mystifying essence that takes control of accidental killers, putting them on "automatic pilot." In this state, they may show unrecognizable qualities because the subconscious is in command.[3]

Some, like the accidental killer who didn't know she was in intensive care, react by fainting and losing memory of the accident. Others react bodily: "I wandered like a zombie around the scene of the accident. I first experienced total disorientation and disbelief. My mind couldn't accept what had occurred. I really felt like I was slipping away." Some go numb emotionally. A woman who accidentally ran over and killed her five-year-old daughter says, "I seem to be in a kind of limbo, not knowing what to feel, to do. I've just retreated into a shell and don't want to come out."

The Denial Function

We attempt to conceal what we can neither face nor escape.[4] The psychologically shocked mind tries to sweep the accident under a thick rug of oblivion. Denial is how Elisabeth Kübler-Ross's terminally ill patients reportedly begin their process of reconciliation to the inevitable tragedy ahead. There is, at first, a need to deny the permanent loss of anything important, be it a loved one, one's own eyesight, or life itself.[5]

Dr. Mardi Jon Horowitz, director of Langley Porter Neuropsychiatric Institute's Stress Clinic in San Francisco, describes the origin of the sadness that people feel in relation to loss: "Any painful stress event has an element of loss that conflicts with the universal wish for permanence, safety and satisfaction. The loss may be another person, an external resource, or an aspect of the self."[6] Accidental killers can lose all three things in a single moment. Each symptom of psychological shock—from sleepwalking to disbelief—can be viewed as a different shade of unconscious denial, affording a safe harbor where the conscious mind can function, tucked away from a truth that would immobilize it.

A Shocking Moment

Fatal accidents are filled with shock-producing elements such as blood, the wet crunch of a body against metal, screams, and the stare of empty eyes. One accidental killer describes what she saw:

> I was driving to the store early in the morning, and a little boy ran out into the street. He was chasing his ball. He bounced off my fender, and the way he landed was on the windshield,

on his belly, and his body was spinning like a record on the windshield. He was so little, so scared. Every time his face came around, we looked into each other's eyes. Both of us were terrified, and we were both helpless to stop what was happening. He was pronounced dead at the scene.

A career railroad engineer describes what it is like to hit a person with the cab of his train, a misfortune he has experienced more than once:

One time I was pulling the brake and blowing the horn at the same time. I didn't realize it, but I was screaming at the top of my lungs the whole time.

You can feel the impact, even through a 2,000-horsepower diesel locomotive. You can feel every bit of it. It makes a noise, and although it's not deafening, it's a noise that runs right through you, and it's a sound you never want to hear again. You know immediately that a life is gone.

Besides the gore, the instantaneousness of a violent accident has a lot to do with putting the accidental killer into psychological shock. Many believe that if they had had even seconds to prepare, they would have been able to avoid the accident. One study of a group of sailors who had survived a collision at sea found that it was the suddenness of the trauma that caused their widespread postaccident psychological problems.[7]

Heightening the damaging effect is the fact that even in the split second of the accident, accidental killers are aware of their role in it. If any part of the sequence of events that produced the accident was a mistake, the trauma will be greater than for a freak occurrence, as preventable disasters are more stressful than unavoidable ones, regardless of who is to blame.[8] Should the error be made by the accidental killer, a load of guilt will exacerbate an already highly charged condition.

Manifestations of Psychological Shock

Designed to buy time so that the mind or body can make the necessary adjustments to prevent an individual from being overwhelmed, psychological shock can take many forms, including amnesia, emotional numbness, and fainting, depending on which parts of the mind or body shut down. Almost always these forms of shock entail the release of the suppressed secret's energy through the subconscious, mainly expressed through nightmares and other sleep disturbances. Most psychological shock reactions seek to dull reality, but adrenaline-powered feats of extraordinary strength also may act as pressure valves to release emotional energy.

The Narcotic Effect

One of the classic ways psychological shock shows itself is the narcotic effect commonly found among survivors of natural catastrophes.[9] People tend to be so overcome by the disaster that they have trouble remembering it.[10] Many have a hard time comprehending how the world and their positions in it have changed.[11] It takes most people at least an hour to respond in any meaningful way to a massive emergency, and some need as much as a day or two to come out of their stupor.[12] Until that time, they remain passive and apathetic. "We moved around like dumb cattle," says one accidental killer describing herself and her companions immediately following their accident. "We just moved when people told us to. Sat down and ate because people told us, when people told us. I think this is the Lord's way of cushioning these blows for us. You're in the catatonic state; you don't really know. Though you're totally conscious, you aren't that responsible. You couldn't make decisions."

Some accidental killers permit the devastating event to enter their consciousness, but their mind neutralizes its feeling response. One accidental killer says, "I couldn't believe it. You read about it, talk about it, possibly even think about it, but you never imagine it could happen to you. It was like I was someone else watching myself." Some accidental killers cannot shed a tear, sometimes a source of guilt and a disturbing thought for sleepless nights.

Amnesia and Fainting

Amnesia is among the most common results of psychological shock. Under its influence, some accidental killers forget only the fatality, while others lose memory of unrelated events as well. The completely blank slate, or total amnesia, is relatively rare. In some cases, memories return; in others, they do not. The only way that some accidental killers discover their loss is to encounter an inexplicable event or detail, usually through a conversation, that brings to light a portion of the time that was wiped out of their memory. Often it happens in a face-to-face meeting with someone known throughout the amnesic period. The vaguely familiar-looking stranger acts like an old pal and has the facts to back it up.

Fainting is a total conscious shutdown. Animals in the wild that are about to be killed often faint when they have no means of escape. This response is thought to anesthetize their demise.[13] The accidental killer quoted at the beginning of this chapter fainted at the wheel. That blackout still acts as a protective device years after the crash. She explains:

> After the accident I was really out of it, but because I was talking and crying, everyone thought I knew what was happening. And my mother and sister came to spend time with me, and apparently we talked about the accident and Dory's death, and, like I said, they thought I was dealing with it. Also, a hospital social worker, who was known as a kind of resident angel of mercy, spent some time with me. So when I came home from the hospital, everybody thought I had had enough of talking about it, and they didn't want to remind me. But I couldn't remember any of that time right after the accident and, of course, not the accident itself. And I felt guilty because I thought there was this kind of conspiracy of silence about it. And as time went on, it got harder to bring it up.
>
> It may have been harder on me because of what Dory meant to me. She was pretty, Indian-looking. She worked at a hat factory, sewing hatbands on hats and she was happy doing that. She could go into a club where everybody was just hanging around kind of depressed, and she could turn it around. She would put music on the jukebox and start dancing and having a good time, and she wouldn't stop until everyone in the place was joining in the party. It was impossible not to have fun around her. She insisted on it.
>
> About a month after I got out of the hospital, an old friend showed up, Dave, with a bouquet of flowers. He was wonder-

ful. He would take me out visiting friends, which was no easy project in a body cast. He was my only social ticket. He was just what I wanted. We got married two months later in my mother's living room, as soon as I got out of the body cast. I wore my mother's wedding dress and underneath it I was in a cast up to the hip.

Dave was one of those people who liked to take care of people. He did the shopping and cooking, besides working. It was pretty much a full-time job for me just to get better, with all my physical and occupational therapy and psychotherapy appointments.

Through therapy I realized that I had forgotten things other than just around the accident. I would also wake up screaming in the night. Dave would be holding me, and I would be sitting bolt upright in bed and screaming. Sometimes I would have bitten my tongue in the same place as in the accident, and the stitches were tender.

This accidental killer's response to the event is based on strength rather than weakness. Amnesia, nightmares, sleepwalking, and other such symptoms result not from the falling away of an unacceptable idea from a weak mind but from its forceful rejection by an ego strong enough to banish it. Strength of character shows in the life choices of the accidental killer: "Just before the accident I came back from out of state to nurse my dying stepfather out of loyalty to my mother, certainly not for my stepfather. . . . He was alcoholic and beat her and he molested me. . . . I left home when I was seventeen because of him."

This woman never regained her memory of the accident. For her it remains a disaster that exists somewhere outside herself, and Dory's death is just another aspect of it. She writes:

As I recovered, I grew less attractive to Dave. There are people who like to take care of other people. We stayed friends, but our marriage ended. I got a job with a company that has enabled me to buy a small house. I've gotten psychologically adjusted to walking with a cane. But my memory block has stayed. I have no desire to see what my mind has locked away.

It's a Pandora's box. Whatever is there, I figure it's there for a good reason.

Another accidental killer found that she could not remember certain things from the time before and after her accident, as if her mind was compensating for the death scene it could not erase:

It was evening. Dark enough so that lights were necessary—not so dark that I could not see shapes of figures. It was on an old road just outside the city limits. There were houses but no sidewalks and no streetlights to help absorb some of the glare from the headlights of oncoming cars. I remember vaguely glimpsing four shadowy figures to the right of my car—four bicyclists—and oncoming traffic to the left. Then, right in front of me in the middle of the road, I saw this child who had fallen off a bike.

The front bumper hit him in the forehead and killed him. At the moment of impact, I could feel myself split. Part of me was there seeing everything, and another part of me didn't want to be there and just flew away. I felt him under the car—and just carefully pulled over to the side of the road and stopped. I actually dragged him 150 feet.

He was five years old. The bike was too large for him. There were no reflectors. He didn't know how to ride a two-wheeler. A witness at the scene said there was no way I could have avoided it.

The little boy looked like he was asleep. The coroner, who happened to be a friend of mine, told me that probably meant he hadn't suffered.

But in the early months after the accident, I was pretty much nonfunctioning. I could not even drive a car for several weeks. Children frightened me. I would come to a dead stop when I saw one. Every time I closed my eyes, I saw the accident.

I went into diabetic shock the night of the accident—and my diabetes had been under control for years. I was admitted to the hospital, and when they let me out two days later, I was still in a daze. Having to support three kids, I couldn't take off from work for very long.

Then I started seeing people in town whom I knew I should know but didn't recognize. One in particular was this man whom I'd been really close with before the accident. I would probably have gotten involved with him, but he was married and I was having none of that. But we got along well. . . . When I met him on the street, I didn't know him.

My kids argued with me about things that had happened and finally convinced me I'd forgotten things, mainly from the two years immediately before the accident and a month or so after.

I was doing my spring cleaning a couple of years later, and I came upon a stack of letters from someone I couldn't remember. She had read one of my books and liked it, and we'd struck up a correspondence. I had to write and ask her who she was.

Like the first amnesic accidental killer, this woman is not disturbed by her mind's hiding information. She says, "At worst it's a little frustrating, but I don't feel the need to be put under hypnosis to uncover what's in there. I don't think I've lost anything essential. Besides, it's fascinating to me to watch how my mind works."

Physical Reactions

In some accidental killers, psychological shock shows itself physically in a response that seems to channel accident-generated energy within the person's body. Some vomit, and others momentarily lose control of their sphincter muscles, urinating or defecating in their clothing. One accidental killer involuntarily performed an exceptional act at the scene of her accident. Perhaps her shock blocked any preconceived notion that she could not do it. She recalls:

I was going for a haircut. Work was on my mind; it had been a bad day at work. I thought if I wasn't angry, it wouldn't have happened. I stopped for the light. I started up again. I never saw him. He'd come across two and a half lanes to the left of me. He cracked the windshield, then flipped over the car. I sat still. A truck driver came and asked me if I was all right.

It took a while to learn how to roll down the window. He pulled the truck sideways to stop traffic.

I thought four things—"Look what you did now"; that I was scared; . . . that "accidents happen"; and . . . "why don't you take off?"

I bent the steering wheel into an oval shape with the sides squeezed together. I picture myself holding on very tight. My claims adjuster couldn't believe it.

Emotional Numbness

Many accidental killers experience an odd emotional numbness toward the accident that they find unsettling. This form of hyper-repression has been termed by some authorities "the most normal and prevalent of defenses."[14] For instance, observers at the sinking of the ocean liner *Andrea Doria* noticed a strange nonchalance about the survivors.[15]

Gerald Glaser, a career insurance claims adjuster, recalls the seeming callousness he has encountered among many drivers in fatal accidents whom he interviewed at home shortly after their crashes. No doubt his role as a professional information gatherer to assess the validity of a claim influenced their behavior.

Lots of times they'd be really fidgety and nervous. They'd do things like thumbing through a magazine or rearranging their knick-knacks—anything to keep from looking at me. But when you'd ask them something, they'd be really defensive and cut you off with something like "He had it coming. I didn't do anything wrong. It was his time to go."[16]

Often mistaken by others as an attitude rather than an involuntary response, emotional numbness can raise doubts about whether the accidental killer cares. Perhaps it is a final defense strategy that comes into play when the trauma cannot be blotted out. Here's how one accidental killer describes his emotions at the scene of his accident:

I was driving to work on the expressway at 11:20 P.M. It was quite dark. I felt something hit the right front of my car. I thought that maybe it was a dog. I pulled over to the shoulder at the earliest opportunity and walked back. There were cars stopped, and I could see their lights. It took me five minutes to walk back, and I had no feeling of deep apprehension. However, I did feel as if it were someone throwing stuff onto the expressway, I might be their next target.

When I reached the lead car, I saw something under the right front wheel and then, gradually, realized it was a person. A jolt of panic shot through my mind, and I guess that was the closest I came to running away from anything in my life.

A woman running across an unlighted expressway ran into the side of my car and was run over by another car. At this stage, when I saw her lying there, the feeling of concern was strictly for myself. As I calmed down, I felt curiously detached from what was happening. I felt guilty about this detachment.

Sometimes this initial state of numbness can lead to behavior that may seem inappropriate:

Adelle and I had been best friends since high school. . . . Both of us married policemen in our town. Our houses were a few doors apart. We learned to duck and cover together when things went wrong, and we could always laugh at ourselves. . . .

Then Adelle's husband was killed. It was a car wreck with him on his motorcycle on duty. The whole town came out to see him buried. The procession tied up the main street for ten minutes.

Soon after that, Adelle moved back to her parents' hometown. And then another accident happened. This time her cousins were both killed in an accident, and their six-month-old baby didn't have a home. So she took the baby.

A year after that, Adelle couldn't take her hometown anymore, so she called me and asked me to fly out and help her drive back. I left the kids with my husband.

We were just outside a little town where we were going to stop and have lunch with my cousin who was a doctor there. We had just switched drivers, and I had the wheel. The left rear tire blew out, and the car went down an embankment. It flipped three times on the way.

When I woke up, I didn't know I was hurt. I had a broken collarbone, and my thigh was bruised. The car was upside down on the desert, and we had had it full of things. Every-thing—clothes and hats and boxes—was on the roof. Adelle was scraped up pretty bad, but her two children who were in the backseat were okay.

I looked around for the baby but couldn't find him. I got out of the car, and there he was, half of him crushed under the car. He was just lying there in the sun. He looked like a little sleep-ing doll. I screamed and tried to lift the car off of him but couldn't. This upset me because I'd always heard that in times of need, you got a rush of adrenaline so you could do things like that. People had stopped immediately when they saw us go off the road, and someone set up a little tent to keep the desert sun off us while we waited for an ambulance. One of the men dug the baby out and carried him up the hill to the ambulance. He'd already been dead a while.

The first thing that Adelle said to me when she woke up was, "It wasn't your fault. I don't blame you at all. You just hap-pened to be driving at the time."

When my cousin the doctor walked into our hospital room, we were giggly. The nurses were shocked at us. We were joking about the bell we rang to call a nurse. It was like an old school bell, and we thought it was like an old cowbell.

Some accidental killers never develop feelings about their accidents. Such a prolonged condition may not strictly be considered psycho-logical shock, but it certainly begins that way and may stay on as shock's residual effect. When a person needs, for some reason, to retain a wall inside, the information is never allowed to penetrate the consciousness.

For instance, a teenage lifeguard who watched a swimmer drown at her feet is puzzled years later by her absence of feeling regarding the death. She complains that she has yet to feel any emotion about the accident, except for embarrassment about the massive newspa-per coverage that implied she was not properly trained for the job. At the scene, she recalls, she worried that the police would get sus-picious because she was not crying. Her guilt was for her apparent lack of guilt.

What happens in a case like this, says Martin Naidoff, a psycho-therapist in New York City, is that the subconscious grieves all the time about what happened. This unconscious grief brings depression, but the accidental killer may not realize this. The former lifeguard says:

> That day of the accident I was kind of nervous because there were only two lifeguards at the time for that many people and there was just so much to look at, so much visual and other stimulation. This guy was hanging around. If I walked away, he would just follow me. And I'm the kind who can't say, "I don't want to go out with you." I'm nice to them, no matter who it is. I can't be rude to them.
>
> So this swimmer was in the shallow end and went under the buoys where there is a drop-off into the deep end, where I was. He got into trouble when it dropped so quick, right in front of the lifeguard manager, who was posted right in front of the buoy. He was only about ten to fifteen feet away from me.
>
> The people standing against the rail, guys, were saying the guy was faking it. I figured they knew him because guys hung out like that, and they'd get drunk and think it was really funny to bug me like that. My first thought was he's drowning, so I started going through the steps in my mind of whether to get the pole or jump in after him, and I had my whistle all ready but they said, "Oh, don't listen to him; he's faking it," and that's what brought down my guard.
>
> All of a sudden, all that I'd been taught was confused in my mind. All the steps that came automatically, that we'd practiced, just fell apart because I didn't know what to think then.
>
> His hands were moving very slowly, so I figured he must have been treading water to stay up. You can't see below three or four feet because of the minerals in the lake, so I couldn't tell what he was doing with his feet.
>
> I was waiting for him to quit any minute, and I kept saying, "Why don't you just knock it off?" and "Are you really in trouble? Do you need me to throw something out to you?" . . .
>
> And my manager, who was supposed to be the best lifeguard out of all of us, he was standing as far away as I was and was flirting with some girls and not looking at the water like I was.
>
> Three or four minutes elapsed—slow motion, looking back. About that time, I called to the other lifeguard and pointed at

the guy and shrugged my shoulders, and he laughed. And I said, "Oh, good. Everything is okay. He's faking it."

About that time, the guy's eyes were looking up at me from just below the water. Then I started walking to the other lifeguard and watching the bubbles, and then the bubbles stopped. But still, in the back of my mind, I thought he must have been hiding somewhere. At the same time, I was panicked because I thought, what if he really is drowning and these guys are telling me a bunch of bull?

I ran over to my manager, and I grabbed him and started pushing him toward the spot and saying, "A guy went down there, and you'd better make sure that he's faking it." I started sending people out looking around the pilings, and it was hard to convince my manager there was somebody out there. He couldn't believe it because he hadn't seen anything. . . .

His little sister came up to me and said, "I think my brother was that guy out there." I said, "I think he was faking it," and told her not to call her mom yet, not to worry her, that we'd probably find him in a few minutes. And she said, "My brother wouldn't fake it. He couldn't swim." I just broke down then when she said that. And I couldn't lifeguard anymore. They had someone take over for me. It was just so terrible realizing that maybe he wasn't faking it and, later on, that there was no doubt. Nothing was in his system—no pot, no booze, nothing.

They filed suit thirty days before the three-year period elapsed and settled out of court for a very small amount because the mother didn't want to go through any more. It was against the county and my name. I felt like a criminal or someone that the public thought should be punished and wanted to make an example of.

I still feel guilty about it, but I don't think about it. I wish his mom could know me as I am and as I was at the time. It was just a very bad judgment but what I thought was the right judgment.

I still have an anger problem, but I'm exercising more. Doing Nautilus and swimming helps. When everything piles up on me, I have to let it out once in a while, but not on my baby—on my poor parents. I go over there and start complaining, and they tell me they don't want to hear me complain, so I get mad at them for not wanting to listen. So they eventually end up listening and realizing I need to talk.

I used to be a good swimmer. I could dive eighteen feet down for crawdads when I was ten years old. . . . Now if a little water gets in my mouth, I panic. My breathing gets screwed up. I used to enjoy the water, and I really don't anymore.

I always think what would it be like to drown and how frustrating it must have been to look up through the water and see me, not being able to get it across to me. I keep seeing me through his eyes. You know how the water's noisy on top and quiet underneath. I think of him going under and back up and hearing all the noise and the people and the life, but under, it's like death. How scared he must have been and panicked and knowing if he slipped down in the quiet black water that I probably would never get to him, that I might never come and save him. And I think of it myself, and it would be a terrible way to die, trying to get across to the lifeguard, whom you depend on to save your life, and that lifeguard thinks you're faking it.

That's the only way it really comes out nowadays. I think I've blocked any feelings I have about the accident to my subconscious to protect myself. Either this or I don't have any feelings. Either way, I'm worried—that someday the feelings will hit and overwhelm me or that I'm just plain cold-blooded.

The Significance of Psychological Shock

According to Dr. Mardi Jon Horowitz, psychological shock is a transition state that is essential to survival:

Whether a defensive reaction is good or bad is a value judgment. Usually they are both good and bad. A defensive reaction gives a person time to have a dose-by-dose reaction—at the expense of not processing some of the information at hand. When one gives it a label like "hysterical," one is suggesting that it is at least in part maladaptive. But there certainly are normal episodes of denial, as when a person with a heart attack does not let himself get too anxious during the recovery period, since anxiety might lead to a racing heart, possibly even a cardiac crisis. A person may deal with different themes at different levels. For example, a person after a trauma may have a lot of hostility activated but not necessarily become conscious of it right away. This does apply to accidents.[17]

As vital a reaction as emotional shock might be, it still is not what could be considered a normal state of mind. To be psychologically sound, an individual must be controlled by a unified ego that is aware of its personal identity based on its history. When that background is unavailable due to amnesia or emotional blockage, the ego has trouble directing because it does not have full knowledge of its own dimensions. When powerful subconscious forces rule, the accidental killer can end up reacting negatively to the past instead of acting positively in the present.

Most accidental killers leave the state of psychological shock rather quickly and start to deal with the other repercussions of the accident. As the psychological shock wears off, a new rhythm establishes itself in the accidental killer's mind: "the accident, the accident, the accident."

2

Preoccupation

It's hard to know where to begin. In retrospect I can see subtle flows building in the substructure of my life long before the accident. The accident acted as a seed crystal or a detonator to set into motion forces which completely destroyed the world I knew.

Afterward, sitting and brooding over the whole thing and trying to find the meaning of why all this happened, the meaning that came into it for me was not to violate principles. And if you do, it's going to have consequences maybe in your external reality. Things are going to happen to force you to look at it until you come to grips with it.

I was driving to an ROTC meeting, all dressed up in uniform. I was running a little late because we'd had company for dinner. I'd had one, perhaps two, glasses of wine. The night was dark. The roads were clear, but snowbanks stood two feet tall on the edges.

There was only one really good place to pass on the road—a long straight stretch in a deserted area. I was behind a tractor-trailer as I approached the passing zone. I stepped on the gas, pulled out, then just as I was even with the cab, I saw them—two men walking side by side in the roadway with a gas can between them. I hit the brakes. I don't know if I swerved. There was a thump as I hit one of them, and the car continued to slide sideways. The car stopped crosswise on the road.

I jumped out of the car and ran back to find the man's companion disentangling him from the guardrail. We stretched him out, covered him with my coat and some blankets, and gave mouth-to-mouth resuscitation until the police arrived and he was pronounced dead.

The clearest memory I have of the whole incident is the taste of blood and the aspirating sound of blood and air as it exited behind his ear. The degree to which I have separated the affective memory from the cognitive memory is surprising to me. For a long time I could not avoid continually reliving that experience, and the taste stayed with me for months. Now I can't recapture it in its totality.

The police were very kind. I felt it was because I had been all dressed up in uniform and was planning on being a doctor, while the deceased and his friend were longhairs and had had minor difficulties with the law before. One person wished me good luck in a very deep and sincere way. It surprised me. I remember at the time I was a little angered by it. Later on I understood.

No criminal action was taken. After the investigation at the scene the police drove me home and returned my license. Except for necessary routines (going to classes, going to work) I spent most of my time staring at the walls. I couldn't talk about the accident, even with my wife. I just stayed in this universe consisting of myself and the man I had killed and whose blood I had tasted, whose death rattles I had heard.

Before I had a certain stance, whether it was ideological or religious, about the Vietnam War and about participating in the military. I didn't even conceive of the possibility of getting a conscientious objector status because they were pretty hard on those things then. You had to be raised in one of those faiths that historically opposed war, and you had to base it in dogma, so the only option I saw was going into ROTC, being paid a scholarship, and being guaranteed a noncombatant status.

In ROTC we would talk about how it's okay to drop a bomb if the reason why you're doing it is worth the cost in terms of pain and death to human beings. Just don't pretend you're not dropping it, because that's what most people do. For them it's video games. But I kept my mouth shut about prodding people's conscience, so when I asked for it, they gave me a CO discharge without any hassle.

Although it may seem bizarre, I've drawn out a pattern to give meaning to the death. It's a very egocentric one, but then on an existential level we all are. I was in ROTC against my own principles. I needed the money it paid me each month. My wife did not support my CO beliefs. My draft lottery number was low, and it seemed the best option. All good reasons to be in, but it created a kink in the core of my being. I was on my way to an ROTC meeting the night of the accident. It was classified as an "act of God." Therefore (so it seemed), God had sacrificed this person's life in order to get me back on the track. To mitigate the extreme harshness of this, I add that while trying to revive my victim (lover, enemy, brother), I prayed that his soul might transfer whatever task it had to do over to me. It was a spontaneous prayer of the heart and had no formulated theology behind it, just an intuitive approach to the circumstances. The accident, and similar hard-learned lessons, have taught me never to go against my principles. I feel there is some balancing mechanism which keeps me on the right track no matter how hard I try to get off it.

After the accident I was too inside myself. I wasn't connecting and I really needed my wife, but I wasn't communicating that. I wasn't communicating anything. I couldn't talk about it with anybody, just be inside of it.

Probably it is similar whenever a person feels she or he has violated or been violated by the Community of Being on a grand scale. In a spiritual sense it feels very much like "accidental" rape. Although accidental, one feels fully culpable and responsible for an act which tears the fabric of reality, resulting in a deep-seated alienation toward all external reality. The internal reality at this point, though, is a gloomy whirlpool of self-accusation and anguish.

I tried to stay in my self-reinforcing loop of pain, but economic survival and interpersonal relationships kept drawing me out into an external reality. Soon after my marriage fell apart. My wife went elsewhere to fill those emotional needs which I was denying. That added another dimension to the pain I was feeling, so we separated. During that summer she lived with another man and I cooked, drank, and survived at a resort in upstate New England. It seemed to be a love-hate thing. I needed so much at that time, and I would not allow people into that space inside. I'd lash out or run. The pain was so bad at times that I actively wanted to take heroin or something which would negate the reality I was experiencing. Fortunately it wasn't readily available. I found an abandoned piano in a barn and went and drank and played it and cried every night. I played out so much pain on the piano—and I can't even play it. I talked through so much on the piano that I couldn't have expressed in other ways.

It wasn't until four years after the accident that it started coming up again. It was almost like peristaltic action, as waves of physical constriction and emotion would pass through me. I had one really bad day when I just cried uncontrollably and beat the furniture, not really knowing why. At this point I made a plan to leave all that I knew behind and to make the pilgrimage in search of self which is required of each one of us. Mine took me across Canada and the United States. I became aware of an intimate relationship with transcendent forces who were concerned for my welfare (God?) and I was able to share my story—to confess—with several people, including my father, in the course of my travels. This period of my life I look back on now as the most important but without the foundation and background of suffering I don't know how much depth it would have had. Each time it seemed that I was being sealed into a tomb, help would come from somewhere. Friends I didn't know I had would just be there for me—extending but not imposing. Of course I felt the need to escape, to get away into a whole new reality which didn't remind me of the pain. When I did, though, it was even worse; there was no one there. In the period of traveling I learned to listen to the inner voices from which I had always run before.

To preoccupy is to engross fully or to take possession of first. It is as if the accident has taken hold of the accidental killer's mind, preempting all else. The beginning period of adjustment to the accident can be comprised of many different parts, as the different injured aspects of the person come forth, calling for work. It can be labeled posttraumatic reaction, traumatic neurosis, hysteria, or obsession. It seems that for many accidental killers, time stops while their mind locates the pieces it will need to sort out.

"In adversity," wrote Horace, "remember to keep an even mind."[1] But for varying lengths of time following involvement in a fatal accident, an "even mind" can seem unattainable. The mind can lock into its moment of terror so that the accidental killer lives and dreams in the accident's shadow. Nothing else can hold the person's attention. Regardless of her daily routine, whom she is with, where she goes, or what she is supposed to be doing, the accident envelops her inner world. Some accidental killers say:

> "Time has helped, but for three years there hasn't been one day that I haven't thought about being responsible for the death of a child."
> "For up to two years after the accident, I *always* thought about it."
> "It hangs around me like a permanent cloud."
> "I remember thinking about the accident daily for years and thinking, 'It's been . . . three years—when are you going to stop thinking about this every day?'"
> "The thing that gets me is that it never seems to fade. Even though I may go several days without thinking of it, when it does come to mind, it's as if it happened only yesterday."

The period following the cessation of shock can bring unwanted visions, invading dreams, and health repercussions. Many accidental killers become preoccupied with death, withdrawn, and disoriented, endlessly questioning the world and its rules. Some suffer eating compulsions, sleep disturbances, nightmares, flashbacks, and other psychosomatic ailments. An accidental killer who shot his brother as a boy says, "I felt minutes of denial and hours of sobbing, a loss of appetite, crying, a feeling of a leaden weight on my heart."

The Function of the Posttraumatic Reaction

To regain one's equilibrium after a sudden trauma, it is necessary to go over and over the event until its force has dissipated. For example, flood survivors who experience extreme danger and personal vulnerability do not immediately recover once the calamity is past. It takes time for them to assimilate the trauma.[2] Temporary fixation on the disastrous event is normal and necessary. It signifies that the accidental killer is coming to terms with what happened and not repressing it. Dr. Marilyn Geller, a psychologist in Binghamton, New York, describes this phase of adjustment:

> We have been taught to value human life, and these individuals are now dealing with the fact that they are responsible for killing another individual. Thinking, "How did it happen?" "How can I go on?" is a very common response to a traumatic event. Initially, this should not be referred to as an obsession; the term implies pathology. If, however, over an extended period of time, the thinking remains intrusive and continues to limit the individual's functioning, then the situation would be labeled problematic. It is important not to label it so initially. In the beginning, it is a coping strategy. The repetitive thoughts help individuals to feel in control of their lives and their emotions at a time when their lives have been turned upside down.[3]

Individuals who go through an acute situational crisis are entitled to feel whatever they feel. Posttraumatic reactions show vulnerability, not pathology. "Nothing emotionally felt is bad, nasty or dirty."[4]

Preoccupation often dovetails with the shock reaction. Most accidental killers function flawlessly at the death scene and appear to handle the accident well for a period afterward. But once the shock wears off, they fall apart. Their physical defense mechanisms (pounding heart, sweating palms, and so on) may be set off by symbols that remind them of the accident.[5] One accidental killer recalls, "On the fourth day, the feelings rushed in, and I felt like an uprooted tree floating down a river of emotion."

There are many other reasons why a period of intense focus on the crisis is necessary. In the aftermath of a crisis, all the accidental killer's resources—anatomical, social, physiological, anthropological, and psychological—that have been marshaled to cope with the traumatic event have to settle back into their normal forms of functioning. This cannot happen all at once, and it necessarily involves the entire person.[6] One accidental killer notes, "Fragments of me are slowly coming back, grating together as they seek a matching—sometimes painfully jarring into place."

There is bound to be some lapse in contact with an outside world that becomes too taxing after a traumatic event has created excitations beyond the individual's mastery. This event has inflicted a severe blow on the ego. Normal activities involved in successful adaptation to the external environment get blocked by the body's instinctual reading of what it perceives as its own failure to escape or prevent harm. The trauma can numb the portion of the ego that normally helps the individual automatically orient and survive.[7]

According to stress researcher Dr. Mardi Jon Horowitz, one reason preoccupation can be so strong is that the expectation of personal omnipotence has been violated. Although people may not realize it, they expect themselves to have total control—an unrealistic but universal secret desire.[8]

The traumatic event also may cause a tendency toward compulsive repetition of some aspect of the event in thoughts (unbidden flashbacks) and emotions, although the accidental killer may not recognize the ties between these feelings and the event.[9] Frequently there is a latent period between the stressor and the time when symptoms begin. And once these symptoms begin, they have a remarkable tendency to persist long after the immediate effects of the event are gone.[10] Unfinished business complicates the process. Whatever tasks the accident interrupted may weigh on the accidental killer until they can be completed.[11]

This absorption is the accidental killer's primary work project, but without that understanding, the individual may fail to recognize it as such and resent thoughts of the accident as oppressive intrusions. It is common for accidental killers to be oblivious to some of their routine responsibilities. One accidental killer says, "At work I find it hard to concentrate. Sometimes I make errors or forget to do things, and no one understands why. I don't want to come out and say, 'Hey, I'm remembering the accident and not concentrating very well.' They don't want to be reminded."

A Pattern of Oscillation

Preoccupation is far from constant. Intense reliving of the traumatic event will be separated by periods when it seems remote. When the mind's capacity for control is high, it is able to ward off highly provocative thoughts about the accident. The accidental killer experiences these breaks as periods of emotional numbness or even disbelief that the accident occurred. But then memories of the trauma keep cycling back into the person's awareness until they have been processed fully. When the accidental killer's resistance is down or something happens to bring the accident to mind, it may trigger a recollection, a pang. This oscillation is a form of "dosing" in which the mind helps the individual to deal with the accident a little at a time. As the process continues, with the assimilation and accommodation it demands, the episodes of reliving the event gradually decrease in their intensity, suddenness, and frequency.[12]

The accident may at times block ego functions, which in turn causes regressions that throw off the economy of mental energy and upsets the equilibrium between repressed impulses and those forces that keep them in check. The accidental killer may act out in unusual ways. The work of fitting the accident back into the accidental killer's life may appear as its opposite to many—that is, the accident may seem to be shaping them to its form, leaving them no choice but to bend themselves around it.

Different Susceptibilities

Many factors help determine how deeply absorbed an accidental killer will become. If the accidental killer believed himself to be invulnerable to danger prior to the accident, he is likely to be overwhelmed by the crisis. Those who could tolerate some anticipatory alarm and could acknowledge that disaster can strike at any moment will have much less emotional disturbance than those who denied the reality of the threat beforehand.[13]

The accidental killer's level of empathy is another important factor, causing more initial upset but hastening eventual recovery. People who can cry for the human condition and have the ability to put themselves in the place of others are better prepared to cope in the long run.

Another important factor is whether the accidental killer has experienced the death of a loved one. If the accident is the accidental killer's first encounter with death, she will have more trouble dealing with it.

Obviously, whatever else is happening in the accidental killer's life at the time of the event also will have an effect on how the person handles the accident.

Children seem most profoundly affected by an accidental death. Because a child's or an adolescent's self-concept is still developing, it is much more vulnerable than that of an adult, which may be better able to attribute the accident's cause to uncontrollable circumstances or to a particular mistake in judgment without identifying himself solely as a killer. A woman tells of the death of her girlfriend when they were both schoolchildren:

It has been twelve years since the accident, but I'm finding it extremely difficult to control my crying and organize my thoughts so I can communicate coherently and meaningfully.

The accident involved a child being hit, thrown, and run over by a car immediately after it made a left turn around a corner. This occurred while several friends were walking to school. All of us had left for school late because I had been very late meeting the other children. All of the children were waiting at the house of the child who became the accident victim.

When I arrived at her house, I heard her father yelling at her and using words including f——— and s———. He was angry because she had waited for me. I felt responsible for this treatment by her father. In addition, because she was walking faster than the rest of us to get to school on time, she was in the middle of the street when a car came speeding around the corner, and the rest of us were on the curb, about three or four yards behind her.

I feel that my role in the accident included (1) her father yelling at her, causing her to walk to school faster and thereby being in the street when the car arrived, thus causing her father to feel guilty afterward, and (2) actually getting hit by the car. If I had been on time, the car would not have been there at the time we were crossing the street. I feel responsible for the parents' and sister's grief and their anger at me.

Initially, for at least a couple of months following, I could not believe the child was dead. I remember feeling exhausted the day the accident occurred, but my mother took me on all of her errands. When we came back from the supermarket, she got out the Scrabble game. I continued to think of the victim as we played. My mother gave me some excuse and then went to her room and phoned the hospital about my friend. I heard my mother say, "Oh, I'm very sorry." I knew then that she was dead, but I thought to myself, "She's not dead. She's okay. Everything's going to be fine."

For a long time afterward, I was convinced that she was really alive but that nobody was aware of it. I became very upset because I thought that she had been buried alive and that she was trying to get out—and couldn't. I became preoccupied with thinking that all "dead" people were able to communicate with the living but the living didn't know it. I talked about this with friends who soon got bored with it and wanted to talk about other things, but I didn't want to.

I remember seeing the movie *The Pit and the Pendulum* on TV about four years after the accident. I went to bed crying because I vaguely remember someone in the movie being buried alive, and I remember thinking of my friend at the time.

There is a feeling that because a peer had a sudden, unavoidable death, I could too. Following the accident for years—I think years—I was afraid that I would get hit by a car. I kept imagining what it would feel like to get hit by a speeding car, and I thought that if I ever saw a car coming at me and couldn't get out of the way, I would fall to the ground, lie flat, and let it roll over me, thereby escaping injury. I remember telling my mother this.

I felt bad because my family didn't seem to comprehend what I was thinking and feeling. Neither did my friends, except those who had been present when the accident occurred. Since the time of the accident (I was ten or eleven) until I was about twenty-one, I never thought of my role in causing the accident. I was at home, and I suddenly thought of the accident, and then it occurred to me, "You were responsible for it. Why don't you feel guilty?" It never occurred to me until that time what my role had been in the sequence of events that led to her death. I really didn't feel guilty, although since then I've become increasingly aware of it, and it's become very painful.

I terminated psychotherapy after going through it for approximately two years. The problems for which I sought and remained in therapy were basically (in my opinion) unrelated to the accident and had mostly to do with my difficulty in perceiving myself as an independent adult. Yet I did not bring up in therapy anything about the accident until a few months before I finished it. My psychiatrist pointed out that my coming late to class and missing classes (both of which were real problems) may have been my way of punishing myself. I don't know if that is the case, but the occurrence of my missing a class or being late for one has decreased dramatically since this was brought up.

I think what I'm trying to say is that the feelings about the accident seem to be the worst and the strongest of any feelings that I've ever experienced.

What made me feel more guilty was the reaction of the girl's parents to me following the accident—i.e., ignoring me or glaring at me without speaking—and generally the grief that I saw in them and the victim's sister. Because I told only two people other than you of my role, most people didn't perceive guilt in me, and so they didn't attempt to alleviate it.

I do feel that children are at a special disadvantage because they aren't aware of any kind of formal resources to help them and don't have the financial capacity to pay for it. Also, it is up to the child's parents as to whether the child should get help and where. As I found out, if they don't understand all of the child's feelings, the result can be more pain rather than helpful. Above all, I would want people to know that a child is at an enormous disadvantage in dealing with the situation. There is no guarantee of safety anymore—parents are not all-powerful in preventing horrible and excruciating death or injury. Adults have to and can come to terms with this, but for a child it's a real shocker.

There is one thing. Although it's irrational, I have a very strong feeling that I owe the victim, that although she has been dead for a long time, her spirit is alive and she is very angry at me and grieving for her family. I wish I could convey to her how sorry I am. I wish I could convey this to her family also.

If she were alive today, she would still be around to enjoy life and her family to enjoy her. She would have been a twenty-two-year-old woman.

I feel that my fear of death, of being terribly injured and unable to communicate, originated from the accident, and I feel that others involved in a similar death may have these feelings.

In her preoccupation with death and lasting belief in her dead friend's continued existence, this accidental killer has reacted in a way that is similar to the way concentration camp survivors perceive their dead. They have a lifelong identification with death and dying, as well as a strong sense of obeisance to the dead.[14]

Psychosomatic Illness

After a traumatic event, many people stay extremely tense and irritable, are tired all the time, and are unable to relax.[15] Horowitz says that this tension results from realizing that the world can be overwhelmingly dangerous and threatening.[16] Nerve-related body disorders are common among accidental killers. A study of drivers involved in fatal accidents found that a significant proportion suffered from either high blood pressure (much higher than before the accident), colitis, or ulcers, all afflictions related to stress.[17]

"I had one headache for thirteen years," reports an accidental killer. "Night and day, day and night. Then one morning I woke up to feel where my head was. I went through a very famous clinic—they could find no cause. I did not tell them about the accident, but now I know."

Another says he suffered a recurring case of hives that went on for thirty years after the accident. Another remembers:

My close friend and I were returning from a business meeting when a nineteen-year-old male driving a one-and-a-half-ton commercial truck ran a red light, striking the driver's side of our car and causing a fatal head injury to the driver. I was relatively untouched.

I have gone through, I guess one could say, a severe emotional trauma. Two very important theories of mine were shattered in one moment. I believed that if you were a careful driver, you could avoid accidents. Also, I believed that if you lived according to the Golden Rule, the Supreme Being would protect you. Neither idea held water in this case.

I first experienced total disorientation and disbelief. I really felt like I was slipping away, like my mind couldn't accept the fact that the accident occurred and that my friend was so seriously injured. Next was the feeling that she was so good, and everybody loved her so much, that she would come out of this all right. That was the stage of praying and literally trying to will her to live. She stayed in a coma, showing daily improvement for four days, before she developed a blood clot and died.

Then came the feeling of defeat. This was the hardest part. The weeks following her death I was in a daze. I returned to work but didn't function.

I started having nightmares about dying. In all my dreams, the act of dying was painful, but once I was dead, I felt at peace.

About this time, I started having physical problems associated with nerves. I had colitis and nerve flutterings in my eyes and ears. These symptoms lasted for about a month.

I said that I would never be one of those who need psychiatric counseling, and I swear I will never come this close to "the couch" again.

Another accidental killer recalls the physical symptoms that plagued her:

I had a car wreck which was completely my fault. I passed a truck in a fog with no visibility and ran head-on into an approaching car. We both swerved to avoid the accident but swerved in the same direction. . . . There was a lawsuit for approximately $1.5 million, which was settled out of court for the limit of my insurance, $50,000.

Since the accident, I have had many changes in my life. The weeks following it were spent mainly at home—depressed, worried, unhappy, nervous. I had my wedding already lined up to be four months after the accident and had trouble coping with happiness and great sadness at the same time.

I worried for my parents and what I was putting them through. I went through a long, guilt-provoking lawsuit and could not get car insurance for anything close to a reasonable price and consequently didn't drive for three years. My husband was very patient with my frequent trips back to the city of the accident, my spastic stomach and frequent trips to the doctor, my temper tantrums, and my inability to drive.

I developed a nervous condition and a spastic stomach, and I gained weight, all of which took some years to get under control.

Compulsions that arise in response to stress are attempts to alleviate anxiety. But the itch of compulsion does not go away with scratching. It only gets worse and confirms that the person's resources are inadequate for dealing directly with the problem. For relief from this feeling of inadequacy, a compulsive person becomes more deeply entrenched in the problematic behavior until she can integrate new ways of coping with her life.[18]

Stormy Nights

Most accidental killers have trouble sleeping at night. Many also have trouble getting out of bed in the morning and experience a lack of energy in the months following their crises. Relaxing sufficiently is the challenge.

A man who acknowledges no conscious guilt after running over a little boy who was crossing a busy highway started losing sleep after his accident. "Every morning for several months I would wake up a couple of hours early and sit there in the dark and think about it, not being able to get back to sleep," he says.

Another accidental killer recalls:

My accident happened at 9:30 P.M. on a rainy evening in November while I was driving home from work. I saw a dark figure dart out from between two cars across the street and run diagonally across and away from me. It was an intoxicated man. I tried to swerve and cut behind him, but I couldn't. I still wonder if I could have missed him if I'd swerved to the right.

The police took me to the hospital—screaming. Words seem useless at such a time. Unless you experience it yourself, you cannot know the despair and hurt.

My nights were the worst time. I had trouble sleeping, especially falling asleep, and I was frightened—sharp sounds, movements, and darkness. I finally did manage to do without keeping a light on in the bedroom.

A twenty-two-year-old policeman remembers his difficult nights:

The incident happened while I was working. Since the time of the shooting, in which I was shot and my partner was killed, I have quit my job.

I worried a lot that something else would happen to me. It was the first time I really knew that I could die at any time. I never gave death much thought before this. I spent four weeks and five days in the hospital—eight days in intensive care and four of those days in critical condition. After surgery I had a 60 percent chance of recovery. Since leaving the hospital a year and a half ago, I've come to appreciate life a lot more. I see the beauty in the whole world around us.

I used to think it was my fault, since I'm alive and he died. I felt maybe I could have prevented it. We were answering a domestic quarrel. I took the front entrance and directed him to the back. I realize now that since I was shot first, I had no control after that. I got opinions from other people and have convinced myself I am not to blame. Once I convinced myself of it, I felt a lot better.

It was a week after the shooting before I knew my partner died. This was the idea of my mother, and I'm thankful she didn't let me know sooner. The shocking news took me unprepared, but I'm glad I didn't know until my physical condition was better.

For five or six months after the incident, I'd wake up three or four times every night. It wasn't easy to go to sleep either. I've gone through many nights of being afraid of the unknown. There were times when I'd just shake from fear, not knowing what I was really afraid of.

A college student recalls: "For almost two years after the accident, I would wake up screaming from scenes of the accident or from guilt about her four children, ages 22, 20, 17, and 13. I refused to drive a car for a year afterward, didn't own a car for another year, relying on hitchhiking for transportation. Writing this, I still feel nauseous."

Replaying the Event

The experience of being part of a sudden death can replay itself in one's mind unpredictably and with force. Freud wrote that a horror that the mind would like to forget often forms the nucleus of a new psychic group separated from the ego and around which impressions collect that reinforce what is being suppressed.[19] He added that people who are upset suffer mainly from reminiscences. When they attempt to remember, they suffer partial amnesia or are overwhelmed by uncontrollable recollection. When they attempt not to remember, unbidden images break into their consciousness.[20]

According to researcher Kai Erikson, sudden death "does not retreat into some discrete compartment of the mind. . . . It remains with one, becoming a part of the very air one breathes and a dominant figure in one's imagery . . . an advance look at hell. And the sight does not go away easily."[21]

One accidental killer notes, "For weeks I had daytime nightmares, reliving the accident time after time. I couldn't shut my mind off." Another says:

I don't brood on it day in and day out, but it's just something that when you least expect it, the whole thing can just flash back in your mind—mostly when I'm driving or when I'm by myself. I kind of live out in the country, and it'll just all of a sudden pop into my mind if I'm driving down the road and there's no traffic around—a tree-lined road, nothing at all like the street where the accident happened. I'm in that lush green world, and all of a sudden, plop, there it is for no reason. When it [flashes into my mind,] it is just as clear as if it had just happened—that's it, the clarity of it.

A railroad engineer repeatedly sees the face of a suicide victim:

Since the accident occurred in 1975, I have not had any problems accepting the fact that because I happened to be in a certain place, the wrong place, when this individual decided to kill himself, I could not have avoided the accident.

This particular incident occurred while I was operating a passenger train. While en route the train made stops as scheduled, which called for certain stations to be passed without stopping because of a stacked period in passenger traffic. As I approached the station, a man in his twenties appeared from behind the waiting room and without warning dropped himself directly in front of my train.

His face was expressionless, startled, and, I can honestly say looking back, lacking any emotion or fright. The young man was killed instantly, and after the police arrived, I proceeded on my route.

A man who called on the telephone identifying himself as a police detective indicated the victim had been under the influence of a strong drug prescribed by a psychiatrist.

The dreams from this accident were enough to keep me from a restful sleep for about two weeks. I saw the accident over and over when I was in a sound sleep. I kept seeing the man's face.

A woman whose infant nephew was killed in her accident reports redreaming the accident many times, with different ones of her own children substituted for the dead child.

Dr. Mardi Jon Horowitz explains the purpose of such dreams and flashbacks: Until a traumatic experience is mastered, it remains in some special form of memory storage where it sends vivid sensory images to the person's mind, evoking unpleasant emotions. By seeing and feeling the impact of the images over and over, the person deals with each image and emotion in turn, and the traumatic experience thereby loses its intensity.[22]

Signs and Premonitions

Some accidental killers say that they knew their accident was going to happen in advance, and this aspect becomes particularly engrossing to them. One says:

I've always been able to find my way to places I've never been before without using a map, or else somebody will need some gadget to fix something, and I'll always have it on me.

I had a dream about the accident one and a half years before. In the dream I didn't know what it was that I hit, but I knew I hit somebody and it was in the same location—the body was in the same position on the road. I woke up so scared I couldn't move. Then I thought no more about it. Now I dwell on it. I think about it all night long until I go back to sleep—if I go back to sleep. I always had the question that since I dreamt about it, [maybe] I could have made it happen.

This happened when I was in a whole cycle of bad luck. That year my house caught fire. I broke up with my girlfriend. Also, I was riding in a car that smashed into a tree. Plus some girl thought she'd be funny and put PCP into the punch at the New Year's Eve party and nobody knew it. I didn't drink the punch, but I ate the fruit, and it went into the fruit more than the punch. I smoked two packs of cigarettes in four hours.

A week before it happened, I was driving alone at night when I saw a dark hole in the sky, really big, with no stars. The moon was out, and the sky was clear. If it was a cloud, it would have been lit up. I got out at the top of a hill to look at it. It was creepy, completely black. I didn't feel right after that. That bad feeling went away after the accident.

Then a year to the day I drove by the spot where the accident was—I could tell because of gasoline leaks on the road. There was another accident right there. Two years later to the day I went by, and there was a fire. It was like something was lurking there.

Sometimes foreknowledge shaded by emotional upheaval engenders self-doubt with regard to the limits of the accidental killer's responsibility:

In the summer of 1969 I moved into an apartment with a girl I had met in college. I didn't want to go back to Texas to stay with my parents that summer, so Belinda and I got an apartment in a town near the city. . . . She needed a place to live while she looked for work to pay her tuition for the next year.

We had some disagreements but got along okay. I never ~~~ a job, but she got one that she just hated. . . .

I went to visit my parents in Texas, and after a week wnen i came back, Belinda had moved back to her parents' home in the city with no explanation. She called and said she wanted to talk to me, and we made plans to go hiking that weekend.

I drove and picked her up. She seemed in good spirits. We bought some munchies, and she gave me directions. We'd talk while we hiked, she said. We drove several miles out of town and up an old highway. We came to a place on the old road where it had washed away. I tried to turn the car around and misjudged the distance or something. It went over a cliff. My door was already partially opened, and I jumped out. Belinda was in her seat belt, and she was in the car all the way down. She died in a hospital emergency room from her injuries. I was the driver, but all I had was bruised knees.

I have gone through many emotional "phases" similar to those described by Dr. Kübler-Ross in her work on death and dying. For the first few hours after the accident, I was a real zombie—mechanical and rigid in my movements, all my thoughts frozen: "This can't be happening." I never cried until several months later, and then I cried all the time—in the dorm while I was studying, on the way to class, during meals—all the time, everywhere. I didn't associate it with the accident at all, and neither did anyone else.

For a couple of weeks after the accident, I couldn't ride in a car. For a while, about a month, I couldn't stand being alone—even at night. I could fly in airplanes, but from the time of the accident until last year, I couldn't drive or ride comfortably in a car going to or through mountains. In the fall after the accident, my roommate and I took a long road trip. I was so upset going through the mountains that I had to lie on my back on the car seat with my eyes closed.

About six months after the accident, I joined Campus Crusade for Christ [CCC]. But while the crying and feelings of being alone disappeared, the "peace" I found in CCC didn't last long—about four months.

Everything seemed to go okay until the early part of 1973, when I developed severe insomnia and a deep depression. I was afraid I would die if I fell asleep. From January to April or May, I ate very little, stayed in bed, and wore the same blue jeans and black turtleneck that I had worn the day of the accident. I never left our apartment from January to that spring. Even then I couldn't stand to go far for a couple of months. . . . The depression became periodic—suicidal thoughts gradually disappeared—and in the fall I got a job. The next year I was able to buy some new clothes. I had been denying myself anything like that.

I dreamed that someone close to me died. I had this dream a week or so before the accident, and it terrified me. I discussed it with Belinda. We decided it referred to a friend of ours who had threatened suicide. On the day of the accident, my feelings of impending doom grew greater. By the time Belinda and I started up the side of the mountain on the old road, I was sure that one of us would die. Before I started to turn the car around at the site of the accident, I asked her if she wanted to get out while I turned. She said no, and I'm convinced that I knew then exactly what was going to happen. Until today I never told anybody that I think I had foreknowledge of the accident. All these years I've wondered if I really did—and if that makes me crazy or directly responsible for her death.

Magical Thinking and Philosophical Accommodations

To realize that the world can be overwhelmingly dangerous and threatening can make accidental killers tense, apprehensive, and hypersensitive to the extreme.[23] Some lose faith in the idea of order, becoming so timid toward anything physical and social that it is obvious they now regard the world as an unsafe place.[24] Perhaps the most troublesome part about encountering a seemingly irrational world is that it casts doubt on the validity of the person's daily efforts to build a better life.

Science fiction author Harlan Ellison describes this horror in "Bright Eyes," a story of the survivor of some future cataclysm. The character comes upon a rushing river jammed with bloated human corpses. The river "continued unheeding as it had since the world was born. For the world went on. And did not care."[25]

To keep from believing that death can come without evil motive, that the universe may not run according to any particular plan and that its forces are capable of killing without the slightest notice, some accidental killers construct elaborate schemes to make the cosmos comprehensible. These schemes include magical thinking, spiritual theories, and self-scrutiny. As stated earlier, the impact is likely to be stronger if prior to the accident the accidental killer viewed the world as a safe and logical place or held a secret belief in her own personal invulnerability. Once that belief is crushed, some people replace it with the illusion of centrality, feeling that malevolent forces are aimed directly at them. Both views, of course, distort reality.[26]

One accidental killer contemplates a series of tragedies:

I was driving my girlfriend home after a football game when the accident happened. She was a cheerleader and very popular. After a lengthy trial, I pleaded no contest to speeding and careless driving. I was given a one-year probation and lost my license for three months. The other insurance company is suing ours, but we are trying to redirect the suit to the county. We think that since there was no curve sign, I was not at fault for not seeing the curve. It was a dark road, and I'd never driven it before.

Of course, since the accident caused the death of my girlfriend, I at first went through extreme shock. I had feelings of guilt, horror, hatred of myself and others, and just about any other emotion right away. Some of these feelings were so strong they were suicidal, mainly the guilt feeling. I felt it was definitely my fault, since I had been the one driving the car.

A few weeks after the accident, I went to visit my girlfriend's parents. They expressed nothing but extreme hatred of me, and to this day I wish that I could convince them they are wrong about me. I was having enough problems trying to convince myself that it wasn't my fault. I didn't need their negative opinion, too.

Since then a lot has happened to make it worse. A month later, my cousin was killed while on his honeymoon in Hawaii. He fell from the balcony of the thirty-sixth floor. I really didn't know the girl he married, but I went and related my accident to her and helped comfort her as much as possible. She, her brother, my brother, and I soon became best of friends. Our relationship, created by our related incidents, has created a very fine camaraderie among us. That's one bright note.

About a month after my cousin's accident, one of my best friends was killed by being hit by a train. This made me feel like there was a curse on my trying to be happy. This had me very down and blue and had me very shook up inside.

And if that still wasn't enough, another person who was my best friend where I used to live drowned. It felt like I was very old and they were supposed to be dying. I was seventeen at the time.

Magical thinking (also discussed in chapter 4) is the irrational belief that one can cause harm simply by wishing it. Accidental killers often think backward from the accident, believing that they must secretly have willed it.

Accidental killers who believe that good always comes back to those who do good often have difficulty reconciling their accident. One explains:

> I've always thought that things happen to people the way they live. If you're good, good happens to you; bad, bad things happen. If you are sincere and honest and treat people good, everything comes back to you the same as you dealt with people.
>
> I also believe that things happen to people for a reason. If you lose a child, that means that it's an awakening for you to respect and think more of your other children. . . . I'm ashamed of what happened. My family does not know, other than my children.
>
> I try to find reasons for my accident. I'd been drinking too much, but not that day or two days prior to the accident. There must be a reason for me taking a life. To save mine? To awaken me to save others? I have not found a reason yet—unless I do not want to recognize it and will not accept it.

Backtracking

The natural response to preventable disaster is to analyze one's actions to see whether what went wrong could have been avoided.

For accidental killers, this question can become an obsessive cycle of "what ifs": "What if I hadn't been in such a rush? What if I had checked? Checked again? What if I had not been angry? Tired?" A related cycle involves hopeless wishes, the "if onlys": "It is very hard to kill a small child and not continue to go over the events and wonder if you'd done this or that, it could have been avoided," explains one accidental killer. She continues:

> She knew she was in bad trouble when I hit her, and though she didn't say anything, she gave me a look that said, "Help me." Then she slipped down, and the wheel rolled over her. There was no blood, but she was lying on her back still looking up at me with that same expression, only the bottom half of her was twisted completely around backward.
>
> I don't know why I keep reliving it except for—it sounds so stupid—I keep going back and seeing if there's some way it could have been avoided. What difference does it make at this late date? It happened, it's over with, but I keep trying to go through it step by step.
>
> I've always thought there was a reason for everything, but I've never understood what that possible reason could be and why it would have had to happen to that little girl.

As this woman and many other accidental killers find, the answers to their questions are not readily available. The process of freeing oneself from involvement in a fatal accident depends entirely on the ways in which it has become enmeshed in the accidental killer's psyche. Whether preoccupation with the accident takes the form of a need to search out the ground rules of life and death, bodily reactions to the trauma, unannounced tears, or an endless cycle of "what ifs," that preoccupation must run its course before it passes gradually away.

3

Anger

I was on my way to Sunday brunch with friends. It was about 2 P.M., sunny, hot. This retired colonel from the Air Force had run out of gas and parked his van on the grassy median in the middle of the freeway. The police came along and they were giving him a ride to the gas station.

When they parked, the police left their right rear wheel hanging out into the fast lane. I was coming up an onramp into the fast lane and checking my rear view mirror. All I saw was blue. It was the colonel's shirt—some Hawaiian print, dark blue.

He was getting into the back seat of the police car on the traffic side and the door opened all the way out into my lane. I was going fifty miles per hour, and it was a square hit. He was fairly heavy, and I pretty much quartered his body. . . .

The police took me into the station for questioning; they were pressing criminal charges against me for negligent homicide. They kept me there for hours and hours. My family finally bailed me out.

When I got home that night I walked in the door and looked down. All across the front of my blouse there were little bits of dried flesh stuck to it that had been on me all day long, and I had never looked down and nobody had told me. I tore off the blouse and threw it across the room against the refrigerator.

Then I thought about all the people who were leaving me all alone, all the people who knew what happened. And not one of them came to be with me on *that* night. I grabbed a butcher knife and ran outside. For blocks around my house, every car's tires were slashed and every tree had its branches cut up.

Shame and humiliation fueled this accidental killer's vengeance. Though extreme in her response, she is not unusual among accidental killers for getting angry about the accident.

Like anger from any other source, posttraumatic anger over having done senseless harm is born of frustration. Depending on the values and ideas that the accidental killer brings to the crisis, the accident holds enormous potential for constricting future possibilities for getting the accidental killer's needs met. It can destroy the person's faith, target the accidental killer for doubt and suspicion from others, and fixate the mind. Although many accidental killers may not recognize it consciously, they resent the accident's intrusion in their lives.

A powerful emotion fueled by adrenaline, anger is a primitive response to injustice. It may serve to externalize a person's anxiety. It springs up in an instant, sometimes seeming to use the angry person to its own ends. It is capable of flooding the body with passion and causing muscle tension, scowling, grinding of teeth, glaring, clenched fists, flushing, paling, goose bumps, chills and shudders, choking, twitching, sweating, feeling of heat, feeling of cold, dizziness, tears, snarls, and a complete inability to vocalize. Some say that anger makes them feel good, others that it makes them sick.[1]

Some hold anger in, while others express it outwardly. Anger can be healthy when it helps a person to identify the problem externally rather than to turn it inward, where it is transferred into guilt and depression. But anger also may hurt others, and in this way it can generate more guilt.

Not every accidental killer gets mad, for anger is born not just of frustration but of the feeling that the frustration is unjustified. Stoic philosopher Lucius Annaeus Seneca wrote that anger usually involves a conscious judgment that an injustice, insult, or idiocy has been committed.[2]

Dr. Carol Tavris agrees, noting, "Anger depends upon our perceptions of a situation, perceptions of injustice included. . . . We tend to equate what is with what ought to be (people have a curious tendency to act as if life was fair). In order to feel angry, people need to know that they are not alone, crazy, or misguided."[3] Of course, many accidental killers lack such assurance.

Dr. Ann Kliman, a therapist at a leading Boston hospital's crisis clinic, writes, "Anger is entirely appropriate. Anger is not bad or maladaptive in and of itself. It is a manifestation of an energy that demands expression."[4]

According to Dr. Angelo Canedo, director of rehabilitative medicine at New York's Bellevue Hospital, "While at first it may seem maladaptive because people might do things that would be considered antisocial, anger turns out to be a way for people to get a grip on their situation."[5]

But for all its important functions, anger can be an emotion with ugly consequences. Anger can be directed at anyone who can be held even symbolically responsible for an accident. Stress researcher Dr. Mardi Jon Horowitz cites the example of a mother who cuts her hand while slicing the ham for her child's sandwich and feels the immediate impulse to yell, "See what you made me do!"[6]

With varying degrees of rationality, accidental killers attribute the victim's death to some combination of the following sources: themselves, God, a third party's negligence, or the victim. (Anger at the self, manifested as guilt, is treated separately in chapter 4.) The accidental killer's anger also may be directed at people not directly involved in the accident. For example, the accidental killer may become angry at his family if it is not supportive or at the victim's family for filing legal suit.

Anger at God

Accidental killers who subscribe to the belief that a greater intelligence rules everything in their lives sometimes feel outraged at a God they feel has betrayed them. The basic questions they direct in prayer are "Why me? Does my suffering have meaning? What is there for me to learn?"[7] One accidental killer says, "I stopped praying then and there. If there is a God, he is unfair." Another, who called herself an atheist, remembers, "I told God every morning that

I despised Him, that I was glad I hadn't had the privilege to know Him well." After years of depression, drugs, and an unsuccessful suicide following her accident, she converted to Catholicism.

Anger at Life

Involvement in a fatal accident is the first time some accidental killers are exposed to misfortune. The physical, financial, and emotional devastation resulting from such an accident can generate deep anger. One accidental killer describes his anger as follows:

> I'm in constant pain, physically and emotionally. I have lost respect for myself and 90 percent of my confidence. I have all kinds of fears I never had before. My future as a man, husband, father, businessman, and human being seems to be one big question mark. The physical, medical, emotional, marital, psychological, and financial repercussions of our accident seem endless, with little hope in sight. People say, "You shouldn't be alive considering what happened." That only makes me feel more guilty. . . .
>
> My father, who died when I was 12, taught me that there was no limit to what I could accomplish if I put my mind to it. Before the accident, I felt no limitations physically, mentally, or emotionally. I could do anything I wanted to. It was just a matter of what I wanted to do to get it. . . . I felt invulnerable. I didn't plan on being disabled. I don't think about it because it isn't a pleasant thought. If I have any choice at all, I don't wait. I do it now. Tomorrow I could get hit by a bus.
>
> Jim was the brother I never had, the father who died. He was reliable, dependable, trustworthy, loyal, faithful. I could talk to him about anything. I could conceive of anything with him. . . . At the time of the accident, we were planning our first building project, where he would have been a full partner on a chain of fast-food restaurants. . . .
>
> The day of the accident was clear with thinly scattered clouds. Visibility was excellent, and it was 70 degrees. Wind was at five knots. [My wife and I] had flown down for an in-

vestment convention with Jim and his wife. As I was checking out the airplane, there was an avionics problem. The display light in the navigation equipment had gone out. I was very regimented in my flying responsibilities for the trip. I went down the checklist. It took me an hour to clear up the problem with the light bulb.

I got clearance for takeoff. From the time of takeoff until the flight plan was canceled, only forty-four seconds had elapsed. The tower radioed we were trailing smoke. I requested a runway assignment, but they didn't hear me. The wiring was already burned through.

I reached for the lever to cut off the engine. I glanced down at my hand and saw it was bleeding. The skin from the top of it was folded back up on my forearm, as if someone had filleted it. I could smell hair burning. I noticed the plane losing fuel pressure. Then I went blind. My face had melted shut. The doctors said this saved my life because otherwise my lungs would have melted. No pain, though. Throughout the whole thing, until I lost consciousness, I never felt pain because the nerve endings were singed. . . . By the plane's motion, I could tell it was right side up, and I managed to bring it to a stop on the ground.

I reached over for Jim, but no one was there. I yelled out to the wives but got no answer. I kind of groped through the plane to the rear door, and I felt no one there. They were already out. As I dropped from the plane, it felt like the shirt was being pulled off my back, but it was the skin on my back, not my shirt. The earth felt cool. I heard the firefighters already hosing down the plane with saline. Then I blacked out.

The wives had made it out with minor injuries, but Jim never did get out. According to the autopsy report, he died from smoke and heat inhalation and from burns.

When I woke up, I was wearing a body cast. I'd lost three and a half inches in height. I was too sad to move. I didn't want to go outside. Just looking out the window made me cry. I felt alone, like I was down so far no one else was anywhere close. . . .

When the cast came off, my body seemed like someone else's.

I had been 6 foot 1 inch, 185 pounds, athletic build, with sandy brown hair, blue-eyed, with Scottish features. Now I am 5 foot 9½ inches. I atrophied. I lost 30 pounds. My back was broken in eight places, and the one disc that remains to support my upper body is showing signs of eroding. Two 14-inch metal rods hold my back together. The muscles in my back were starting to collapse and put pressure on my arms, and this threw pressure on my sciatic nerve, causing pain in my leg and foot. My right ankle was shattered when I jumped from the plane. I had a series of operations to remove parts of the liver and intestine that were injured by the seat belt and shoulder harness apparatus. Bits of shrapnel and upholstery fabric keep migrating to the surface of my skin over every part of my body. I have a hard time shaving because of the scars.

My wife left me before I got out of the body cast. As I was sorting through her things, I came across a box full of newspaper clippings dating back to just after the wedding. They were all about practical tips on how to get good property settlements from a divorce. There was also the tape recording of the voice of an astrologer telling her what life would be like without me. The wife of a supposed friend overheard him plotting with my wife about what the two of them would do with all my property after the divorce.

I had to declare bankruptcy. . . . I went to court against the manufacturer and distributor of the airplane engine and the manufacturer of the airplane. The investigational procedure took two and a half years. We settled for $750,000, and it took a month for the paperwork to be done. Each insurance company contributed a check for one-third of the amount. The lawyer deposited all of this into his trust account and wrote himself a check for all of it but $10,000.

The bankruptcy trustee was one of these people that's really kind to people, but he didn't know how to run things. He didn't pay my medical premiums, so the insurance company used that excuse to cancel.

My wife's lawyer said I'd better allow the trustee to buy up the estate or they would attempt to prove me incompetent and institutionalize me to get me out of the process. Theoretically, there's no money for her, though. . . .

I still have acute pain. . . . It takes me all day to do things like taking out the trash and grocery shopping. It is hard for me to find a comfortable sleeping position because I can't stand to be in the same position for more than twenty minutes and turning over takes me several minutes. At one point, I was up to sleeping eighteen hours a day, although now it's down to around ten. . . .

I think about Jim, how heroic he was, how he's safe wherever he is and that at least he was spared this pain that I'm going through. I'm not sure I ever really tried to separate my grief over Jim's death from my other emotions. I just know that the events that happened after the accident would have been much easier if Jim had been alive, since he was a great supporter and confidante, and he would have been a good, strong hand holder had he been able to be with me.

I feel detached from who I once was and who I am now. My body feels strange to me. It feels strange to be in pain at the kind of consistent level that I have the pain. I'm obviously not as confident a person as I used to be because I don't feel I have the skills or the capabilities that I used to have. I do feel that I'm more in touch with myself. I feel that my emotions are more finely tuned and more on the surface than they used to be. I obviously have an awful lot of time to think about things that I never had time to think about before.

I believe that there is something . . . that put this great Earth together and something that apparently wanted me to live, and I would not say that I was angry at God. There were certainly times that I wondered and was maybe a bit disappointed.

Now I express my anger verbally. I see a psychologist once a week. I'm talking to a lawyer almost on a daily basis. But there's a point at which people shut you off. They don't want to hear because it reminds them of their own vulnerability. We all come to a point at which it doesn't compute anymore. So I go through a combination of denial and expression of my anger, and between the two is frustration. . . .

I was angry that the pilot's code [which drills it into you that you are ultimately responsible for everything that happens in your aircraft] made me feel so guilty, regardless of the facts. Also, that companies do so much damage by manufacturing faulty equipment. The doctors can't deliver what they promised. I had thirty-five surgeries and still am in pain. Our legal system is an unjust system.

I have performed some acts to consciously let go of my anger. I tried to use a punching bag at an athletic club at which I'm a member, but my back just couldn't handle it. I also have found sleep to be an escape mechanism. And I've found TV to be an escape mechanism.

Anger at the Victim

Outrage at the person who died can come from two primary sources: the circumstances that brought on the accident and the accidental killer's own need for separation. "Why should I have to suffer because of his carelessness?" asks a woman whose car was broadsided by a motorcyclist running a red light. "[It was] nice of him to die on me," says another woman, who did not see her victim running across the road at dusk. And a college student whose car struck a truck driver standing in the middle of a blind curve trying to estimate whether his vehicle would fit under a bridge asks, "How could he do something so stupid?"

If the accident's circumstances do not provide a reason, some accidental killers get mad at their victims because of classic conditioning. According to Dr. E. Tory Higgins of Columbia University's Department of Psychology, "This is a normal response—to dislike them . . . for having caused a very negative event."[8] Higgins also notes that people tend to attribute blame defensively and to derogate the victim in order to distance themselves. "What happened is so terrible you fear it could happen to you, and so you make yourself think you are very different from the other person: 'I'm not like that, so what happened to that individual couldn't happen to me,'" he notes.

Anger often is stronger when the accidental killer did not know the victim in life. Without the bonding of memories—shared laughter, conflict, and understanding—the victim remains forever linked to one of the accidental killer's worst life experiences.

Some accidental killers generalize this negative feeling, beginning to dislike anyone who resembles the victim. After her auto—bicycle accident, one accidental killer remembers having intense reactions to children on bicycles. "They were just out there, vulnerable. They could do unpredictable things, and people would suffer," she says.

Some victims clearly bring about their own demise,[9] and some accidental killers resent being used as a weapon of suicide:

> I have driven since the age of thirteen. I'm forty-eight without a single ticket. I've always been proud of my driving record, never have hit an animal, never lose my temper, always excuse the actions of other drivers. I always say, "Relax, you have the rest of your life to drive, so take everything in stride."
>
> He was intoxicated. He was all in black. At first I veered to the right, and then I veered to the left, thinking he was going to proceed. As the car began to skid, he stayed on the hood. I wasn't even going the speed limit.
>
> It has been seventeen months since the accident, and they have two years to file charges, according to law. The state police filed an eight-page report finding no fault because the dead person was drunk and should not have been trying to cross an interstate highway. The police report also stated that I was above average in trying to avoid hitting the person, according to my skid marks and the condition and position of my car. The police said, "Thank God he died instantly." It was better than if he had been left a vegetable.
>
> After the car stopped, the man fell off by the car door. I thought, "Why doesn't he get up and yell at me? If I go out of the car, he's going to get up and hit me."
>
> They say that time heals everything. It was unbearable for weeks to think I took a life, I killed a human. I'm ashamed of what happened.
>
> He had no right to do that to me. He put me through hell.

Another accidental killer recalls:

> Laura and I drove to a ski resort about fifteen minutes from her college to meet some friends for drinks and dancing. We

stayed most of the afternoon. As we went to leave, she did something that has forever stayed with me. In the car as we left the lodge, she kissed me. I asked her why. She said she just wanted to.

Three minutes later, we slid on slick ice and went into a ditch, hitting a tree. Her head went into the windshield, and she was knocked unconscious.

An ambulance came and took her to an emergency room. I rode with her. All the while, she moaned softly. I wished that the ambulance would get into an accident so that I could die, too.

I was charged with failing to have the vehicle under control, fined $15. There were no other legal proceedings.

For a long time, perhaps even now, I have not been sure if she died because I had been drinking that day. Although I was not drunk in terms of the law, I am sure it had an effect. For some months after her death, I was very erratic in my behavior. Although I did manage to complete the spring semester, my social life was abnormal.

I took to carrying a wooden club around with me, both in my car and especially to dances at the college where I had been a student. One evening I had to be asked to leave by the security guard. The college was small enough that all the girls knew of me and of the accident. I'm sure they put up with behavior from me that would have otherwise been unacceptable.

I remember for some period feeling resentment of her because she was so unprepared, so vulnerable to injury because she was sitting sideways on the car seat. When we struck the tree, she had no chance.

Anger at One's Family

Some accidental killers direct their anger at their loved ones to avoid aiming it at themselves. Others are enraged by loved ones who give what the accidental killers consider insufficient responses.

Following an accident that claimed the life of his first son, an accidental killer's rage was so intense that his mother was stirred to write:

Several weeks after the baby's death, I watched my son grow red then blue with fierce wrath. I watched him as he fought to restrain himself from hurting anyone else. It was like twenty Mexican firecrackers exploding inside one body—but contained. He finally walked out of the house and chopped wood. I sat down and wrote this poem:

> When yellow, red, and blue
> infuse my vein
> like thunderbolts
> my sinews leap aflame.
> Each muscle burns
> contracting now
> with pain.
> I struggle to contain
> the searing sparks—
> clenched fists
> clenched teeth
> contorted mouth and brain—
> until my soul is blistered,
> spirit seared.
> The surface flames burnt out,
> I'm calm again.
> I ache to see the radiance of the moon
> unfiltered through the ash and smoke of noon.

The accidental killer himself says:

This was totally unexpected. I was used to good fortune, not tragedy. It brought me down to earth. I thought of a whole lot of things—why me?—and externalized a lot. I verbally rejected my wife and a friend, criticized them for their relationship quite a bit, went out and chopped wood, accused them of deserting me. There were things to be angry about, but not to the extent that I was.

My wife was as supportive as she could possibly be, but I didn't let myself see that. I felt real alone, more alone then than I have ever felt.

Even my folks were far away; they weren't directly abandoning me, but they were distant physically. What hurt the most was the sense of being by myself in this whole thing, and Jacob's being gone was a large part of it.

He was my first son and my favorite. Just his being gone was so bad, but there wasn't anything I could do about that, so what I did do was lay into Shauna [my wife] and her friend. I focused a lot on that, and I think it was to take a lot of heat off myself and my own involvement in Jacob's death.

Jacob and I spent a lot of time together. I wasn't an absentee parent with him like fathers can be. I'd drop anything to spend time with Jacob. I'd feel a lot worse if I hadn't had time for him.

The day of the accident, I had just bought a motorcycle, and we went down to pick it up. Shauna drove the car home, and I took the bike. On the way, we stopped at an air-conditioned restaurant to take a little break. It was really hot, and Jacob drank his favorite drink, a chocolate shake. That turned out to be his last one.

When we got back, Shauna took the baby into the house, and I unloaded the trunk. When I got through, I noticed Jacob standing by a willow tree in the front yard. I got into the car to park it, pulled back, and started to pull forward into the parking space. In the meantime, Jacob had evidently run and sat down on the driveway beneath my line of vision. I felt a bump, and I hit the brakes. It was a horrible feeling.

I pulled Jacob from beneath the car, carried him into the house, and laid him on the kitchen floor. He had a broken arm, and he was slipping in and out of consciousness. He still had it together enough to look up at me at one point and say, "I've got to get out of this."

Within ten minutes, the ambulance was there, and I rode along with Jacob. I could tell that Jacob knew I was there. I was real upset. I couldn't go in the emergency room with him, but he wasn't there long. It was just a few minutes after they took him in that they came out and said he'd died.

I had friends with me there. Shauna and this man that she was friendly with and other people were there, too, and we all gathered around and hugged one another. Prayed. We buried him on our own mountain property with a service that we and friends created and carried out. This was a tremendous help to me.

I was not mad at myself but at life, fate, or the way people were reacting. I suspect I was dealing with a lot of guilt in myself. I personally was involved with my son's death. If it hadn't been for me, it wouldn't have happened. I was definitely a catalyst in the death of my son. And I still don't like the fact that I had something to do with it. Not that I know what I could have done about it. My anger was focused all away from myself. My anger was focused on other people.

It seems that when Jacob was killed, Shauna needed more support than I could give her. I was sort of incapacitated myself, and she turned to Robert knowing that we had an open relationship. I asked her not to do that. I told her I didn't think I could handle the stress of that at that time, but she wasn't up for renegotiating just then. Later she was, but not then. And that's where I began to feel some abandonment personally— not just some, a whole lot. . . .

Robert tried to extend himself to me, but he couldn't, and I wouldn't let him. He was a whole lot more of a friend to Shauna than he was to me at that point.

I kind of went crazy on our property up in the country. Twice this happened. I just got fixated on what was going on and these two people in my life, and I would go out and find a bunch of boulders and just throw them. Big rocks, maybe a foot across. I would throw them and yell and curse. I would do a violent thing. I would just fantasize that it was his body there on the chopping block, and I would just chop wood and pretend it was him. I'm not exactly very proud about that.

Another time I came in the house and turned the whole house upside down. I turned over furniture and threw things. I came into the house and found these folks on the couch, Shauna and her friend, sitting close together, and just turned the couch over right on top of them, and continued through the house and turned everything else over, too. Devastated the place. I can remember being a little careful, but not much. I just let out every bit of violence that I was feeling. . . .

There were quite a few incidents like that, particularly the first year after Jacob died. . . .

There was another time I moved out . . . intending to start over again. Shauna came and talked me into coming home. In my own figurative way, I really killed more people. It was at least four years before I reconciled my feelings. . . . It isn't even real clear to me how I worked out of that.

Anger at the Victim's Family

Fatal accidents often generate lawsuits. Accidental killers who feel no culpability are insulted by such claims and by what they view as a mercenary attitude on the part of the family to capitalize on the death of a loved one. "If it was me, I couldn't enjoy the trip around the world or the new car or the new house knowing where the money came from," one accidental killer says.

A registered nurse voices her outrage:

My husband hadn't wanted me to go to the store, and my mother hadn't wanted the kids to come along, but we all piled in anyway—me, mother, and the two girls.

We were coming home from the store, barely a quarter of a mile from the house. Two teenage girls were riding on the right side of the road, side by side, on bicycles. They were playing tag.

I pulled to the left to give them plenty of room; no one was coming from the other direction. They just had almost hit an elderly couple.

Then, suddenly, one of the girls pulled directly in front of me. I slammed on the brakes and pulled nearly off the left-hand side of the road, but she still ran into the right front bumper of my car.

She and the bike flipped, causing her to hit the back of her head on the road, causing a depressed fracture at the base of the skull. This caused the skull to sever the brain stem. There's nothing you can do about a smack on the back of the head. She was unconscious, but she looked okay except for a scraped knee and a bump on the forehead. Her friend screamed at the girl, "Why did you do such a dumb thing?"

I got out, thinking she wasn't badly hurt . . . only to find her not breathing. I started mouth-to-mouth resuscitation—her heart rate was okay—and continued it for over fifteen minutes. No one stopped for a long time or called an ambulance. I was yelling between breaths for someone to call one. I could hear my younger daughter asking why the girl didn't get up. It seemed like hours until the ambulance arrived. Her body started going into spasms.

There was only one attendant, so they asked me to come in the ambulance and help, which I did. Just before we got to the hospital, she arrested. We did CPR, and her heart and respiration returned. However, forty-five minutes later, she died.

Her mother came into the emergency room, and I could hear her screaming the girl's name, which happens to be the same as mine—"Carol, Carol, Carol"—over and over again. Then she came up to me and said, "I know that God is going to take care of my daughter." I wanted to scream at her that her daughter was already dead, because I knew by that time.

The first week I was in shock. I couldn't believe I had killed someone, my fault or not. It reassured me when people told me it wasn't my fault, but it also made me angry. I was full of grief and disbelief. I knew in my heart I'd done nothing wrong, but I was heartsick. I remember thinking I'd scream if one more person said, "At least it wasn't your fault." It didn't make any difference whose fault it was. The child was dead.

One week after the accident, my four-year-old son came down with encephalitis, and I was pulled out of shock as I sat by his bedside watching him tremor. My grief had shifted to fear that I would lose my own son. For weeks I had daytime nightmares, reliving the accident time after time. I couldn't shut my mind off. I slept poorly and little. I was on Librium for a while.

I had nightmares for months. There were always disfigured

bodies much worse than in the accident. I avoided the road of the accident, as it always caused me to relive the whole thing. It was the main road from our house to town, so I went out of my way for months just to avoid it.

When we moved away a year later, I felt I had left it behind me, no more nightmares of driving down that road. Then, this last August, I received notice that the family was suing for loss of income and medical expenses. I was crushed. I had worked so hard to save their daughter. The police told them how I had worked on her despite my shock, and they had expressed their appreciation through their priest at the time of the accident. At first I was heartsick and then angry. Their attorney came out and took an affidavit; he went back and told them they had no chance. My anger has cooled by now, and my grief has been made much less because of their attitude.

An eighteen-year-old accidental killer says:

I would break out in a cold sweat and find myself overcome by trembling of the hands—and still sometimes do—when the subject was mentioned. I was much calmer before this ordeal.

I was tired of people telling me that it wasn't my fault and I shouldn't feel guilty. It wasn't all guilt I was feeling. I had a strange feeling of outrage at that old man, knowing that he was dressed in dark clothing. And it was obvious that he didn't walk well, since he carried a cane. He shouldn't have been crossing a busy highway after dusk.

I was shocked when the family decided to sue. They shouldn't have let him out there. A few times, I have found myself driving by their house as if I'm looking for revenge.

I have gotten extremely upset when people have asked me whether I had been drinking or not. I was totally sober and level-headed at the time.

People would also imagine without knowing the full story that I ran down a defenseless old man in cold blood. People have also tried to joke about it with me in a sick way.

Fortunately, the anger of accidental killing tends to wane with the passage of time. But until accidental killers are able to release their anger and forgive the offender, be it themselves or someone else, resentment will hold them back.

Anger turned inward is guilt, an even more difficult problem to solve, as it pits the two halves of the accidental killer against each other: the one that acts versus the one that watches.

4

Guilt

I was nineteen years old, had a job at a title insurance office, a '66 used Impala and a fiancé in Vietnam. And of all days, my "accident" occurred on Christmas Eve, 1970. Holidays are still hard for me.

Our office has a luncheon at a local restaurant for all of the employees and closes at noon. At about 4:00 P.M., I was on my way home. All of a sudden, upon coming around a corner and starting up a hill, my car straining to make it, my life changes. I was in the inside lane and traffic was terrible. The outside lane was stopped. All of a sudden I heard a "thump" and noticed something blonde at my right front fender. I hit the brakes, stopped the car, and ran around to the other side where I immediately fainted. I had not been drinking.

The next thing I knew a nice man was helping me up, and I noticed a child lying in the street. I returned to the car and got a blanket from my car to cover her up. I looked up and there was my dad. How he made the ten-mile trip so fast I didn't know and I didn't really care. Finally my dad and the officers came to tell me what had happened. The girl lived across the street and had been playing with her brother and friends. A car in the outside lane had stopped to let out a friend and the driver was chatting (under a "No Parking" sign). The child thought traffic had stopped to let her cross the street, so she ran out between two stopped cars and into my car. Ironically, my dad even knew the driver of the stopped car and at one point was so angry he would have hit the man if the officer hadn't stopped him. The officers said they had about twenty witnesses so they cited the driver of the parked car for parking in a no-parking zone and causing a fatality.

When I got home my mother yelled and screamed that the people would sue and they would lose everything and how stupid I was. I sought refuge in my basement bedroom. I locked the door and cried for three hours.

My dad had left. When he came home I found out that the girl had died of suffocation. She had been eating an apple. When she ran into my car, it lodged in her throat. There were some internal injuries, but she might have survived if she had not been eating.

Six months later my dad died of a sudden heart attack. To this day I feel that was my punishment for what I had done. I found out a few years later that the little girl's brother had been one block down at the crosswalk and was unable to speak for several years after seeing his sister killed. The child's mother called several times during the next couple of years to ask my mother how I was doing.

To complete the story, it was the first fatality in my state for the holiday season. One aunt and uncle on their way to town heard about it on the radio. They, along with other relatives, began calling constantly. I watched the accident replay on the news reports for what seemed to be a million times. This tragedy made the front page headlines. I couldn't face my family, friends, or job. I had an awful time writing my fiancé and telling him I was a murderer. Even today I still have a terrible feeling driving up that street—it is a main road in town. I have never driven up it on Christmas Eve since 1970. I still cry to think about it, and now I'm married with a seven-year-old daughter and a three-year-old son.

When I went back to work, it took all I could muster to walk in that door. I remember my boss approaching my desk first thing in the morning. He asked me to come into his office. I just knew I was going to be fired. Instead, he offered his condolences and asked how he could help.

Nothing has ever changed my feeling that I murdered a

seven-year-old child and ruined a family. I still feel guilt and pain, and I wish there would have been someone to share this with who knew and understood my feelings. If I went into my feelings totally I would have to have this delivered by a truck.

In his treatise *On Guilt, Responsibility and Punishment,* philosopher Alf Ross theoretically absolves the accidental killer of guilt, but theory does not change what people feel. He defines guilt as "to have brought oneself, by a transgression, into the situation where one must expect to be greeted with ill will and reproach, inward-directed anger."[1] By its very nature, an accident implies the interaction of forces beyond the accidental killer's control. In Ross's view, because there was no transgression, the accidental killer is exempt from guilt:

> The killing may be due to an unfortunate accident, say, a stray bullet on a shoot. The act itself is undesirable, but here there are circumstances in the mental contexts which excuse it. Its perpetrator in the supposed case intended no evil and has not acted in a thoughtless manner. In these circumstances we do not impute the killing to the man who fired the shot. We excuse him, which is to say precisely that we do not accuse him of the deed, do not hold him guilty of it.[2]

As irrational as it may seem to others, most accidental killers hold themselves directly or indirectly responsible for the victim's death and have much difficulty forgiving themselves. There are few guidelines for them to follow. The legal definition of the term *accident* may or may not imply human fault depending on its interpretation. But the judges who deliver the punishment of guilt for an accidental death do not sit on any bench. They hold court inside the head of the guilt-feeling person. "There are still difficult times when I regress into the past and remember the incident and damn myself and pray for forgiveness," explains an accidental killer. Since guilt is self-referential, sensitive persons often experience it without justification, while others who should feel guilty do not. Ignoring objective reality, many accidental killers apply much higher standards to themselves than they would to others. The process is often unconscious, resulting in feelings of low self-esteem or depression. Ross elaborates on this propensity for undeserved guilt:

There is nothing to prevent a man being guilty without having any feelings of guilt; or conversely, not being guilty in spite of having guilty feelings. The former is true of many psychopaths, the latter of people with a neurotic obsession with guilt.

The intensity of the feeling of guilt and the way of alleviating it also varies with different types of personality. There are men of an introverted, brooding type who not only experience guilt as the worst kind of pain—sorrow of heart and vexation of spirit, as Isaiah said—but also consider it their constant duty to keep this feeling alive. A person of this type will not only be tortured by the special pain of guilt actually incurred; his painful broodings will, perhaps in most cases, relate to purely imaginary guilt. Where, say, he has been the cause of some accident but without being guilty of causing it—it was sheer mischance—he will continue to speculate over what he might have done to avoid it, and be unable to stop accusing himself, thinking over the possibilities, judging himself guilty. Perhaps a child ran suddenly into the road from behind a parked vehicle, so that he, the driver, ran over and killed him. If he has driven with all due care, he is not guilty according to the general view which is also that which he would apply to others. A normal man will accept the same judgment as to his own act. He will be distressed over what has happened, distressed that he was a pawn in the complex play of events that led to the unforeseeable accident.

But the man obsessed with guilt cannot be content with this. In imagination he will go over a whole range of "ifs" which might have prevented the accident. If he had left home a little earlier, if he had driven a little more slowly, if he had braked a little sooner, and so on. And despite all the rational arguments against it, he will be unable to rid himself of the feeling that, in spite of everything, he is guilty. It may end in him taking his own life.[3]

The Cultural Roots of Unfounded Guilt

Ross's description of a person suffering from guilt fits many accidental killers who would never consider themselves "the brooding type" or "neurotically obsessed by guilt." It is not enough to have lacked malicious intent; many blame themselves for not having seen the accident coming and prevented it.

Why is there such a preponderance of seemingly unjustified guilt? One may only speculate about the effect of the Christian religion on guilt formation, even among those not directly trained by the church. Partial responsibility may lie with the stance taken by much of organized religion that emphasizes legalism while ignoring Christ's message of loving liberation from exploitation of all kinds—but especially that of the law. Guilt is a natural by-product of Western society, which has high ideals that are often understood to be unattainable. New York psychologist Dr. Stanley Rustin states:

> If for years I've told myself "thou shalt not kill" even in an accident and I incorporate that, the religious setting will affect me. If, conversely, the person incorporates other values, such as fate, he doesn't feel fettered through religious experience. The person with that set of values would say, "It's unfortunate, but that was that person's fate to die. He shouldn't have gotten out of bed that day."[4]

Guilt-ridden value systems are hardly confined to churches. Guilt-inducing methods of child rearing and the use of guilt as the primary means of social control throughout life are dominant features of U.S. culture. Early on, the vast majority of children are stripped of their right to be valued inherently; instead their value lies in what they can buy back through obedience to systematic injustice. Industrialization played a role because it helped to develop people's feelings of mastery over nature, which prompted them to delegate any mishap to an identifiable error. Not all cultures hold this worldview so strictly. For example, the Spanish language does not allow for the assumption of guilt without one's conscious intent. Instead of "I lost the pen," for example, someone speaking Spanish would say, "The pen lost itself to me."

Many accidental killers' need to punish themselves is so strong that they beat up on themselves emotionally for what seem to others to be small details. One accidental killer notes:

> I got the feeling, because I had known LeeAnn for only a few months and her coworkers had known her for years, that they couldn't see why I should have such a hard time dealing with her death.

The accident was an unusual occurrence. LeeAnn's car was hit broadside by a man in a high-speed chase running from the police. The man was coming from out of town, then decided he could lose the trail of the police if he turned and came into town. The police had set up a roadblock on West Avenue, the route LeeAnn was taking home. A policeman had LeeAnn move off to the side behind the roadblock—to be kept safe. As it was, the fleeing man attempted to fool the police and did not try and go through the middle of the roadblock. Instead he tried to go around it, thus hitting LeeAnn. She died four hours later.

That evening she was supposed to come to my house for coffee. I was not there when she arrived, so she went on home. I kept saying, "If I'd been there, her timing would have been different." The man who killed her was charged not only with auto theft and running from the police but also with manslaughter.

When I first heard of the accident, I was shocked and full of disbelief. When I got to work that day, I called my friend's place of employment to confirm the news report. When her coworkers told me my friend had indeed been killed, . . . I still found it hard to believe. The only other person in my life that I knew closely to die was my grandfather—when I was six years old. As I began accepting reality, I was overcome by guilt.

In a matter of hours, I was rebuking myself for not keeping the date with her the night before. I could not get hold of her to tell her of the change. My mind kept repeating "if only" phrases. Intellectually I knew "if onlys" would not change life and that fate had taken its course, but emotionally I was making myself suffer. It took about three months before I quit thinking of her on a frequent basis.

I only knew her about ten months, so perhaps that is why. I sent flowers to her home, but no one acknowledged them, not until I ran into her coworker in October and she said thank you. Perhaps that is why I quit thinking of her so much—the two incidents happened in the same month—acknowledgement and forgetting.

Since October I think of her occasionally. The "if onlys" have subsided, though I still tend to believe that if some part of that twenty-four-hour period could have been changed, she might have avoided the time of her accident.

Another woman feels guilty for a similar twist of fate in an accident that killed her friend: "I was the passenger. Lisa was crossing a large, busy intersection on a green light when she was struck on the driver's side by a truck running a red traffic light. My guilt came by the fact that I should have driven but had a last minute change of plans."

Guilt's Impact

There is no way to overemphasize the effect of guilt on a person's life. The elimination of guilt is the goal of most psychoanalysis. Psychotherapists refer to it as the essential obstacle to human progress and development, the number one blockage to growth. One accidental killer puts it like this: "I believe guilt, not so much death, is what makes the accident so hard for those left behind." It is abundantly clear that it is primarily the amount of guilt a person feels that determines the accident's impact. If guilt is heavy, the accident is a major problem. If it is absent or minimal, the person recovers quickly, though grief and sadness may be temporarily severe.

As stated earlier, most people feel guilty only if the system of rules they break is one in which they themselves believe. In calm consideration, the truly guilty feel just as much astonishment and indignation toward themselves as they would toward anyone else who had committed the same act. But for some accidental killers, guilt works its way backward from the accident. They feel as though they must have done something wrong because tragedies like theirs should not happen unprovoked if the world is to be trusted.

The emotions guilt brings are difficult to live with for any length of time. Among these are feeling unworthy, defective, unlovable, full of contempt, paranoid, and angry. The person also may suffer from one of several eating disturbances. What else but guilt drives murderers to confess voluntarily? Sophocles wrote in *Oedipus Rex:* "The greatest griefs are those we cause ourselves."[5] The captain of the *Andrea Doria,* an ocean liner that sank, killing sixteen, was said to be plagued by guilt for years after the calamity, severely criticizing himself for having made wrong decisions. Similarly, in Arthur Hailey's *Airport,* an air traffic controller cannot forgive himself for taking too long on a bathroom break during which a subordinate causes a midair collision. The controller is continually haunted by the scream of a little girl that came over the radio seconds before impact.[6]

Different Reactions to Guilt Feelings

As with every other aspect of accidental killing, each person reacts differently to guilt. Guilt consciousness seems partly to be a matter of how far people see their responsibility extending. Those accustomed to working their will on the world tend to have a harder time excusing themselves for accidents than those with more modest self-expectations. It is as if powerful people are accustomed to taking credit for success and so also take the blame. A propensity toward guilt also may indicate high moral standards. The decent, conscientious person suffers the most. Indeed, strong guilt reactions could be seen as a profound reverence for humanity, a cherishing respect for life.

Some accidental killers see their victims as very different from themselves and dehumanize them along racial, sexual, and class lines to the point where the death does not consciously bother them. Guilt rests heavily on the subjective values of the perpetrator, as two accounts show. Both focus on the accident's cost to them—a lawsuit, a jail sentence, and a spurning lover.

The first accidental killer says:

> I like to trade cars—buy them old, fix them up, and sell them. That day I'd bought this old pickup, and I didn't have time to change the tires before I had to rush out to work. The two back tires were slick, and I had bought two new ones, which were in the back. On the way home, about 12:30 A.M., I had a blowout and sideswiped another car. And the gal who died happened to be my cousin's former girlfriend. She had just left a bar with somebody she'd met that night.
>
> There was a lawsuit, and I was convicted of second-degree manslaughter. But I never served any time. What was awful was the civil suit. They wanted $150,000. My wife and I had four kids. I knew this could wipe me out financially. It went on for fourteen months before the hearings were over. I started

drinking my wife's nerve medicine by the bottle. One time I stopped the car and almost jumped off a bridge. Luckily, my wife grabbed me and pulled me back. I just knew I was done for financially. The pressure was intense. The insurance paid the settlement, but the legal fees wiped me out. I moved away from that area as soon as it was all finally over.

A young policeman speaks:

In my job, I know I could do it (kill someone) consciously if I had to and not care, but not accidentally. I was on duty in a city patrol car. I had recently (about two months before) broken off a live-in relationship that I had with someone I really cared about. She was a clerk in the police department, and she started dating . . . the other officers. This was on Father's Day. I started my shift at 4 P.M. About 7:30, I heard a rumor about her and another officer. Being the skeptical kind, I drove by his house and saw them together. I will say what most men find impossible—that I am sensitive and I care. I take relationships and promises very seriously. I was deeply hurt and began to cry—not your typical macho type.

Just at that time, I got a radio call to respond to an active fight a mile away. While crossing a large intersection, going a little too fast and not thinking clearly and crying, I hit a drunk driving a small pickup who turned left in front of me. I hit him broadside, the passenger side, almost full speed.

The passenger near the door was injured. The driver was in critical condition for two weeks, but the person in the middle died—system failure, possibly due to a head injury. I guess the most important thing was that I was in the middle of a very traumatic crisis when this accident happened.

So far the legal outcomes are resolved. My friends were good for the "don't worry about it" pep talks, good (sic) to make jokes about it. They also point out the bad qualities of the person who died.

A certain girl (we had been separated for three months) dropped by to say she was sorry. This made me very angry. She spent a lot of energy rubbing it in that I killed someone just because I was upset when she left. I think by now I've kind of blocked it out.

In contrast, other accidental killers are absorbed by the question of whether there is anything to feel guilty about, whether the accident was avoidable. These people devote a lot of energy to examining the circumstances of the accident. One reports:

It was a car wreck—two cars and an extra-wide trailer. I was driving my car and attempted to pass the trailer. At the same time, the trailer pulled well over the line and didn't leave enough room to complete the pass. I applied the brakes and attempted to fall behind. When I did this, I slid off the road into a ditch and into a car on a crossroad which had stopped to fix a flat tire. The five occupants were standing outside the car, and my car struck them. They were kids. They flew like dolls off the front of my car.

That was thirteen years ago. I went through three years of very difficult times immediately after the accident. There was a lawsuit which would be set up and delayed repeatedly. Then there was the terrible guilt of having driven a car that killed one person and injured three others. I also felt such remorse. I empathized with the parents of these young people, as I have five children of my own. I also felt pain when my children's friends found out about the accident. Several said, "Your mother killed someone." This caused considerable anxiety.

I still relive this procedure and second-guess what I should have done or not done to avoid the accident. I was taking someone to a county seat of business, and I repeatedly admonish myself for even offering my car. I have doubts about my role in the accident—could it have been from poor judgment on my part versus the fact that it was a freak accident.

This close scrutiny seems to come out of an empathic response, the trait that defines moral behavior. Psychologist Stanley Rustin characterizes highly empathic people:

I would think the people who are shocked by being responsible for the death of someone else are people who, for the most part, are very caught up with the humanistic concerns, maybe more artistically inclined. And we can see this in what I call the "feral children" in the city of New York. I worked with these kids for a couple of years. They don't have the capacity of empathy or compassion. So if they rip somebody off, they mug somebody, and they inadvertently kill that person—and you see it all the time on the eleven o'clock news— somebody is arrested for committing a murder . . . they look very calm, composed: What's the big deal? Those people who are shocked, who are traumatized, are people, I think, who have the ability to put themselves in the other person's place or [that of] the person's survivors—the widow, the widower, the children. They say, "My God, I'm responsible for leaving three kids without a father." I would definitely call empathy a healthy trait.[7]

An empathic accidental killer remembers:

I really thought it wouldn't bother me to think about the accident in detail again, but it did. I began to have nightmares. I cried and cried and was depressed for about a week. I almost threw this questionnaire away. That's one reason why I'm getting in touch so late—I couldn't face reliving that experience again.

I was involved in an auto–pedestrian accident. The accident occurred about 11 P.M. after we had been to a party. The two people with me had been drinking, but I had not been. I was mad at them because I couldn't drink at the party, since I knew I had to drive home. We were driving in the skid row part of town when a little man ran out in front of the car.

It was dark, he was wearing dark clothes, and he was in the middle of the block. His name was Danny. I don't know if it was determined if he had been drinking that night, but he was given a ticket for jaywalking. He suffered a broken hip. He died three days later of pneumonia. I knew Danny was going to die, although everyone told me he was all right.

I was angry with the police for being so nice to me. I thought they should have taken care of Danny. I was in shock, and the police called for an ambulance for me. I flipped out; I thought the ambulance was empty because they came back to tell the police Danny had died. I refused to go to the hospital because I didn't want to be there listening to him dying.

My friend who was with me the night of the accident came down the next morning and called the hospital. I sat on the floor of the bathroom with all the water running. I didn't want to hear her cry out when she learned he had died. He hadn't died.

Going to visit him was the hardest thing I have ever done. Diane and I were sobbing so hard. Diane is the friend who was with me. I wondered if he heard what I was saying. He kept saying over and over again, "Don't cry lady; it wasn't your fault." That didn't really help then, but it has in later years.

There were numerous things that happened that helped. The wife of one of the policemen investigating the accident was an old high school friend. She told me a lot of stuff the police had said. One of my customers was a doctor. He read the autopsy report and told me all the things wrong with Danny. He said he could have been hit by a bike and died.

When I wanted to visit Danny in the hospital and to explain what happened, friends told me to stay away, that by going to the hospital, I was leaving myself open for a lawsuit. When I feel bad, I remember Danny telling me not to cry, that it wasn't my fault.

A teenage farm worker discusses his guilt feelings for letting a friend die of a heart attack:

At the time, I was working for the gentleman who passed away. He was a farm laborer. On the particular day of his death, a coworker and I were unloading hay bales off a trailer into a bin where he was stacking them. All at once, he said he needed a rest, but before he could sit down, he collapsed on the floor. Not knowing that he had suffered a heart attack, I called the closest neighbor, and when he arrived, I called the rescue unit. I realized later that I should have immediately called for an ambulance. Within a few hours, I learned this man had died. The shock of this didn't really stick for approximately three hours. I was overwhelmed by a sense of disbelief. He always seemed to be a healthy man—a bit overweight but not sickly or near death.

I was with a coworker. I described the incident shortly after I first heard that he had died. He too was shocked. So we talked to a member of the rescue squad. He indicated that the two of us did all we possibly could, adding that only a few months earlier, members of his squad could have done little more than we did. We were both fifteen at the time. The squad had only recently participated in a CPR course, so they just learned how to handle a similar case.

I talked with an attending nurse, who also said we did all we could. Even a brother to the man who passed away told me he appreciated all we had done. Still, I felt I should have known what to do, even if it appeared my ignorance was shared by most everyone in the general population.

I felt guilty for a time, but support from relatives and this man's doctor soon helped me return to the state of mind I had maintained before he passed away. Within a matter of a few weeks, I'd say, I was pretty much as happy as before the accident. I accepted his death as something I was unable to prevent, considering what I knew at the time, and I knew it wouldn't help me to worry anymore.

The Guiltless

As prominent as guilt is for many, certain circumstances and sensibilities can preclude it. A man who rated his unavoidable accident fourth on his crisis scale after a personal injury, marital unfaithfulness, and the death of a parent when he was age forty-three reports:

I felt no guilt. I was driving on a blacktop narrow road at night. It was very dark. It had been raining. The road had many hills and curves. There was a car behind me, tailgating, trying to pass. His bright lights were reflecting all over my car. I came over a slight rise in the road and immediately in front of me was a figure prone in the road, crossways to the car. I had only a split second to react. Fearing that my wheels would crush his head, I elected to try to straddle him, left wheels to the left of his head, right wheels over his legs. The underbody of the car did not clear him, and he sustained injuries that caused his death days later. I later found out he was a farm boy who had left a tavern highly intoxicated and presumably had passed out in the middle of the road. This upset me for a while, but I recovered rather quickly.

A man whose accident happened fifty years earlier while working as a bicycle messenger expresses a similar feeling:

> I was riding, carrying a heavy, fifty-pound load, and was in a hurry. I entered an intersection with a green light. I was riding close to the curb. Immediately upon reaching the opposite sidewalk this elderly man stepped into my handlebars. We both sprawled into the street. The police came. He said it wasn't my fault. The man was taken to the hospital, I assume, and I was taken to the police station. Because my accident was followed by an immediate assurance that I was not to blame for the death, I was able to set the incident aside and live a normal life.

Accidents can be very disturbing even when guilt is not consciously acknowledged. One accidental killer states:

> I was driving home from my work as owner/manager of a drive-in theater. I was approximately three miles outside of town. The evening was dark, and I was proceeding probably about forty-five or fifty miles per hour at a legal rate of speed. All of a sudden, my lights picked up a dark outline immediately in front of me—then a face turned and looked at me. The impact immediately followed. He was a male, probably about thirty years of age. The impact tossed his body approximately seventy-five to eighty feet. Death was instantaneous.
>
> The accident took place in 1956. . . . I was so shaken that I was unable to walk down and look at the body. Two nurses happened to be driving just behind me, and they went and examined the young man and then came back and reported their findings to me. . . .
>
> He had been wearing very dark clothes and undoubtedly was drunk and had fallen down in the middle of the highway. I was unable to see him until just immediately prior to the incident,

when he apparently stood up in my lane of traffic. I was completely exonerated. . . .

The immediate aftermath was traumatic. I had no particular feeling of guilt, as I was found to be blameless. However, I was strongly affected emotionally by the fact that I had been responsible for the death of this [man]. It was probably about three months before I could concentrate fully on my regular and routine daily affairs without constant haunting thoughts of the accident. To this day, I probably will have a dream about once a year. In it I generally see the person turning and looking at me just at the moment of impact. Fortunately, the human mind has an ability to repress unpleasant memories of this nature.

Guilt-Producing Consequences

Some guilt develops from the accident's effects on the victim's family. One accidental killer explains this type of guilt:

A logging accident happened on July 27, 1959, in which my brother-in-law was killed. Early on a Monday morning while I was running the yarder and he and another man were setting the chokers, an empty choker hit him in the head. He never regained consciousness.

I was the one running the yarder, a machine that has drums and cables on it. One line hauls the chokers back and the other forward. Signals are sent by radio with a beep sound, so many beeps for stop, go, and so on. The choke setters are perhaps up to eight hundred to a thousand feet away, so a person can't see them. I heard the sound of the beep to stop, but the accident had already happened.

After carrying him out of the brush up a steep hill using a stretcher, the ambulance attendants took him to the hospital, so everything was taken care of in the emergency line. The crew and I then went home. We didn't go back to work for a week, during which time the funeral was held.

I felt guilty because I thought that perhaps I should have let someone run the yarder besides myself. People indicated that inexperience was the cause. Also, a movie the church showed about accidents and their causes didn't help. Many people said that I didn't have enough experience to do the job, as I'd only worked five months for this operation before the accident happened. I never did go back to work for the outfit. In the first place, my wife didn't want me to work in the woods—she was against it 100 percent. I really felt I should go back and try to do the best I could. But my wife was pregnant with only five months to go, so I decided against it. In the meantime, I thought we should have moved to a different location. Jobs were hard to find. I've worked the past sixteen years as a tire mechanic.

The property that my brother-in-law owned was all in his name—no will and five children. The court took over the operation of the business and property. Most people wanted his widow to sell the logging business, but some encouraged her to keep on, which proved to be a disaster. All the children were minors, so until they came of age, the court controlled the property and equipment. Finally, part of the property had to be sold to pay off debts that had developed over the years. Meanwhile, the five children divided the property. The outcome doesn't look good at this time.

We live only a few yards apart. In fact, our property and theirs join. It's hard to visit or drive past and see how things have gone downhill. I think to move to another community would help in my case. Since I haven't tried it, I don't know if it would do any good. When people marry and have children, they should provide a will. Probably it would be better not to work for a relative.

Guilt for Indirect Responsibility

There is no need for an accidental killer to be present at the scene. For example, a bartender may allow a customer who has had too much to drink to drive home. By extension, the owner of the establishment and the liquor manufacturer also could be considered to have contributed to the accident. Even though these distant connections often go unnoticed, some people feel guilty about deaths that occur as a result of their involvement somewhere along the line.

One example is police officers who kill in the line of duty. In such cases, officers are acquitted by grand juries 90 percent of the time. Police departments across the country insist that they have the right to discipline their own officers and generally have been successful in resisting oversight by the courts. Often, however, the punishment for physical abuse or murder of a civilian is much less than that for tardiness or insubordination.[8] In such a context, fatal accidents can gnaw at the consciences of those involved even if they receive official exoneration.

Doctors comprise another profession with largely hidden guilt. Physicians who malpractice whether from failing skill, overwork, failure to pay attention or any other reason are rarely censured by their peers. In the six years between 1970–75, for example, only eight physicians in the United States were disciplined.[9] Professional denial is immense. Only one article in *Cumulated Index Medicus* (1976 to 1983) under the heading malpractice acknowledges the possibility of personal guilt feelings, or any feelings at all, on the part of the practitioner. It lists guilt along with anxiety and fear of financial ruin as potential problems.[10] The remaining several hundred articles discuss ways to avoid malpractice suits.

Businesspersons can suffer guilt over workers' deaths on the job. Safety consultant James Mallory says that one company's board of directors "cried like babies" when a defective metal shackler about which he had warned them jettisoned a fifty-pound piece of metal into a worker's chest. He also recalls arguing with a company president about a ditch that needed shoring up. Soon thereafter, the sides caved in, drowning two workers in sewage. Although the president was defensive when speaking with the consultant, the man's brother confided that the accident "was killing" him. Mallory says that his only recourse when faced with a recalcitrant administration is to report the company and get its insurance canceled. "I've gone through sleepless nights myself wondering if I could have prevented deaths," he admits.[11]

Responsibility for some accidental deaths is hard to trace. For example, who is responsible for the fact that the U.S. death rate by fire and explosion among blacks is the highest in the world?[12] If freezing apartment buildings that force inhabitants to warm themselves by any means necessary can indeed be seen as operant variables, who is to blame? Contractors who construct shoddy housing? Government officials who look the other way? Elites who keep wages low? All may be considered guilty of contributing to dangerous situations.

Direct Guilt

Although guilt may be theoretical and vague in some accidents, often it is easy to trace. Improper driving, for example, is a factor in 90 percent of all auto wrecks, and faulty maintenance figures into the other 10 percent.[13] Mistakes that cost lives can be extremely hard to admit. One accidental killer reports:

To start with, it has been nine and a half years since the accident, and I find it difficult now to honestly relate what some of my true feelings were, although there are some that time cannot erase. I would have to put guilt feelings at the top of the list and then remorse.

At that time, I thought I could handle those feelings by drinking and using narcotics, but I just sank into an even deeper depression. I could not admit it at the time, but I was an addict and an alcoholic way before the accident occurred. In fact, I had just stopped at a bar one block away from where it happened to get a six-pack of beer. I also had codeine with me at that time, but lucky for me, I didn't have enough time to drink any beer or take any codeine before it happened.

This happened on Mother's Day, and the woman I hit was a mother, so on that day every year, I tend to think about the "what ifs," although I realize that doesn't bring a life back. I deeply regretted this woman's death and what her family had to go through.

I was on my way to take my mother her present. I saw a couple standing in the median of a four-lane highway, then the woman ran into the traffic to get across. I hit the brakes and swerved to the right-hand lane, but to no avail. She died the next day.

I retained a lawyer as soon as I learned that she died, and he said I could be charged for involuntary manslaughter. The following day we went to court, and I was found guilty of a basic rules violation. The judge fined me $100 plus costs, but he did not read the full report to see that there was a death involved in the car–pedestrian accident. He had already sentenced me, so he could not add any other charges. The legal part was over. I felt guilty mostly because I was driving faster than I should have been.

Until guilt is resolved, its intensity rarely fades. An accidental killer elaborates on his unresolved guilt:

I killed a young student who was getting off a public school bus which I was driving. I was trying to be "cute" and brush him with the left front fender. The left rear wheel passed over the boy. He was a young, good-looking blond kid, about thirteen. I got out of the bus and ran around when I felt the bump. The blood was spurting out of him like a fountain. There was no ambulance. After the police came, I continued with my route.

At this time, I was either age fifteen or sixteen, a junior in high school in a small town with a population of about three thousand. The high school class had twenty-eight graduating seniors. I am now age fifty-two. I was a descendant of an old southern family in this community. They were in the [Ku Klux] Klan for years. It was during World War II. That's why I had a driver's license at age fifteen. The matter was covered up as things are in a small community with people of some standing. At times I felt very bad about this, but I tried to push it out of my mind as much as possible.

It was a hellish ordeal. I had, at age fourteen, received the second highest Boy Scout award for heroism for saving a companion from drowning. I was what would be called a "good boy"—I had never stolen or taken advantage of girls, was elected most popular in the high school class (after the accident), etc. My regional scoutmaster came to see me after the accident. He said, "Bud, you saved one life and you lost one, so now you're even by the board." This made no sense at all, that since I had saved one person's life, I was entitled to take another's. I had refused the $2,000 scholarship that went along with the scout prize because I thought I had just done what anyone should do, like if a lady drops her purse, you pick it up.

I do not recall any hostility at all toward the victim—the

hostility was against me—why did it happen to me? I was not an evil wrongdoer. What was particularly difficult was that it occurred during the teenage period. I was also the product of an unhappy home situation—an alcoholic father, a prominent person from another community who had lost absolutely everything in the Great Depression and subsequently committed suicide while I was in the Air Force. No one, including my mother, could handle his drinking. They were basically separated, except that he would come home on weekends. He would show up drunk and ruin Christmas every year. He was supposed to be such a big shot, but not one person from the town came to his funeral, outside of family.

As to the accident, perhaps one of the most difficult things was going to the boy's funeral and looking in the casket. I decided to do this. One schoolmate within ten months of the accident during a typical high school joshing about something remarked, "You didn't know you were going to kill that boy either, did you?" This hurt me very much. There were the usual legal statements but no trial; it was declared a simple accident. This, too, was difficult because I had just never lied and the accident summary was glossed over. For perhaps five years, every time I saw a school bus, this horrible thing would go by in my mind. Even today when I see a school bus, it may enter my mind for a few seconds.

As I enter middle age, sometimes I say, "Bud, you really haven't done too bad. You began at age eighteen with nothing. Now you have a $90,000 house with a $20,000 mortgage; a $48,000 rental dwelling with a $24,000 mortgage. . . ." On the other hand, I have through the years entertained thoughts of suicide. My marriage is far from satisfactory—in fact, most of the time [it is] very distasteful.

By ultimatum from my wife, the drinking, which indeed became a problem, is restricted to a couple of times a year when I can get off by myself and just drink solid for two or three days. The suicidal tendencies are still here. Feeling very sorry for myself after all the stuff I've had to handle, I do not think I'd really mind being dead. I believe in God, and I feel He has helped me during my hard times. I know, too, that there are so many more people that have a lot more hardships to bear than

I. Life, really, has not been much of a fun thing. What bearing the accident had or has on my way of thinking is something I just don't know. I feel God has helped me through other crises in my life; why He put that on me, I don't know.

Guilt Resulting from Having Been Stressed at the Time of the Accident

Research shows a strong relationship between stress, personality, and accidents. Stressed people are prone to temporary emotional upsets because they become so absorbed in a problem that they don't pay attention to what's going on. They also may be antagonistic and impulsive, thus losing the benefit of their better judgment.[14] Some accidental killers blame themselves for having been so stressed that they lost sight of what was going on around them.

One accidental killer acknowledges his discomfort about not being at his best the afternoon he ran over a little boy:

The accident happened just after leaving a corner with a red light. I was driving down the right lane of a four-lane road and was passing a car which appeared to be stopped for a left turn. The passing lanes were full of stopped autos waiting for the light. As I passed the car, a nine-year-old boy pranced out from behind the car. He took just three steps between the time I saw him and the time I hit him with the left front of the car. He disappeared for an instant and then was thrown well out in front of my car. I stopped as quickly as I could and moved up where my car could protect him from being hit again. The accident occurred as I was driving home from work, and I was a little agitated at the time because of freeway traffic.

I have a very active mind. After the accident, my mind was preoccupied with thoughts about it and the effects of it. . . . There was no rational reason for this because I came very quickly to the belief that the accident was strictly that—an accident. My thoughts were mainly of concern for the parents of the victim. They lived in a new apartment on a very busy street and may even have given him some money to go across the street to the candy store. He was jaywalking on the way back when I hit him. While I did not feel guilty as a result of the accident—at least I don't think I did—the result was still a number of months with some loss of sleep.

The parents hired a lawyer but settled out of court after witness depositions were taken. I had no concern at any time about legal or financial impact. The investigating officer told me the next day the tire marks indicated my speed was within the legal limit. I was sorry for the parents because I thought hiring a lawyer reduced the amount of money they would get from the insurance company.

An Air Force officer who was driving behind me stopped and stayed for about two hours, being very noncommunicative with me. I found out later from the insurance company that he had apparently seen the boy before I did, and he wondered why I had not stopped and why I was not cited. I was needlessly agitated before the accident and sometimes feel it might have contributed. Because of the legal implications, there is usually no personal contact between people whose lives meet as the result of an accident. I do not know what impact this had on the boy's parents. By the time the matter was fully settled, I had no interest in them at all.

It had no effect on my family's organization. There was no correlation between my happiness and the accident. Before I participated in this study, I didn't think the accident had much impact on my life, but now I think it had more effect than I have been willing to admit.

The Victim's Role in Guilt

One important factor in the way guilt is experienced is the deceased's participation in the event. In some cases, the accidental killer feels victimized by the one who died. A woman describes an accident in which she became someone's instrument of suicide:

This was a long time ago, so I'm not sure how good my memory is, but it was about noon on a Sunday morning. I was driving to my mother's for Sunday dinner after church. She lived in another town, so I was on the highway. I was going pretty fast, as fast as the speed limit allowed, when a man ran out of the bushes and into my car. There was nothing I could do, and so

I just pulled to the side as soon as possible and went to see about him and sent someone for help—he had already died.

This was back during the Depression, and it happened right outside a camp of transients. The man's friends told me that he had been drinking that morning and was very depressed. He had been trying to run out in front of cars five or six times all morning, and they had been running after him and pulling him back. Finally, they had given up. I never felt any profound effects from this accident, although, of course, it was very upsetting at the time.

Participation on the part of the victim does not always alleviate guilt feelings, especially when the victim cannot be held responsible for his behavior. An eighteen-year-old prisoner at a correctional institution confesses his guilt over not keeping better watch over his best friend, a fellow inmate, who died taking drugs supplied by the accidental killer:

I'm a white male, born August 16, 1956, at an Air Force base. I feel that if I were to be cut, I'd bleed red, white, and blue. David, the deceased, and I grew up in the same town and went to the same schools. We were never really close but got to know each other better and liked each other better the more time we spent together. I used to go to his house a lot. We watched a lot of football games together. . . .

John, the friend who really questioned my giving David the cleaning fluid rather than telling me not to give it to him, did so because he felt David was not playing with a "full deck"— that is, he felt David was not mentally able to handle the effects of the cleaning fluid. I felt the same way and gave it to David only because he asked me for it. I should not have—but [I did].

I gave David a moistened cloth which was soaked in the cleaning fluid and left him with it on my bed. John and I went to the bathroom, which was only about fifteen feet away from my bed. We were standing in the bathroom entrance smoking when we saw David fall back on my bed. We ran over to him, and I tried to lift him up to a sitting position. When I touched him, I knew something was wrong. We tried to revive him by artificial respiration, but nothing worked.

I believe he inhaled the cloth. When he inhaled the fumes, he probably got light-headed, and while he continued to inhale, his hold on the cloth loosened to where on the next inhale of breath, it went down his throat. I'm not positive if he died from the cleaning fluid or from the piece of cloth being lodged in his throat. It really doesn't make any difference in my mind. Since the accident, I've had recurring thoughts of the accident and the part I played. I'll be engaged in some other activity, and all of a sudden thoughts of the accident pop up! I'll think about it, then search for something else to divert my thoughts.

As I have never related this experience to anyone else except you, I've had to deal with it on my own. I'll continue to do so, as there are very few people I'll open up to. I've thought about why I wrote you in the first place and why I'm writing this at this time. Maybe it's the hope of relieving the burden held so long inside! . . .

My emotional reaction at the time of the incident was concern for David's life. The following day, I started thinking about it in detail and the part I played in it. Why, after knowing David wasn't 100 percent upstairs, did I give the fluid to him? If I hadn't, then he would still be alive. It kept nagging at me for a long time. Even to this day, I still feel guilty and sorry. I hope David knows that I am sorry and I'd change it all if I could.

Guilt for Coping with the Accident and for Having Needs

Some accidental killers feel guilty about being able to cope with the aftereffects of the event. One reports feeling guilty for the praise people gave her: "The one thing that made it hard for me was having someone say they would never have coped as well as I was. They made me feel guilty for coping. I wondered what they expected me to do."

A few accidental killers say that they felt guilty for having the complex emotional needs the accident generated within them. One explains it this way: "I wanted others to support me, not because they were my friends, but because they thought I was right. I wanted to control what they were thinking. I felt guilty about wanting this."

Guilt for a Suspected Subconscious Motive

This is perhaps the most difficult guilt to dispel. Often a nagging doubt arises when the action that constituted the accidental killer's part came out of a subconscious motive. Although they had no will to kill, these accidental killers find it almost impossible to convince themselves of their innocence. If, as Freud asserts, something as small as a slip of the tongue may be caused by unconscious motives, might not an action resulting in death also be caused by such motives? The question becomes "Is there a part of me I don't know that wants to hurt?"

According to a psychotherapist who wishes to remain anonymous, "That's the tragedy of the person who is still alive. You just can't tell them that their subconscious is innocent. The real tragedy of the living person is that they have to realize that for themselves." He goes on to tell of a young man who was involved in a car wreck that killed his mother. Growing up in an intense love-hate relationship with her, the son felt that he had subconsciously caused the head-on collision. Drugs, therapy, and institutionalization did not help him, and within two years, he committed suicide.

Guilt as an Explanation

The search for a logical explanation for what happened underlies the guilt of some accidental killers. This guilt has little correspondence with objective reality, resting instead in personal philosophy and secret belief. The need to locate a cause, even at the price of bearing guilt, is part of the way in which many accidental killers try to order their sometimes chaotic environments. A teenage boy who was instrumental in the death of his friend describes "this overriding sense of guilt which came from my suspicion of some unconscious wish within myself to do harm. I perceived myself as possibly wishing subconsciously to hurt the person or scare him for some reason. I guess I needed a reason why this had happened."

Some go so far as to blame themselves for seemingly unrelated details. A mother whose child fell out of an unlocked car door on the way to school feels guilty for having been involved at all with a car pool, although the presence of other children was not instrumental in the death. Others blame themselves for having agreed to run errands that placed them at the scene of the accident. According to sociologist Irving Goffman, this type of guilt springs directly from the Western view of the world:

> Given our belief that the world can be totally perceived in terms of either natural events or guided doings and that every event can be comfortably lodged in one or the other category, it becomes apparent that a means must be at hand to deal with slippage and looseness. The cultural notions of muffing and fortuitousness serve in this way, enabling the citizenry to come to terms with events that would otherwise be an embarrassment to its system of analysis. The punishing part of this belief is that luck is perceived as coming from outside, whereas failure is seen as a personal act.[15]

People are afraid of a world with no justice. Many have such a great need to believe in fairness and order that they are willing to suffer acute anguish rather than question the foundation of their existence. This self-blame relieves anxiety and restores a sense of control and safety, keeping at bay the intolerable conclusion that no one is responsible.[16] It also provides protection from the idea that future victimization is possible.

Guilt from Magical Thinking

Guilt sometimes grows out of magical thinking, the belief that one can cause harm to a person by simply wishing to do so. Accidental killers who experience this type of guilt in effect hold the unseen forces of fate responsible for treating them fairly. One woman notes, "I was twelve years old and an only child. When I learned my mother was pregnant, I prayed every night for something bad to happen to the baby. I could never forgive myself when my mother miscarried."

Survival Guilt

Survival guilt affects many people who live through cataclysmic disasters. These people have the notion that a certain number of people are destined to die each day and that by sacrificing their lives, the victim tipped the scales in the survivor's favor. The survivor wonders why she should have been the one to live.

Similarly, guilt can stem from the Hindu belief in karma, the idea that every deed returns to the doer fourfold and that fate is the cumulative result of one's actions. According to this view, accidents do not exist. Therefore, the accidental killer's prior behavior somehow must have caused the accident. This was the primary problem for an ROTC student who felt that by joining ROTC, he had violated his principles and somehow had set himself up for the accident. No doubt guilt was a major motivation for the young man's decision to join a notorious religious cult in an attempt to pay back a perceived karmic debt.

Guilt as Meaning

Unearned guilt also can fill a need to connect with the tragedy and find emotional meaning in it. Dr. Joseph Nicolosi of the St. Thomas Aquinas Center in Encino, California, notes:

> The reason people are going to blame themselves for an accident in which there is no reason to feel responsible is an attempt to find meaning in the event. Let me add that people who do blame themselves and seem not to have a reason will tend not to hold on to that guilt for a long time. It's a transitory way of dealing with the tragedy. They are trying to meaningfully tie themselves to the event. Events are sometimes so haphazard, so random, so crazy, so meaningless that people would rather suffer punishment that they don't deserve than to be face-to-face with something meaningless. By blaming themselves, they tie in their personal reality with this meaningless external reality. They make it meaningful. They somehow relate to it on a feeling level. That's what meaning is. Meaning is a feeling connection between ourselves and our environment, and sometimes guilt, even though it's a negative and a painful feeling, is still better than no feeling, no connection.[17]

A woman who felt that her eighty-six-year-old father's death by heart attack was connected to the concussion he suffered three days earlier when she skid the car into a tree says:

The death of my father and my involvement in that death has been the most shattering experience of my life. The finality of death and the fact that it cannot be reversed has always frightened me, and the thought that I may in some way have been responsible for another reaching this final act of living is beyond consolation. After the accident I was convinced that no peace could ever be mine because this burden was too great. Time does not heal but is a salve to the troubled mind.

From whatever source the guilt of accidental killing may come, justified or irrational, secret or obvious, direct or vague, it is difficult to resolve. But to get on with their lives, accidental killers must grant self-forgiveness. Unresolved guilt is the root of the quiet debilitation known as depression.

Appendix: Not Quite an Accident

As we began this book, we encountered a problem: Some of the people who answered our questionnaire had taken a life by choosing society's directives. Among these were drunk drivers and military personnel who had killed during wartime.

Dangerous behavior results from the disregard for life that is the fiber of a competitive system. Many fatal accidents come from attempts to win validation and to prove oneself. No one forces people to drive drunk, and no one forces them to enlist for military duty, excepting unemployment's incentive. But U.S. society does strongly encourage these choices. Drinking alcohol is a popular form of entertainment that is promoted and accepted in this society. Public transportation is not widely available, and in many cases, the only way to get home from a party or bar is to drive. The military offers careers to poor youths, and advertising promotes the advantages of joining the armed forces. A military career also is traditionally seen as a test or validation of virility.

Psyches formed inside an advertisement jungle without instruction in resistance to its powerful commercial messages cannot make what can be called free and responsible decisions. Everyone wants to be accepted, valued, and loved. What is honored in public is aspired to in private. Promotion by authority becomes an unconscious motivation. A nation's character is molded through the values it permits to be exalted.

Public opinion about drunk driving has changed greatly in recent years. Today most people hold drunk drivers accountable for any harm they do. But it is unclear whether such a shift has occurred regarding those who participate in war. How is it that those who kill by drinking and driving generally are blamed while those who kill in conflicts rewarded?

The United States has been called the "alcoholic republic." Fourteen percent of all U.S. adults, an "astounding number," according to Dr. McGrath, have at some time been alcohol dependent, making alcoholism the single most common psychiatric disorder.[1] Alcohol is the nation's second most deadly drug after nicotine.[2] Some people turn to alcohol because of a sense of alienation and hopelessness. Rorabaugh writes:

> Today we Americans see all too clearly and painfully the contradictions between what we are and what we believe we ought to be. Institutions seem incapable of fulfilling our old ideals of liberty and equality. Our belief in perfection torments us even as it drives us to greater efforts and our failures bring us to methods of coping with life that are scarcely different from those of the alcoholic republic. So we remain what we have been.[3]

Basically, drunk drivers have confused the boundaries between work and play. Embedded in our thinking about such drivers is the image of the "killer drunk," a hostile and antisocial threat.[4] Contrary to popular mythology, the most likely victim of the drinking driver is himself, as the majority of fatal drunk driving accidents are single cars running off the road or into objects.[5] But though some of the reasons people drive drunk may be understandable, there is no good excuse for needlessly endangering lives. Ann Russell of Mothers Against Drunk Driving says, "Given the verifiable impairment that occurs when an individual drinks and drives and the frequency with which DUIA [driving under the influence of alcohol] offenders repeat their offense, the grounds for considering such acts as accidental become very shaky."[6] Indeed, such fatalities are no longer legally considered accidental in any state. Whether a drinking driver is personally condemned or absolved seems to depend on whether others identify with the person:

> Drunkenness as an unusual, episodic event in the life of a stable person is a comic event, classically introduced in comedic scenes in drama. Only when the drunken behavior is perceived as a consistent, compulsive event, filled with recurrent threat to self and others does it become frightening and "tragic." The social drinker retains the aura of Everyman while the drinking driver is now "pathological," marginal and deviant.[7]

Whatever their legal status and however they are seen by their friends, drinking drivers who kill someone suffer greatly, at least the ones who answered our study. A student driving home after an afternoon of drinking and dancing hit a tree, killing his girlfriend. Although he was not legally intoxicated at the time, he feels sure that his earlier drinking had some effect. Ten years later he says, "I have no right to ease my emotions by forgetting her." Another, whose best friend died when he drove drunk at one hundred miles per hour, says:

> I never felt so low in my life. I would have at that time, and still would today, trade my life for his if it could only bring him back. Most people could not understand why I could not care less what was going to happen to myself at the time. After the accident, all I could think about was how horrible I felt for being responsible for my best friend's death. I wanted to kill myself. There is no need to shower the person with guilt and shame. His own conscience will be constantly reminding him of the horrors for the rest of his life. I know. My reasoning was that there was no punishment equal to the terrible crime of being responsible for the death of a human being, especially that of a close friend.

Like the drinking driver, the soldier is duped by society's picture of the glamor of war. In this century, only the heroic Vietnamese have been able to expose this fallacy in a war as "odd as it was brutal,"[8] a war that showed that "to kill with impunity is no simple matter."[9] An entire generation in both nations was marred. Accidents happen in wartime, but massacres are not accidental. Yet no one planned to murder infants when they enlisted or submitted to the draft. The massacre at My Lai was not an isolated event. It exemplifies a war that aimed to annihilate a population united against invasion. A veteran writes:

> How to start? Your study concerns the accidental killing of another human being. Perhaps you will find this letter out of place. But I'm avoiding what I have to say. I shot and killed a young woman. It was not an accident. Often I feel as if I had died. I cannot describe any further or I will vomit, with feelings welling inside of me as I watch my hand write this. This occurred 13 years ago, in South Vietnam, at the time they call

Tet, the anniversary of which will occur at the end of this month. She was not a noncombatant, but it does not matter. This event has, according to certain experts, "traumatized" something or other. I don't much care. Sometimes it seems I cannot walk ten steps without being aware. . . .

Nightmares, once guaranteed, occur only infrequently now. I always sleep in a lighted room. This is a precaution I've learned, as for years I woke up running—sometimes into walls, radiators, once my stereo set. It's very embarrassing if someone unfamiliar to me is nearby. . . .

All in all, I live in a small pleasant world. But often I feel as if I'm a separate person, inside myself, looking through my eyes as one looks out a window, moving my head as one operates a machine. While, as I said, I sleep in only a lighted room, I feel very comfortable in darkness, very aware, very confident.

My only residual feeling of any real consequence is that I have a vast hostility that used to scare me. But I know now that it has no specific direction, other than perhaps myself. I don't think I'm schizophrenic, but I don't really care.

The only people here that I've ever talked to about this were my girlfriend, one or two old girlfriends, and some Catholic nuns in a convent nearby, whom I call anonymously, which is how I sign this note, which will be mailed from a distant city. I simply want to be left alone.

5

Depression

In October 1978, Dan, my sixteen-year-old son, accidentally shot and killed his best friend, Steve. These were two clean, neat young boys who spent every waking moment together. Many of their friends had discovered the world of parties and girls. But neither Dan nor Steve drank or smoked. They spent their days fishing or hunting—they both had guns. We lived in a good neighborhood.

One evening they had a fast-load contest, and the tragedy was the result. Thank heavens Steve lived long enough to verify Dan's story, or it would have been called murder.

Dan suffered intensely. He crawled into a shell. . . . When I came home from work at night, he would be sitting in a dark room—no radio, no TV, no books, no toys, and, most of all, no friends.

Dan stayed out of school for a month. He's been a long time recovering. He still has nightmares, one of which involves our family hiding the body.

We started getting anonymous phone calls in the middle of the night. My husband usually answered. A man's voice would whisper, "You're going to die." My husband was very upset. He knew it was the boy's father.

One evening my son visited a friend who lived across the street from where Steve used to live. He returned home at 9:30. He had just come through the door when the phone rang. He answered, talked for a minute, hung up, and began crying. We asked what was wrong and who it was. He wouldn't tell us.

The phone rang again. My husband answered. It was Steve's father—he was drunk. He stated that my son had killed his son, and now Dan was going to "get his."

My husband spent the night walking the floor with a loaded gun. The next day we moved to a vacant rental across town taking only our clothes with us.

We've had some problems with Dan. He's frequently moody or angry. He didn't graduate. He doesn't seem to have any plans for his life. . . . He seems to lack any pride, and he should have some. He's good-looking, reasonably bright, and capable of doing almost anything. And yet, he doesn't do anything.

Depression is lethargy whose only act is withdrawal.[1] It is like being locked in a prison and not knowing that the walls are self-constructed. It comes in with a whimper; quietly, the depressed person lies down.

Physically, depression is repressed energy. When a person feels inadequate to cope with an overwhelming environment, a biological mechanism turns on to protect him from overloading. Withdrawal and inactivity shield the accidental killer when he cannot avoid excessive stimuli.[2] There seems to be a need to limit input after a person is overwhelmed on a sensorial level, as by a major accident.

One study of drivers involved in vehicular homicide accidents found that a third of these people got depressed, with the depression lasting from one month to several years.[3] A man who accidentally killed someone who ran out in front of his car says:

I've had a deep depression and loss of confidence in dealing with day-to-day problems. Also, much anxiety occurs over any decision making. I'm much more aware of accidents in the press. It's very difficult to enjoy any activity such as eating out. I have a desire to be alone, which is the opposite of normal behavior. I have a constant case of "what ifs"—What if I had been driving slower? What if I'd left a half hour later, earlier, etc.? I'm worried over the welfare of my loved ones—insecure in that many aspects of life seem very fragile. I have extreme empathy toward others in my position. My confidence has been shaken in unrelated areas.

I have little confidence in my emotions. I cry watching TV or feel elated for no reason. I can go a week or more without thinking about the accident, then it seems like yesterday. People do not improve day to day. You have good weeks, bad weeks. Sometimes you can rationalize that it was fate, that your life is back to normal, and then the next day feel depressed so as not to be able to function. I feel frightened much of the time.

A depressed person feels lonely, bored, miserable, hapless, ashamed, worried, and useless.[4] Depression is a feeling that life is hopeless, nothing matters, existence is misery, and there is no remedy for these feelings. It is a tangible deadness inside. "I feel like I don't know what I believe or like about much of anything anymore," one young accidental killer says. He continues:

I took a group of ten people on a canoe trip in the boundary waters of Canada and the United States. While camping, some of the kids went swimming, and after a while the girls in the group noticed that one of the boys was missing. We searched the island where we were, and others proceeded to the water when that failed. We found the boy in the water and started CPR and artificial respiration immediately. This went on for forty-five minutes, but we couldn't revive him.

At the moment I knew it was hopeless—that is, when I knew the boy was dead—my heart sank down into my stomach. With this death, I was shown the ugly side of life.

I was in a fraternity the year before, but when I went back to school, I stayed away from there. I didn't go to any football games. I ended up taking two classes incomplete. The whole semester was depressing.

I don't think I've felt guilty about the death except that the real spirit and drive have been sucked out of me. Maybe this is a result of guilt. Somehow these feelings are my realization that the boy was just sixteen years old. Did he really deserve to die? What am I still around for?

Depressed people go limp. Many feel a lump in the throat, a gnawing emptiness in the stomach, and a heaviness in the chest.[5] They may move like robots, just going through the motions and lacking any motivation, although usually going ahead with daily tasks. They do not experience the same intensity of love for their families as before. Cheerful people seem naive, remote, or dishonest to them. At times they still may be able to laugh at jokes, even to laugh at themselves briefly, but not nearly as much as before the depression. They feel depleted, ready to quit.

Severely depressed people cannot snap out of it. The depression may be so painful that it immobilizes them. They may be disappointed in themselves to the point of self-hatred. Conversation, sex, eating, and expressions of love and friendship bring no pleasure or satisfaction. Those suffering from depression may not want to make decisions for fear of being wrong. It may be easier for them to mumble and not be heard than to speak up or to repeat themselves. They may sleep for long periods of time. Sometimes they are so numb that they cannot even cry.

Signs of depression include not getting dressed all day, staying home from work, and canceling invitations to parties. One accidental killer reports, "My personal hygiene went by the wayside. I was in a definite slump. I neglected my children. I couldn't clean or cook or do anything associated with my day-to-day activities." She continues:

> I was driving on a residential street about half a mile from my house. Halfway down the block, as I rounded the bend, I saw two children playing in the road. I slowed my car down to about twelve miles per hour. As I came closer, the children moved to both sides of the street, one to the left and one to the right. For some reason, the boy on the right darted in front of my car. I stopped immediately and just in time. I cleared my vision after the boy on the right backed away from my car. As I started to proceed, I went about ten feet and my car hit something. At this point, I didn't know what it was. I just sat in the car and screamed as I watched a man come and pick up a little boy from under my car, put him in a car, and take him away. I found out from the police that he had run from the curb after hearing his mother call him. She assumes he thought she was telling him to come to her. There are many more details, but this is basically what happened.

The traffic court hearing was canceled four times. Then the

family sued for $6 million. I started to despise them. My insurance company settled out of court, and I was found not at fault by the court.

I considered divorce. I thought it would save my husband from having to go through this with me. He tried to help me but didn't know what to do. My depression became so bad that I didn't go out of the house.

One time I had an anxiety attack where my eyes hurt and my stomach turned and I got dizzy. My doctor knew it was emotional, but I thought something was wrong with me. Also, I made my husband sell the house, and we moved in with my mother across town so I wouldn't have to go by the place where it happened. I felt personal guilt because I have never been able to figure out why I didn't see the little boy run in front of my car.

I always walked from the day after the accident. I would walk for miles. I did this for about a year. As I look back, I see myself almost running all that year.

This accident rules my life. I can't get into a car as driver or passenger without getting anxious and thinking about it. I will never get back my level of happiness before the accident. I feel like so much of my independence is gone. I drive only for someone else, never for myself. Therefore, I don't go to the places I used to enjoy.

Many, like the camping guide whose charge drowned, see the accident as a turning point and believe that life, which was good before, can never be the same again. The guide notes, "I had dreams; I believed the world had mystery and hope in it before the accident. This took the spark out of my life."

A teenage accidental killer expresses a similar attitude:

I will never forget that day. It will constantly haunt me. I imagine the hardest part of it all was attending the funeral. The family was not expecting me to attend, and they were quite surprised. It was not too hard to talk to his girlfriend, since we already knew each other. I could not face his mother. We talked over the phone. I knew that no matter what was said, she would always blame me, and I accepted it. Bill was an only child, and his mother raised him by herself. Since I grew up with about six different sets of foster parents and did not know what kind of relationship mothers and sons have, I knew I could never realize how much she hurt.

But then again, she would never know how much I hurt and would continue to hurt. She told me she wished it was me and not her son, and at the time I agreed with her. Now it is two years later, and I still wish it was me. But whenever I do think of the accident (which is often), I just feel that Bill would not necessarily want me to forget about living and accomplishing for two people instead of one—which I try to do.

It was a traumatic experience that will never fade away. I have gone through feelings of guilt, shame, suicidal thoughts, disgust, a hell of a lot of stress and anxiety, and most of all remorse. Immediately after the accident, I kind of withdrew from life, got lost, living in a shell and communicating with others only when necessary.

Psychologically, the accident was damaging, and the scars will remain permanently. I felt that people had the attitude when they saw me of, "Oh, there's so-and-so. He's the one who killed his roommate in a car wreck." I often cried, and even now I occasionally do. I try to overlook it and realize I'm living for two people. But I never will forget the accident or the guilt feelings involved.

Depression versus Mourning

Depression and mourning are not the same things. Mourning is a pouring forth of anguish about some unfortunate external condition, whereas depression is a personal self-abnegation for perceived shortcomings. Mourning heals; depression does not.

Dr. P. J. McGrath, associate professor of clinical psychiatry at Columbia University's College of Physicians and Surgeons and a research psychiatrist at New York State Psychiatric Institute, explains the distinction between depression and mourning:

> You can have an intense state of grief or sadness, which is not depression. And that's an important distinction. Freud made the distinction

first when he differentiated between mourning and melancholia. I don't think that people who are grieving, who are appropriately sad about a tragedy or a loss, necessarily need psychological evaluation. But I think people who are depressed should be evaluated because depression is a treatable illness.

And, of course, there are blends because an unfortunate life event can trigger depression. It is difficult because appropriate feelings of loss can shade into depression—like the people who say, "I'm depressed because I lost my job," and the fact is that two years later, they're still depressed and they can't go out and start looking for a new job.[6]

One accidental killer is very clear about the difference between grief and depression. Although she listened constantly to the problems of others, she was relatively alone with her own:

Not even losing my own baby was this bad. It was a different kind of grief. With the baby it was because I had the Rh factor, but I wasn't the first to lose a baby on the first try. After this accident, it seemed a very long time before I got back my level of happiness, maybe longer because I could not have children of my own for so long. We had been married four years when it happened. We adopted two beautiful children. Then two of our own came along. Note that I rate the death of my little girl just after the accident in severity. I didn't go into a real bad guilt trip over losing her.

It was after World War II. I was going to the next town. I had taken a friend to a heart specialist. We were going down a dead-end street. I saw children playing hockey and stopped for them to clear the road and then started on. A child ran out from between two cars, and I trapped him. I never saw him.

I had to go to jail that night after the accident. They said, "We'll let you sit in the office, not behind bars." We put up bail. They threw the case out at the hearing. A witness said there was absolutely no way it was my fault. Only faith kept me from breaking down.

One very big mistake I was making was that I did not talk about it. It happened away from my home, so few people around me knew it—so I certainly didn't bring it up. But I should have talked more to family. The two friends who were in the car with me lived far away, so I couldn't talk to them. Therefore, I buried it deep inside. I had shock and a depression deeper than I had ever had before or since. I had an outgoing nature and was a happy person—all this was gone for some time because I suffered with those parents insofar as one can who has not had it happen to them. I did not dwell on it if I could help it because I believe you must look at the positive as much as possible.

But I feel I did very well outwardly because I had many friends, was very active, and helped my husband socially. He was then chairman of the board of an insurance company.

I must explain one thing. I am the type of person who not only has sympathy for people, but I have empathy. I love people. I do listen. It always surprises me when someone comes and wants to talk to me. I'm so grateful for this. Since college—I noticed it in the dorm—someone was always in the room talking out an inferiority complex. And then when they left, I would have to study. And up until my husband passed on, he was the same way. And if someone asked me not to tell my husband something, I wouldn't, and the same was true for him. He didn't tell me either.

I wish I didn't think of others first so much. I'm not bragging, but I had no children at the time and wanted some. I thought of the parents, . . . [but] it was the grandmother I saw first. She was kind. She came and put her arm around me and said, "It's not your fault." The father was angry at the hospital.

A friend told me, "If it will help any, the mother has been seen on the bus going downtown shopping, and the husband's back at work." I tried to write them after the trial. I wrote, but she would not talk to me. I wanted to know they weren't blaming me.

I mostly wanted to hole up in the house. I'd wake up and pull the covers over my head and not come out. Then I'd pull myself out and go out, doing anything. The pain would swell up in me. It felt like I would fall into a well. I was grateful there was no breakdown. I believe I would have taken my own life if I had been at fault.

A Question of Predisposition

Not everyone becomes depressed after accidentally killing someone. What separates those who do from those who do not? Depression is a "mixed bag of problems,"[7] and the confusion is multiplied by the effect of a traumatic death. Dr. Mardi Jon Horowitz notes, "The question of how much is predisposition and how much is the effect of immediate stress is hard to elucidate because every syndrome will be composed of both sources of influences."[8] The subject is so cloudy that the term *traumatic neurosis* was not included in the official nomenclature of the 1968 *American Psychiatric Association's Diagnostic Statistical Manual of Mental Disorders (DSM-II)*. Any mental problems that occurred after a crisis were categorized by their symptoms as if nothing had triggered them.

Certain characteristics are common among accidental killers who get depressed. Those who were anxious beforehand are subject to depression, since they tend to rate their self-worth entirely on external conditions and are deeply affected by failure. It is as though they are incapable of weathering threats to their self-esteem.[9]

Family background also is important. Any stressful event evokes a reaction of intermingled elements stemming from both unresolved childhood conflicts and responses related solely to the crisis. Sometimes it may seem that parental predictions of failure were right.[10] According to Kardiner, "The . . . situation, with all the accompanying horrors, rather colors the intensity of a neurosis than gives it its essential character."[11] The traumatic experience is filtered through the accidental killer's characteristic way of viewing things. One accidental killer recognizes the contribution of his family history to his postaccident depression:

Because of problems growing up with a jealous older sister, I have always lacked self-esteem and confidence. The accident did not improve the situation. I was never very happy growing up, and I guess I have always had a death wish.

My father died when I was fifteen. The next year I was kicked out of school and left my friends to go to a military school. The accident happened on Christmas Eve during my first year at military school. It was almost more than I could handle.

I was driving with one passenger in my car at night in a residential area. I approached an intersection at a high speed, my yield. I struck another car in the right front and spun it around. Two of the three occupants were thrown from the car, one badly injured, one dead, one with minor injuries. I saw the yield sign and did not try to slow down. I did not see the other car until just before we hit. My passenger was not injured. I broke my collarbone.

Nine years later, after being married, I went through analysis with my psychologist to try to unravel the basis for my unhappiness. This is when I first learned how my sister had affected me. I feel like I made real progress in the area of family problems, but the accident was never discussed. I really don't know why I didn't bring it up—whether I thought I'd gotten over it or it was just too painful to discuss—I really don't know. For so long it has been a cloudy picture in the back of my mind. I used to remember the bloody pictures from the lawsuit and feel sick. Somehow I learned to turn them off, blank it out.

Depressed people are accident-prone. Depression draws a person's attention from the outside world, causes drowsiness, and slows response time. Those who are depressed tend to fear their environment, acting with disorganization, inefficiency, and an inability to coordinate their activities.[12] The children of psychiatrically disturbed mothers, for example, have a much higher accident rate than those of more mentally healthy women because of the mother's lack of attention to her children.[13] The accident-prone personality is practically a syndrome of its own.[14]

Dr. P. J. McGrath proposes an alternative to the theory that people are involved in accidents, either as victim or perpetrator, to punish themselves:

It is known that even mild depression, and probably anxiety as well, interferes with cognitive functioning. By that I mean the thinking and concentration abstract reasoning involves, and it is a common thing that someone who is depressed or anxious—we've all experienced this—tends to be distractable. They have a hard time concentrating.

They don't remember things readily. And it is not hard to imagine that impairment of thinking could very readily translate into accident proneness. If you are forgetful, you may well not take the normal precautions you would when you're doing a project around the house or when you're driving on a wet road. You may not be able to concentrate well, particularly when you're driving or working with machinery, and so on. It can be a simple thing—for example, climbing a stepladder around the house.[15]

Christmas Depression and Accidents

Depression and the substances taken to escape it make for a deadly combination at Christmas time, when the accidental death rate rises dramatically.[16] Traditionally, this is when people in the United States sense most acutely the contradictions in their lives. James Greenstone notes:

> We continue to buy into the fairy tales. We listen to the promises made by parents who did not believe them when told by their parents. And as we do, tension increases. Stress mounts as we try to be sure that this time the fantasy will really be all that it is supposed to be. We look for the spirit of the holiday and we come up short. We expect togetherness and we get loneliness. We want things, gifts and the like, to testify to our worth and we get nothing worth having. We fail to notice, to recognize, that all we seek is not "in" the season. It is not the things outside of ourselves that can make any real and significant difference in a life filled with problems, trauma, or the day-to-day situations that plague us all.[17]

According to Leslie Lieberman of the Safer Travel Through Education and Prevention Program of Contra Costa County, California, somewhere between 50 and 60 percent of all accidents involve the use of alcohol or drugs.[18] Dr. P. J. McGrath comments on the holiday-alcohol connection:

> Seen clinically, people who are distressed often self-medicate with alcohol. . . . Some of the people are not even particularly aware that they're anxious, but they're drinking excessively, and some of it is to block awareness of unpleasant things. The "ideal Christmas" is part of the problem. What happens at the holidays for a number of people is that they become acutely aware that something is missing from

their lives. The holidays remind them that they didn't get along with their parents. Or it reminds them of a divorce or of children from a first marriage, or a child who died, or any one of a number of personal or family problems. Christmas is held up as an ideal family time, and everywhere you look there are people enjoying this supposedly family holiday.

A lot of times people will seek various ways to deal with that. They'll overdo the drinking, they'll immerse themselves in mad Christmas shopping, buying presents for everyone they can think of—anything to try and bring more of that joy into their lives. But in fact what they're doing is running away from a realization of some emptiness in their lives.

Probably it's applicable to most people—that is, this big issue of the holiday bringing a recognition of some ongoing problem in their lives. It brings it to the forefront, whereas previously they suppressed it.[19]

That Christmas should be a time of fatal distress exposes some of the cracks in the foundation of U.S. culture's thinking—that any one way of being is ideal, that all false hope can be packaged into a single day.

Depression and Unresolved Guilt

As we noted in chapter 4, people who are "only doing their job," such as police officers and soldiers, pay a steep personal price for killing someone in the line of duty. The wife of a man who shot a felon while on duty as a corrections officer reports how this event affected her husband and their family:

He has gone through a lot. He could not stand working in the jail. The other felons knew who he was and what he did. So he transferred to the Public Works Department. His biggest problem, when he has nothing else to think about, is to feel sorry for himself. He'll say, "You blame me for killing that kid, don't you?" He makes a good officer and misses his work and buddies. The department wouldn't transfer him off the decks— "either get in there and take it or transfer out."

He is one that cannot go hunting because he could never kill an animal. He was in the Army at seventeen, in weapons, then for the past eighteen years in the reserves, the patrol, the police department, then the jail. So you see, he's carried a gun for a long time.

My husband warned the boy, firing warning shots. . . . [He] was justified. State law says a police officer may lawfully use deadly force when necessary to effect the retaking of an escaped prisoner who has been committed or arrested for felony charges. The outcome of the inquest was a shooting justified by state law. A Rehabilitative Services hearing said the discharge was justified and in compliance with procedures, with one exception—the shooting violated the department's prohibition "under no circumstances shall a firearm be drawn or discharged as a warning."

It was hard when the [victim's] family called our home and threatened us or when they kept driving by our house. If they saw us in public, they would yell, "Killers!" The victim was also into drugs and supplied a lot of high school kids. Our son attends high school. He had to put up with a lot of smart remarks from the toughies. . . . I still get phone calls from the mother and the grandmother.

The former officer says:

You'd think it would start to go away, but damn if I don't always seem to think about it. Seeing their address or the same name, any little thing like that reminds me of it—always when we go past the street where it happened.

It was a normal day. I was happy. It was a sunny morning. I was transporting four inmates to court. Three were on minor charges, and one was in for three counts of felony rape and assault. I didn't have them in handcuffs because that particular judge didn't like to see them in handcuffs in his court. So you walk behind them. You don't treat them like animals. As we arrived at the court, the inmate with the felony charge tried to escape. If his friend had told me, the kid would be alive today. I chased him for about two blocks shouting out warnings to halt. I also took out my gun and fired several warning shots. One shot finally hit him in the head. He was 150 feet away. I didn't think I could hit him from that distance.

He was an eighteen-year-old kid, blond hair, blue eyes. I ran up to him and crouched down. He looked up at me and said, "Mommy." Then he died.

State law states an officer may use deadly force to stop a fleeing felon. What it [doesn't] say is what happens when it's all over. I feel guilty, but I cannot explain these feelings. I am still not back to the point in my life where I was before, but I cannot explain why. . . . Maybe someday it will go away. It only took one minute, and your whole life-style is changed. It's lousy.

The victim's family has said they're coming to get me, and I know it's true. His cousin is getting out of jail in a few months, and they say they're sending him after me. But I'm not selling my house and moving. If they're going to get me, they might as well get me here. If I moved, they would know I'm scared. . . . I have a very high tendency to check and make sure the old car is the same as I left it the night before. I check under the hood for bombs.

Not a day goes by that it doesn't cross my mind. I'm afraid I'll never get over it. I always seem to think about it. To tell the truth, I wish I hadn't agreed to talk about it. I didn't know it was going to make me feel so bad.

A Shift in Self-Concept

What separates those accidental killers who become depressed from those who do not is whether they incorporate the accident into their self-concept. Many people's self-concept is quite susceptible to outside influence. People do not think of themselves as either good or bad. They rate themselves separately in different areas based on the feedback they get from others.[20]

The key psychic damage that accidentally taking a life can do is to convince a person that she is inept to a lethal degree. The difference between thinking "the world is a dangerous place" and "the accident wouldn't have happened if I hadn't messed up" is the difference between holding faith in oneself and losing it. It is much easier psychologically to face a terrifying world than to live free from external threat in self-contempt.

Sometimes the accident can catalyze an already negative self-concept. An accidental killer who believes that he does not deserve happiness may be overcome by guilt. A psychologist speaking in confidence describes a client who felt responsible for her lover's death in a car wreck: "She took the death as a confirmation of what she already believed about herself—that she didn't deserve a relationship."

It is equally debilitating to believe that the world is against you in particular as it is to think that you are against yourself. Both result in a feeling of helplessness, which is the primary ingredient in clinical depression.[21] For a nondepressed person to get depressed following a traumatic event, that person must feel as though she has no control and expect that this will always be true.[22]

According to several studies of victimization (in this case, the accidental killer is considered a victim, since that term includes those who suffer because of their own actions), victims who react with a perception of unique vulnerability may be more likely to experience a shift in their self-image. Their external world may still be regarded as rather benign, and they may perceive other people as remaining relatively invulnerable. What has changed is their view of themselves. They may have a more negative self-image and believe that they are deserving of negative outcomes in the future.[23] Accidental killers who look at themselves more negatively by blaming themselves and feeling helpless have a much more difficult time regaining their former sense of invulnerability than those who maintain a positive self-image.[24]

Dr. E. Tory Higgins, professor of psychology at Columbia University, explains why he believes that an outside event is incapable of causing depression on its own:

> The main thing is that with mourning, it's not really you. Something out there is bad. You don't like that. But it's a person coping with something bad out there. Depression is much more of a problem. You don't have a healthy person coping with something bad out there. You have internal problems that are totally separate from what's out there.
>
> With mourning and support from friends, one can quickly overcome the loss, but once you get melancholia, the outside world can't do much about it. Things could go well out there. You have friends that are supportive. But you don't believe it.
>
> Depression seems to come when the accident highlights a gap be-

tween people's current picture of themselves and what they would like to become or think they ought to be. These conflicts lie dormant in a fairly large segment of the population until some crisis activates them.

You wouldn't expect everybody to have the same kind of affect. Everybody is going to feel upset and sad—that would be natural or accepting of some degree of responsibility—but if the symptoms are much greater than that, it probably means the event has a significance that goes beyond itself.

The difference between mourning and melancholia is that when someone has melancholia, there's a significance, a subjective meaning that is more than just the event. You don't just feel bad that your spouse died. You may feel worthless or unlovable or guilty, all of which doesn't have anything to do directly with the fact that your spouse died. An exogenous event is causing some internal conflict independent of it. You have a vulnerability, but you don't feel it until the event.[25]

Socially Induced Depression

Self-perceived failure is not the only cause of some accidental killers' depression. A person who depends heavily on feedback from others will suffer greatly from their disapproval. This is harder to avoid than it may seem, as the accident also creates a sensitivity to judgment by others. People who normally would not be affected by criticism may be vulnerable to it after an accident. "[The accident] already involves feeling shame, loneliness, worrying about what others think, and what others are saying," E. Tory Higgins notes. "It feeds into what is already there. [Criticism] has a much greater effect because it feeds into the person's history."[26]

Depressed people make about half as many interpersonal interactions as nondepressed people. When other people exhibit both positive and negative behaviors, depressed people pay more attention to the negative ones.[27] The person's bad moods invite social ostracism. Friends may reject the accidental killer upon seeing no improvement in his mood.[28] Accidental killers also may have tremendous emotional needs because of their guilt. They may set others up to reassure them or may talk compulsively about what happened. None of this makes for good company.

One accidental killer recounts how he suffered from approval; his account also reveals ineffective ways of school and interpersonal relationships:

> It was in October. I was driving a new Jeep CJS pac.....
> six people. It was clear when we started out, but a thunder-
> storm hit from out of nowhere. The road got slick and slimy. I
> was trying to climb a clay hill, and when we came to a stop
> halfway up, the jeep slid backward. It was out of control, and
> it rolled. We folded up the cloth top and got back in the jeep.
> No one was hurt. I decided to turn around and get us out of
> there. We went about thirty feet, and the front tire slipped
> into a hole. The jeep toppled and the roll bar crushed my
> best friend's head. He died on the way to the hospital in the
> ambulance.
>
> I continued to go to school afterward, which was good and
> bad. Since I lived in a small town and everyone knew me and
> what had happened, going to school gave me a chance to get
> away—which was good. But I did get poor grades in school,
> which did not help my self-image. I began to use drugs and
> alcohol in excess as a means to escape. . . .
>
> My friend that was killed was married for three months and
> then divorced about six months prior to the accident. I was
> going out with his ex-wife up until about a month before the
> accident. She has made it difficult for me. We tried to get to-
> gether for a while, then we would break up. She didn't think
> he was such a great guy when he was alive, but now she puts
> his picture on the mantelpiece and talks about the things they
> used to do, like the world revolves around him. We have been
> off and on ever since.
>
> You just wouldn't believe the pain. . . .

Another accidental killer describes how her accident and the social ostracism that followed triggered a lengthy depression:

> We had all graduated from college the year before. I was pretty
> independent, career oriented. I liked my job. Cheryl and her
> husband had been married about six months. We were all
> going camping on the Fourth of July at this hidden camp-

ground that none of the tourists knew about. The entrance was hardly marked, and it was hard to find. . . .

It was getting to be dusk, and we had passed up the entrance once already. I was circling back and beginning to get a little bit frantic because I was afraid that once it got dark, I'd never be able to find it. She and I had a map, and we were trying to find the entrance. The road was very dry. It had recently been graveled, and there was a lot of Fourth of July traffic on the road. I got anxious to get to the campsite before dark and sped up. As I came around a corner, the car slid on the gravel. Then the left front tire slid into the ditch. I overcorrected to get the car back onto the road, and it rolled over two or three times.

I crawled out of the car through an open window. It had landed on the roof. I couldn't find Cheryl anywhere. I looked and looked. The car had rolled down an embankment and rested against a fallen log. I finally found Cheryl under the car. I felt her hand. I guess I knew then that she was dead, but I ran down the road to look for help. I still had this crazy hope that she was still alive.

I ran down the road and flagged down a car. It didn't take long before someone stopped. I looked pretty bad. I was bleeding, even though I wasn't hurt that much. Two guys in a pickup truck stopped. They had a CB in the truck, so they called for the sheriff and an ambulance. They took me to a little store to wait for the sheriff and my friends, whom they had gone to notify at the campground. It was the longest wait of my life. The deputy finally came to talk to me and told me that Cheryl was dead. I cried for a long time. When my friends all walked in, nobody said a word. Cheryl's husband drove me home. We were silent the whole way.

I was afraid to call my parents and tell them what had happened, so I got my roommate to do it. My folks have always helped me when it was convenient for them. Like when I was learning how to drive a car, they paid someone to teach me rather than do it themselves. They offered to fly me down to be with them, but I thought they should have come to me. I didn't want to leave my friends either.

I felt that I shouldn't have been driving so fast on a gravel road. I try to shake these feelings off, think about something else. I was single and my brothers were no longer at home. I did not feel like a member of a family unit at that time. . . . I doubt I will ever get back to the point I was before the accident.

At first after the accident, I didn't feel too terrible. I had several friends who were supportive for about the first week. I went to Cheryl's funeral and generally tried to get back into my regular life-style. I went back to work after a few days. After the first week or so, however, my friends abandoned me.

I was not especially happy in my job as a catalog clerk at the library. . . . I couldn't seem to function well. My superiors were critical of my work, and although I felt that I was trying very hard to do good work, the quality continued to decline. I became very depressed. I had no friends outside of work, and I was frustrated with my job and my job performance.

My roommate was very popular, and her hostility was apparent to all of our mutual friends. . . . She started acting really ambivalent toward me and saying that things weren't working out, that I wasn't keeping up my end, but I assumed it was because of the accident.

The day I moved out was really tense. It was polite, but we didn't say anything or say good-bye. I had to find another roommate, someone from work. She was nice, but we weren't really friends.

My roommate and I had had basically the same group of friends. After I moved out, whenever I would see someone on the street and ask them over for a beer or a sandwich or something, they would always say they were going over to her house that night. It was pretty well understood that if they were with her, they couldn't be with me. . . . In a lot of ways, I was completely isolated. I thought everyone hated me for the accident, and I hated myself. . . . I'm trying to get over it, but I suspect it will take a long time.

I bought a car after the accident, since my car had been totaled. But in the first year I owned it, I put only a thousand miles on it. I never drove anywhere unless I had to. I was terrified. My heart would race if I ever had to drive on the highway and exceed thirty-five miles per hour. The first time after the accident that I tried to go camping, I couldn't stop throwing up, and I knew there was nothing physically wrong with me.

For almost two years after my accident, I was very lonesome. I had a boyfriend most of that time, but our relationship was superficial and unrewarding. I had trouble making friends and maintaining relationships. I felt every criticism and negative comment was a personal attack. I had a very hostile reaction to any joking comments about my shortcomings. Basically, I was miserable and probably unpleasant to be around.

I knew my friends had not forgiven me for the accident, and I didn't think that I deserved to be forgiven. I felt like they thought I was some sort of monster. I was sure no one loved me, and I thought I was a terrible person. I began to hate myself, and I was sure everyone else hated me, too.

I met and began dating my husband in July of 1978. I think it was a real turning point for me. He was the first person that I could really talk to, the first person that I had really talked to about my accident. He listened. He didn't make judgments. He was a real friend.

Since getting married, I still experience bouts of depression, but they are not as severe as they were in the past. I have developed a few close friendships in the last year, and the loneliness I felt for so long has been replaced by at least some degree of comfort. I think that I have become overly dependent on my husband. Recently I have tried to become independent and self-reliant. This has been difficult, and I suspect it will be a slow process.

It wasn't until about eight years and two children later that something my priest said—I'm not even sure what—made me feel that God had forgiven me and that I should forgive myself. My old roommate is friendly now when I see her around town, but I wouldn't want to be friends now. I haven't discussed the accident with anyone except my husband. I wouldn't mention this to anyone.

Isolation

The power of the broader social climate over accidental killers' self-perception shows in the experience of a youth who was isolated after his accident. His accident happened in post–World War II

England, but he later moved to the United States. He describes his situation as follows:

> My mother ran a school at home, and summers my brother and I would be home from boarding school. My mother had given us hunting rifles, and we used to go out shooting squirrels. Later my father blamed her for letting us have guns. My parents were apart, and he would always do things to turn us against our mother.
>
> This particular morning we were playing cowboys and Indians in the living room, and my brother hid behind the couch. I was aiming at him from the other end of the couch, and I pulled the trigger. It had been my responsibility to put the gun away, and I thought it was empty. I was sixteen at the time.
>
> I squeezed the trigger and shot my brother in the temple. I heard no sound. This bothers me to this day. I can't understand why I didn't hear anything. I saw a small circle of blood on the side of his head, and I knew exactly what had happened. I ran into the kitchen and told whoever was there what happened, and then I ran out the back door and jumped on my bike and raced to a tree where I used to go and sit. I just sat there praying and shaking. And I prayed to God that if anybody was going to die, it should be me. I felt betrayed when this did not happen.
>
> I don't remember what happened next, except that I had to testify at an inquest, and I had to be there for the whole thing, except the part where they described the injuries to the body. But even at that part, I was standing out in the hallway where I could hear. The inquest was very hard for me. Nobody spoke with me about it because it's just over and done with and it's best to forget about it.
>
> My brother was a happier child. I had been a brilliant child. At age seven, I was learning Latin, French, and German. The moment I shot my brother, that part of me died completely. I felt persecuted, felt people were talking about me.
>
> My father made a big thing about the death of my brother. It's bad enough for someone to die without starting to blame people. No one was aware of what these things did to me.
>
> Now I drive a truck. I don't speak with anyone. I don't like

the people I work with, but I don't have to. I'm very alone, into myself, and I prefer to be. I'm not cut off from the world; I haven't climbed into a shell. Watching TV, if I see something emotional to me, I get an intense hurt welling up inside. I don't cry, but it feels like I am. It can happen all night. Also, if I see a child fall, I get an acute pain. But it doesn't last long.

This depression is exceedingly severe. I've been threatening suicide so long now that people see it as crying wolf; they don't see it as depression. Why I contain it I don't know. . . .

Last Christmas my wife left me and took the children. I curled up in bed with my revolver, and she called the suicide prevention line. She didn't know they would send the police, but they circled the house and told me to come out. I told them I was alone in here and not breaking any law, and they could come in and get me if they liked. They went away after a couple of hours. . . .

What I really want is to be loved, and I don't feel I am. Not a deep love. I have my children's love, but kissing them every night is not quite the same as having a wife love me. . . . Through my own doing, I alienated myself from her. . . .

The leader of the Urban League was assassinated on his porch. They lived down the street from me, and I wrote a letter to the bereaved widow saying I hoped she didn't move away because I found in my own life that running didn't help. I ran from shooting my brother, and I ran from England. My life hasn't achieved for me whatever I'm striving for. If someone else had left the gun loaded, [my guilt] would have mitigated, but it was all [my fault] by two mistakes. I can cry at sad movies but not at my brother's grave. I went back to England, back to his grave, and wanted to cry badly. But I couldn't.

Depression, Drugs, and Suicide

According to Dr. P. J. McGrath, suicide's appeal to depressed accidental killers "comes out of fear or guilt, and that's a very common story. Anyone who's been really depressed has thoughts of not wanting to live."[29] A few accidental killers do make serious suicide attempts, but a far greater number seek escape and self-destruction through drugs and alcohol. Sometimes accidental killers with no prior drug use become heavily involved in drugs after the event. A mother describes her college-age son, who was involved in an auto wreck: "His car skidded on an icy road, crashing into another vehicle and killing the driver instantly. He was not at fault, but he blamed himself. He dropped out of school and started taking drugs. Today he is an admitted alcoholic."

An accidental killer (a nurse anesthetist in the U.S. Navy) tells her story of drugs, alcohol, and suicide:

> Something like this cripples you and takes over your whole outlook. Your self-esteem goes out the window. I just kept saying, "Won't someone please punish me and get it over with?"
>
> The accident happened eighteen years ago, on May 16. Billy, the boy who died, would be thirty-six now. He had fallen into a hold of a ship, and he had multiple critical injuries. During surgery, I switched to a new batch of gas. This resulted very rapidly in death. I turned off all the gases except oxygen. If I had just put him on room air, he would've been okay. We did all the last-ditch procedures, but to no avail. We simply could not figure out why the boy died.
>
> The next day, a young child was brought to me with severe oral injuries. Every time I induced her, she'd turn blue. After two or three attempts, we all looked at one another in complete shock. The oxygen tanks were analyzed as 99 percent nitrogen. The whole crew walked around numb for days.
>
> This was considered an anesthesia death and was investigated thoroughly. The direct responsibility was on my shoulders. The outcome released me legally and professionally. However, the impact remains very much with me. The incident was kept hush-hush around the base. I felt it should have been told as it was. But the grapevine works just fine. I felt sorry for the people who filled the tanks. . . .
>
> I have a red-hot temper. I've considered myself a modified manic-depressive all of my adult life. I had learned to live with it. But this was so profound and such a misery. I knew the depression would pass—just try and hold still until it did. This time it was unrelenting. Along with this was a great amount of fear and anxiety doing my job as an anesthetist. Any little snag would absolutely tear me apart.

Having easy access to drugs, I'd use Dexedrine during the day as a mood elevator and booze during off-hours. The medical profession is dumb when it comes to their own colleagues. They kept telling me, "It's done; put it away," as if that's all there was to it. I had expressed a desire to consult a psychiatrist, but this was answered with, "But you're a nurse yourself" or "You're probably ovulating" or "You're becoming menopausal." So I continued my own "treatment." They did give me some mild tranquilizers, which did about as much good as frog spit.

Ultimately, I had to give up anesthesia, which disturbed me greatly. I switched to another ward, but anesthesia was still my first love, and I would still come around and find out what was going on.

After retiring from the Navy, I really fell into depression. My mother died a terrible death from internal bleeding, and my husband and I were having trouble learning to live together again. I was Navy, and he was civilian. His attitude regarding this incident was one of ridicule. He's not a very sensitive person. I got to the place that I knew I could not go back in time. I didn't want to go into the future, and I sure as hell didn't want to stay in the present.

I overdosed with pills and booze and was on my way out of this world. This was no namby-pamby attempt. I knew what I was doing. My husband came home much earlier than usual and found me. He called the rescue squad and so forth.

Being absolutely miserable, I finally went to see a psychiatrist who placed me on Elavil. I have been slowly working my way back to life. I still waiver sometimes between wanting to live and wanting to die. Right now, I'm keeping on keeping on.

Depression's End Result

Can the accidental killer learn from depression? Does it in any way contribute to growth? Dr. P. J. McGrath does not believe so:

My view of depression is pretty much a medical one, and I don't view depression as anything positive. What has something to do, I think, with people's hopelessness in depression is that when they're down, they can't remember what it is like to feel that life is worthwhile. They are so desolate, bleak, and hopeless that even people who aren't actively suicidal will say, "I would never think of killing myself, but if I were run over by a car somewhere, I wouldn't care. I don't want to live, but I wouldn't actively do anything to end my life."

People with serious depression sometimes learn, but not as much as you would think. That's because in general we tend not to remember pain. Probably our brains are set up in such a way that pain tends to be forgotten.

I had a friend who said, "Of course you can't remember pain. If you could, there would be no families around with more than one child." And people often say that the memory of pain is often dim and it's very hard to reconstruct. That's true of physical pain, but I think it's true of emotional pain as well.

When people are depressed, it's pretty clear that they're not getting anything out of it, and they don't come back and say when they've recovered, "Well, I really learned something from being depressed. Even though it was a terrible experience, I'm glad I had it. I've grown from it." They say, "I hope it doesn't happen again. It was awful. My life was shattered by it. Please help me not to have it again."[30]

Social Tension

"I needed people more than at any other time in my life, but people avoided me. Maybe they just didn't know what to say," one accidental killer recalls. Another says, "People quit visiting me. I guess they were uneasy." A third reports, "It hurt when people avoided me. I felt guilty, alone, and frustrated." A fourth elaborates, "People talked about me behind my back, acted like I wasn't there, and made me feel unwanted and unloved. My girlfriend spread a rumor that I did it on purpose. People should comfort the accidental killer and tell him not to worry, that it wasn't his fault. If you have something nasty to say to that person, just keep your mouth shut because talking will make him feel worse."

The discomfort people feel around accidental killers comes from many sources. Hearing about the accident can stir their empathic horror and demand that they confront the idea of death. The accidental killer may become a reminder of the fragile thread from which the living hang. The ostracism that often follows an accident seems to be more a reflex than a conscious choice.[1] The accident may challenge the "just world hypothesis," a protective device whereby people distance themselves from tragedy by blaming a victim for her own misfortune, especially if that misfortune victimizes another person. While taboos concerning profaning the dead may protect the victim's name, a full load of judgment may fall on the accidental killer.[2]

Other factors characterize interactions between accidental killers and those who care about them. The ambiguity of the accidental killer's role is confusing, being at once that of perpetrator and that of victim. Do accidental killers deserve a hug or a kick, comfort or blame? There is no clearly defined socially acceptable script for an accidental killer's friends to follow.

To understand how one feels toward an accidental killer, one must know the precise details of the death. It may seem rude or intrusive to seek these facts, but not doing so may lead to an even more awkward situation. If the circumstances do vindicate the accidental killer, one risks demeaning him with pity or saying the wrong thing. For many people, these are more than sufficient reasons to steer clear of the accidental killer.

Dr. Stanley Rustin, a psychologist and professor of psychology at Queensborough Community College in Bayside, New York, speaks of the importance of social feedback:

> Whenever we're rejected, for whatever reason, if we have any brains or feelings, we feel depressed, angry—particularly if we feel the rejection is unearned.
>
> None of us talks about social reactions in general. We talk about how particular friends, colleagues, and relatives react. If we do something wrong, we don't worry about what society thinks. I worry about certain people and what they think if I worry at all.
>
> But the toughest reflection of that society is the person himself— because an individual is an amalgamation. What helps to shape the self-concept is a combination of responses from parents, friends, colleagues, children. It depends on who gives us that input.[3]

Some social problems stem from the tremendous emotional needs of accidental killers after their crises. Some accidental killers set themselves up for rejection by being hypersensitive, and others invite castigation because of their sense of guilt. A man whose car collided with a motorcycle recalls:

> I felt it was all my fault—that I was completely in the wrong— although neither of us was found to be at fault. Right after the accident, if someone mentioned something about another accident or about another motorcycle accident, I felt very self-conscious. They meant nothing against me, but it just wouldn't

occur to them. It still makes me feel a little funny, especially when someone talks about motorcycle accidents.

It is no surprise that social problems should arise around accidental killers when negligence is implied. The accidental killer has just participated in one of the most stigmatizing losses imaginable, for negligence is seen as negatively as murder or suicide. The situation is ripe for self-doubt and suspicion.

Accidental killers may be invaded by an unhealthy complex of disturbing emotions: shame, guilt, hatred, and perplexity. They also tend to repeat some aspect of the accident compulsively, going so far as to reenact the tragedy emotionally in other situations. Many are driven to talk about it over and over,[4] and this, along with erratic behavior, sometimes turns away those who could help. A father who accidentally killed his young son recalls:

> After the death happened, people seemed unable to predict the way I'd be. . . . I was kind of crazy for a while. I lost touch with reality. I think that's scary for a lot of people. It scares me now when I see other people like that, and I think I intimidated a lot of people.
>
> In one sense I intimidated them because of the act that I had been involved with, and I think a lot of people in my life had difficulty processing that. "This man ran over his little boy" went over and over in their heads about me. And they had a hard time figuring out how that happens. Whatever people do with that, they had a hard time doing it.
>
> In another sense, emotionally I was really unpredictable for a long time. I got angry, and I didn't care who was around. I haven't ever really actually cared who was around when I did those things, but I was doing them very intensely and in violent ways.

Some accidental killers become irrationally sensitive, seeing insult where none was intended. One accidental killer pointed angrily at the newspaper that contained the story of her accident. Adjacent to the piece was a photo of a fawn bounding into the woods, showing its white tail. "This," she stated with disgust, "is saying I'm as good as a deer's behind."

Others interpret people's actions in ways that seem to reinforce their sense of guilt. A boy who accidentally shot his brother recalls, "Some young people my age appeared to be scared of me, and I perceived they feared for their lives."

Overwhelming Concern

An accidental killing can rivet the attention of a small community on the plight of both the victim and the survivors. Though well intentioned, this intense scrutiny is often embarrassing to the accidental killer. A woman who was known and respected throughout her area explains how the attention she received as a result of an accident that claimed the lives of her two sons affected her:

> You never run away from it. I think this is the hardest part. . . . For instance, one time I was in church. I noticed a couple clear across the church looking at us—total strangers—and I asked my husband if he knew that couple over there, and he said yes. I said, "I knew you did." I think that's about as hard a thing as you can face—that you never get away from it. No matter where we went, we'd see someone look at us and nudge one another, and you knew they were telling them who you were. I didn't object, for that is human nature, but you did feel you were constantly being watched. So you felt like you had to be very careful of your behavior, of your expression, and soon that bothered me, especially until we moved away.
>
> My husband was superintendent of schools in this small town of five hundred people and had resigned just two or three days earlier to go to Harvard to get his doctorate. The day of the accident, he was to let the school know; he sent a wire asking for time to consider and telling why. . . .
>
> The worst thing you feel is that the children trusted you. They were chubby, dark-eyed, attractive little boys. . . . They were always in the spotlight because of their father's position. They were very much wanted. The family was the highlight of my life, more than doing a lot of outside things.
>
> Since the accident was forty years ago, it is hard to say just what I did go through. Strange as it may seem, I never did feel a great sense of guilt because I knew I did the best thing I could under the circumstances. I would consider it a freak accident.

My only guilt feelings were in that I knew those little boys trusted me completely, and I felt I betrayed them.

The accident happened in 1940. It drew national attention. It was coming up on a presidential election year. We were going to town because Gracie Allen as a joke was running for president, and her headquarters were to be in our state. . . .

It was the Dust Bowl days. We were six women and two children, one child on a lap in the front and the back. Shortly after we left home, we ran into a strip of dust so dense it cut off my vision. I was going fifty, under the speed limit. I slowed down but was out of it almost as quickly as I went into it. Many people had just plowed fields, and the patch was about an acre long.

Within a mile, I came to another dust cloud. Thinking it was little, too, I started to go through it. At first I didn't slow down, . . . but when I had absolutely no visibility—not even the front of the car—I put on the brakes and pulled to the right to avoid anyone coming from the other direction. . . . I pulled right into the overturned body of a big truck pulling a prize bull from a fair. That truck had already run into two cars that had managed to stop just before colliding. No one was hurt in those cars or truck. . . .

Glass was shattering and sprinkling down on all of us. For a few seconds, no one made any sound. The women in the front seat were knocked unconscious for a few minutes. One had a broken arm. Two of the other women in the backseat got out for help. One woman was severely injured. She caught her toe under the back of the front seat but hit the door handle and was thrown out of the car, breaking her kneecap and badly fracturing her upper arm, which pierced her side. As she was thrown out of the car, the edge of the door scalped her. They claimed the dust in the scalp wound saved her from bleeding to death! Another had a broken nose; another had a gash on the chin.

I had a light concussion and multiple deep bruises. . . . I had shoved the steering wheel into the car all the way. The bodies of the women flying forward crushed the children against the dash and the front seat. Of course, they caught the full impact. Both had fractured skulls and never regained consciousness.

There was a great outpouring of love. In a small town like

this, everyone felt the tragic blow. Much kindness was shown. Two women came in and cleaned the house and with relatives cleaned out the boys' room of toys, etc. People brought food. People would come to see you, and you knew they wanted to ask questions—you could see it on their faces, those quizzical eyes—but they didn't know how to do it. You just had a sense of knowing when people had questions in their minds, but they didn't want to hurt your feelings. I just wanted to say, "Ask! Ask what you wanted to say," because you had this feeling of a void between you. Most of the time I would be the one to start the conversation just to relieve the tension.

The mortician had an awful time because so many people wanted to do something. He said he could hardly do what he needed to for people coming and wanting to help. So he did send some to pick up a death certificate or on any errand because people wanted to do things so badly. . . .

There were no legal suits. We did try to submit a bill to the state legislature to collect damages. But since we were not in the state and could not afford to hire someone to press our case, it was thrown out of committee and called an act of God. . . .

One of the things my husband explained to me right off is that God didn't want this. He made the world, and it isn't perfect. We are not perfect, and situations happen beyond our control. . . . I could not stand it when people would say it was God's will. That upset me terribly. . . .

One thing that helped me was that one of the women in the car had been married quite a few years and had had surgery to get pregnant. But the umbilical cord was wrapped around the baby's neck, and the baby died. She knew that that was the only child she could have. She wouldn't let people help her, locked the door, and wouldn't come out or speak to anybody. In a town of five hundred, you just don't do that to people. You just don't act like that. I'm sorry for her, but it helped me to know I wasn't going to act like that. She lost people's sympathy. I did my crying in private. I just felt like we had to get out and face the world and get going. . . . It wasn't easy, though.

Silence

The thought of broaching the subject of the accident is unnerving to many, even though it may be begging to be mentioned. "I froze up whenever I would walk into a room that was buzzing with conversation and people would all stop talking," one accidental killer recalls.

A camping guide who felt responsible for the drowning of one of his charges remembers a distant civility that he felt conveyed an attitude of unspoken condemnation. "It's not what they said; it's what they didn't say," he says. "Their body language and gaze told the story." Another accidental killer who was surrounded by sympathetic friends speaks of his frustration:

> It was frustrating because they had the attitude that because they were my friends, they would stick by me no matter what. That wasn't a good enough reason. I wanted them to understand there was nothing I could have done. But it was hopeless. I realized I wanted the impossible—to control the feelings of others as well as my own. I was too aware of everything; I read innuendo into it all. I didn't want them to feel sorry for me, and I didn't want them talking behind my back. I wanted them to come out and ask me questions, but they would never bring it up. I realized that if anybody was going to bring it up, it was going to be me.

Insensitivity

Even in the best situations, where people are trying to give support, they often blunder in the accidental killer's eyes. One accidental killer describes this type of situation: "I think the hardest part is having to talk to people who are trying very hard to help. But they stare blindly at you while you are talking, and they say well-meaning things like 'Why are you doing this to yourself?' And then you begin to question your own sanity."

An accidental killer recalls her discomfort around a tactless friend:

I know this friend did not intend to hurt me, but so many times, even two years after the accident, if we were talking to someone who was from out of town or someone we didn't know really well, she would bring up the fact that we had been in an accident. It was always like a bolt out of the blue, with all the guilt sweeping back over me again. I am grateful that during the last year she seems to have stopped doing this as much.

Another accidental killer explains that she did not like hearing people discuss her accident as if she were not present. "In the office, my coworkers were talking about the accident," she says. "I couldn't stand to listen. I had to speak up—but not nastily."

Some accidental killers feel that the accident has marked them for life. "It was like everybody who saw me was saying, 'Oh, that's him. He's the guy who killed his roommate,'" one survivor says.

Another expresses his annoyance at hearing the assessment "Teenage drivers will just never learn." He says, "I was not negligent. Even though a lot of older drivers are just as reckless as teenagers, you never hear anyone say, 'Middle-age drivers will just never learn.'"

Some people who did not like the accidental killer before the accident see it as an opportunity to insult the accidental killer. One accidental killer notes, "A person I didn't like at school called me an old-lady killer." Another recalls an especially bold affront:

Dad owned a large oil shipping company, and I was driving one of his trucks at the time of the accident. The hardest thing with people that have this happen is that some days you have people looking at you and saying, "Well, I don't know why he couldn't have done such and such, and that wouldn't have happened." Well, it just doesn't happen like that. Who in their right mind would want to run over two other people? Looking back, I never thought growing up that I would kill two people. I will never relish the day that I had to call those two boys' parents and tell them I was sorry that I had killed their sons.

One day I walked into this mechanic's shop, and he said to me, "How much did it cost your daddy to get you off the hook?" If he hadn't been so old, I would've hit the guy.

At the scene, this accidental killer felt ashamed:

> I could not go anywhere from the police cruiser, and it was
> really hot. So I got out once and was put right back in. . . . It
> was very embarrassing because everybody who walks by thinks
> that you're a killer, and the police kept reaching in to get stuff
> from the glove compartment, talking directly to you so they
> could make what I would assume is a preliminary observation
> as to whether you'd been drinking. . . . But the people who
> come look in at you, and the looks they give you can burn you
> to the quick. I felt like a zoo monkey.

Later on he felt exposed:

> After the accident, my dad had me driving again, and I'm sure
> some who didn't know me personally thought, "Good God,
> what is R. W. thinking about? Here this driver has killed two
> people, and he's got him right back in a gas truck driving
> through the middle of town. The stupidity. They ought to take
> his license away from him." You think those thoughts. Whether
> other people actually were or not, I had no idea. You think that
> everyone is looking at you; it's just like your nose grew about
> a foot. . . . It took a while to get over that.

Some accidental killers have to defend themselves against financial
scams:

> I didn't have auto insurance and became the victim of a black-
> mail attempt. Danny [the victim] had told me, the police, and
> hospital personnel that he had no relatives. Yet when I went to
> the funeral home to try and untangle the insurance mess, I
> learned there were two nephews—supposedly! They had
> changed the welfare funeral, and now there was a large bill.
>
> I should explain here. We were all dressed up the night of
> the accident, so it could have appeared that we had money—
> which none of us did. I contacted the "nephews" to see if they
> could sign my insurance paper. They insisted I come to their
> house. I was afraid of them and told them they could come
> where I worked. They did. It was a horrid experience. The one

made me explain everything; he was blaming me. He told me he would sign my paper for $10,000. He said he needed to be reimbursed for his great loss. He kept bugging me for several weeks. I was afraid and angry.

Finally, I told him I had consulted a lawyer and I was going to sue him because of the emotional upset his uncle had caused me. He left me alone after that except for one time. He wanted $75 for the grave marker and then he would sign my paper. A day later I got a notice from the state that everything was okay. I've not seen him since. As close as I can figure, they were two men who hung around the slum area, knew Danny had no relatives, and decided to try to make a fast buck.

Sometimes close friends say good-bye because of an accident. One woman remembers her best friend's rejection, which hurt much more than desertion by the man she had been dating:

I was a sort of pariah or, at least, no longer "neat" to be with. I could understand when my boyfriend said he just wasn't up to meeting my needs because I knew he was correct. What was harder to accept was my best girlfriend's decision that this accident had made me a loser, and she was sorry but she couldn't be friends with a loser.

Sometimes acquaintances of accidental killers or even strangers will prod for explicit descriptions of the accident. A railroad engineer recalls, "A few people have a morbid interest in a fatal accident and try to get all the details. They are not sensitive enough to realize that anyone involved in this type of an experience may not want to talk about it, and so they are consistently trying to bring up the subject."

Another accidental killer says, "Some people asked questions that I considered to be morbid, and I told them so." The difference between morbid curiosity and an honest need to understand the details is the questioner's concern for the accidental killer.

Often accidental killers are irritated by empty words from people who mean well but do not know what to say. One young man tells of his annoyance at hearing, "Oh, I know how you feel." He says,

"It makes me really defensive, and I have often said, 'How in hell do you know unless you have been in the same situation?'"

Some of the most resented words come from people who try to blame the accident on God. One accidental killer remembers, "People said, . . . 'God meant it this way.' I wanted to slap them. I'm sure that people who believe in God meant to be comforting, but there are limits."

Sometimes friends ask accusatory questions such as "Don't you know how to hold a gun?"; "Didn't you check behind the car?"; or "How could you not have seen him?" Others ask probing questions such as "What does it feel like to kill?" And still others bungle an attempt to be sympathetic by saying, "What a horrible thing to have to live with the rest of your life!" One accidental killer painfully recalls her husband's joke, "How many people did you kill today?"

Children who accidentally kill can be especially vulnerable to insensitive remarks by others, particularly if those remarks occur in a group setting. A man who was six at the time of his accident remembers his ordeal:

One Saturday morning we went out to get wood. I took my .22 short rifle just in case I'd see any rabbits. Two of our neighbors, Mr. Hernandez and his son Miguel, went with us. Miguel was about fourteen and spoke very good English. I always admired him for that. As a matter of fact, sometimes he'd interpret for me when I had something special to tell my teacher.

It was a productive morning. We all worked hard, and while most of us chopped the wood, Uncle Julio hauled about five loads of wood to our respective houses. We finished about noon, and then we all sat around on the ground under some trees to rest and drink water out of our canteens. Someone remarked, "Ricardo, where are the rabbits?" We had been so busy chopping wood that I'd forgotten about the rifle. It was still leaning against the tree where I had placed it earlier in the morning.

I gazed at the rifle, but I was too tired to go out rabbit hunting. However, I did feel like having some target practice. I picked up the single-shot, loaded it, and aimed at a tin can on the opposite hill. However, my arms were so tired they began to tremble, and I decided not to practice. Instead, I'd invite others to shoot. As I turned around to invite those sitting behind me, the gun went off. Miguel Hernandez fell backward without making a sound. Mr. Hernandez and Uncle Julio rushed to his side and unbuttoned his shirt. There was a hole in his chest, right over the heart. Mr. Hernandez felt for a pulse. *"Está muerto"* [He is dead], [he said]. . . .

It was too late for a doctor. Uncle Julio sent someone to notify the sheriff's department. Within the hour, several sheriff's deputies had arrived to view the body.

Before the week was over, a hearing was held at the courthouse. . . . I was the only witness to take the stand.

After the hearing, we walked home, just one block away. A heavy overcast added a touch of gloom to the dreary day. The rain began about the middle of the afternoon. That evening, as we were having supper, Mother answered a knock at the door. It was Mr. Hernandez. He was invited in. His visit was short but long enough to ask Mother to help him pay the funeral expenses. The following day, Mother sent her brother with $200 to the Hernandez home. Within a few days, the Hernandez family moved away, and we never heard of them again.

I didn't go back to school until the following Monday. . . . Purposely, I went late that morning. I walked into the classroom quietly, with a feeling of embarrassment, almost afraid. I barely breathed. All eyes were upon me. No one said a word to me, not even the teacher. . . .

At recess time, I lingered in the room just long enough to permit the class to go out ahead of me. When they were all gone, the teacher urged me to hurry out. I did, shuffling slowly down the long hallway to the rear door of the building. As I stepped out onto the playground, I was greeted with an angry chorus of *"matón, matón, matón"* [killer, killer, killer]. I was dumbfounded and confused. I had no idea how to cope with such an attack. Suddenly I burst into tears and ran all the way home.

Late that afternoon, a bilingual truant officer came to the house to talk to Mother and me, assuring us that nothing like that would happen again. He urged me to return to school the following morning.

I did return to school, but with a feeling of loneliness. I felt unwanted and shunned. Little wonder that to a certain degree I became a loner. I no longer played baseball with the rest of the boys. I kept to myself as much as I could. I was always happy to go home at the end of the school day.

Rumors

A fatal accident is an ideal subject for gossip. Unfortunately, the facts can become twisted and exaggerated beyond recognition. One rural area's rumor mill went wild when a colorful local personality accidentally killed another young man. The accidental killer was highly visible because of his business as a party disc jockey. He recalls:

> I never did get bothered by rumors because you never know if the person who supposedly said it really did. And you know the rumor isn't true, but you don't know who added how much. . . .
>
> At eight o'clock the night of the accident, I was at a friend's, Johnny's, and we were watching TV and eating popcorn and drinking coffee. We were giving his sister a ride home. . . .
>
> I saw lights that didn't look right, so I slowed down. It was a two-lane highway. Somebody was making a U-turn. Then I saw the taillights in front of that car. It was a parked van with a gas can in front of it. The car that made the U-turn had pulled over to help him but was leaving. I got past the gas can, and somebody was coming from the other direction that he (the victim) recognized, and he ran out to flag them down. I went, "What was that?" I knew what it was, but I don't think I wanted to believe it, and I said, "I think it was a deer."
>
> I didn't think so at the time, but a couple of days later I realized I was in shock. First I just went over to the side of the road and curled up in a ball. The wife of the guy was screaming in the background. The police cruisers all came. Before I went to the bank on the side of the road, I went back to check on him. I didn't even bother to do anything because I was positive he was dead. His face was on the ground; his left leg was

ripped off, but there was no blood. He died in an instant, so he didn't suffer. He only got to the passenger side of the car.

I wasn't in that good of shape. I was in shock, but I was still in control of myself. I had to give the impression that I was all shook up, couldn't talk, just for my own sake, because I know the cops and how they think. I acted catatonic, answered by nodding to questions, like if you waved your hand in front of me I wouldn't see it. I had to tell that story five times—once at the hospital, the police department, once on the road, once in the cruisers, and to my mother. . . .

They took my license for a couple of days until they saw how the blood test came up. I never heard any more about it after that. . . .

The funeral was almost as bad as the accident. I was the first one there along with the minister and a couple of the mortuary guys. Every police cruiser in the county was there. It was outside in the cemetery. Of course, they're going to come over and look at the person who did it. I would too. . . .

The guy's mother had been at dances I did at the school there. She blamed me for it. She never had talked to me before, and that day she had been acting as if it was my fault. But the next day she came and apologized, and she's always talked to me ever since then. But her husband, he always talked to me before that. He hasn't talked to me since. I don't think he knows how to face me.

I'm used to rumors. I'm always used to people seeing me play; because they don't know me, they make up things good or bad. The guy who died was small, had a moustache, long hair, and smoked pot. He liked to sell drugs to the wrong people. A lot of people congratulated me—which I really didn't appreciate because I didn't do it on purpose. The week before the accident, his wife had asked him to make his funeral arrangements. He had been suicidal. They had been seeing a counselor. Some people said that his wife said he just jumped out in front of me. I couldn't tell if he was facing me or not.

There were rumors that there were drugs. . . . Another rumor was that I was going 120 miles per hour and that I was drinking Jack Daniel's. There was even a rumor that when I hit him, his head flew over to the fire department—and that's a mile away from there.

The Victim's Family

Reeling from their loss, the victim's family is often incapable of forgiving the accidental killer, who may personify their sorrow. But understanding on the part of the victim's family is what accidental killers long for. They want the family to know that no harm was intended. Thoughts of the family dominate the minds of most accidental killers. Confronting the family is for many the most difficult thing they have ever had to do in their lives. They realize that they may be the last person in the world the family wants to see. If direct communication is not an option, they must try to resolve their feelings themselves. Some write letters expressing their regret; these letters often go unanswered. Whatever form this encounter takes, it is central to the accidental killer's recovery.

A friendly relationship between the family and the accidental killer prior to the accident is no guarantee of postaccident acceptance. In some cases, the friendship makes coming to terms with each other more difficult. A teenager who was involved in a fatal accident describes how the parents of the boy who died remained in denial:

> It would have been a very uncomfortable and emotional experience to talk to Jerry's parents. However, since they avoided us, this denied us a chance to say we were sorry and to try to put an end somewhat to the situation. Little opportunity to process the pain resulted in a great lack of closure. I felt unable to share in the grief process due to being an apparent cause of that grief. I found there was little communication between the people involved and the victim's family, and it was very unsettling. The total atmosphere was one of pretending it did not happen!

When there is no resolution, thoughts of the family can linger indefinitely in the accidental killer's mind. "I had never met my girl-friend's parents, or even spoken with them, when I had to call them and inform them their daughter was dead," explains a man who was a college sophomore when his car skidded off the road and into a tree. He continues:

> When I talked to her parents, I told them my grief was as much as theirs. Her father took the news silently.
>
> For years afterward, when my business would take me to the city where her parents lived, I would try to make myself go and express my sadness to them. I could only bring myself to drive around the block where they lived and look at their house.

Some family members lose control of themselves when confronted by the accidental killer. A secretary who ran over a little girl remembers the child's uncle coming to pay her a visit: "In front of my husband and my children, he became very abusive. Luckily my husband was there and was able to get control of the situation. I was quite hysterical. I realize, looking back on this incident, he was just as upset and distraught as we were—perhaps more."

A railroad engineer remembers a beating following a fellow engineer's accident: "It was a little baby girl; she had crawled out through the fence. He [the engineer] clipped her on the track. The father was hysterical. He beat up the engineer so badly the police wanted to know if the engineer wanted to file assault charges. He refused. The father was put under a doctor's care."

Sometimes families would rather not see the accidental killer ever again. A woman who backed her car over a neighborhood child says, "The mother of the child had been my friend, but I have not seen or spoken to her since. She has no desire to see me."

A man who lives in a small town thinks continually about the next time he will meet a member of the family of a motorcyclist with whom he collided:

> The biggest thing that still bothers me is hearing the family's name mentioned or seeing one of them or something connected with them. The fear and guilt come back, and I usually find myself trying to avoid them instead of running into them or talking to them. I have no idea how they feel toward me, as I haven't talked to them.

One thing that really hurts me is that the other son of the family . . . will not wave or even acknowledge me when I meet him on the street. I suppose this is normal and it hurts him when he sees me, but it still bothers me.

Publicity

Accidental deaths often attract a lot of media attention. Many accidental killers are shocked to hear their names broadcast in connection with the death only hours after it has occurred. When inaccuracies are reported, the situation is even worse. A woman who backed her car over a neighborhood child describes her experience:

Television and newspaper accounts held me responsible and pictured me as a reckless driver. They quoted me as saying that I thought I hit a chuckhole, which I never said. Many people asked me if I looked back before backing out.

My car insurance was canceled, and the company tried to get out of being responsible, since I had just bought the car the previous day from a private party and had not yet signed any papers. So I was getting long-distance calls from their central office, and they were recording my statements over the phone. I finally got a lawyer. . . . It was finally all settled, and my insurance is going to pay, but all of these things made me feel more guilt.

My children also went through a trial at school. . . . The evening after the accident, the child's father returned home from being out of state. I was experiencing real fear, not knowing what he was like or how this death would affect him. . . . I could not stay in my house for two nights, and I was afraid to be left alone.

Sometimes the circumstances of an accidental death are difficult to discern, which can result in reporting errors. Deeply troubled by his involvement in the death of a fellow officer, a thrice-decorated policeman did not like the newspaper coverage of his accident:

It was a four-to-twelve shift when we got a red call. Two officers were in pursuit of a stolen '62 Chevy Impala. They'd tried to pull it over for a defective taillight, but he'd driven off and they pursued. It was a kid driving. They chased him for fifteen minutes, and they saw he had an object in his hand, which appeared to be a gun. They put it on the radio that they thought he was armed. He rammed two cars off the road—there were twenty-one officers in pursuit by this time—state and county deputies got involved. He made a threatening gesture every time someone got near him. He had no intention of stopping.

We thought there must be more to this than just an old stolen clunker. We expected to find a body in the trunk. I stopped him when I was northbound and he was southbound. Two cops in front of me were trying to intercept him. We had him surrounded on all the streets, but instead of stopping him, the car in front of me let him go by at the last minute. So I cut him off, and the kid and I both pulled up on a lawn.

I told him to freeze—to stay in the car—but he started to open the door. I was afraid he had a shotgun. . . . I kicked the door shut and told him to come out. The second time he came out, I figured he had a gun. He had on a long blue windbreaker, and I couldn't see his hands. He was young looking, had a baby face, and looked frightened. When I told him to put up his hands, he jumped me and tried to pull my gun away. It went off when the barrel hit him on the side of the head.

Once I'd hit the kid, the other officers jumped in. I saw his car inching forward, so I jumped in and put it in park. Then somebody said, "There's a cop down here." He was lying down about twenty-five feet away in front of his car. There was just a tiny spot of blood on the collarbone. The bullet had ricocheted off the collarbone and cut the aorta. . . .

The search of the kid's car revealed that what was thought to be a weapon was a marijuana pipe. . . .

The grand jury records show that of the twenty-one officers at the scene, twenty gave exactly the same testimony in separate accounts. Also, the instructor who wrote the manual on the use of force for the state testified that I had done everything by the book.

I was given the week off, and I didn't think I would go back to my job. I didn't know it, but my wife had called my captain and said if he didn't get me back soon, I was never going to come back. He called and demanded I come back the next day. . . .

I wished I could've taken [the other officer's] place underground. I wanted to go to the wake, but I was told by the department not to. . . . I called up the widow, and she said she knew I was a good cop just like her husband and that if I didn't go back to work, they would lose two good cops.

The newspaper sensationalized [the story]. I would never have recognized the story if my name hadn't been in it. It showed the kid as a poor, misguided kid, talked about how it took twenty-one cops to get him. It criticized me for having drawn my pistol. My wife happened to work for the paper, and she blew her stack at the reporter who wrote the story: "I know my husband, and I'm telling you what he's like, and he's not like this." Gradually, as the reporter did more research, the stories got better. . . . It was annoying that they didn't take the time to get the proper information in the beginning.

Accidental killing is an occupational hazard for railroad engineers. One engineer explains how media coverage of such accidents affects the killers:

People still use the trains as a way of suicide. The media still put these stories in the paper locally and also include the engineer's name in the story. The union has tried to stop the names being put in the paper, but the police release the information. All your neighbors and children's friends see these articles and make remarks. It is very hard on young children.

A local newspaper carried a story giving my name and the town in which I lived. It also stated, "As yet, criminal charges have not been brought against the engineer." Needless to say, I was enraged, but fortunately neither myself nor my family was exposed to crank phone calls from despondent friends and relatives of the deceased. That does not, however, nullify one's apprehension about being exposed to such calls.

Employer and Teacher Problems

Some employers have a negative attitude toward accidental killers, especially if the accident occurred on the job. One railroad engineer notes:

> Operating trains as a railroad engineer on an express train, I had two deaths in two weeks. The first Sunday, about 5:20 P.M., was a male sleeping on the tracks. The second Sunday, about the same time, was a female, later identified as the girlfriend of the man I had killed the previous week. She stepped out from behind the station platform. I never saw her face, only her back. She extended her arms outward. I placed my train in emergency, continually blowing my horn. When I was approximately twenty to thirty feet away, she placed her hands over her ears. I never knew it was a girl until afterward because her hair was not too long. She wore a white, loose, long-sleeved shirt, some jeans, and western boots.
>
> The company didn't help at all. They stated, "No work, no pay." I really think the news media, in their sensationalism, distorted the facts and made kind of a human interest story out of it.

Another railroad engineer remembers:

> In the spring of 1975, I was operating a locomotive at approximately forty-five to fifty miles per hour. The locomotive was one that did not have any cars attached to it, and I was alone in the cab. As I was proceeding in a westerly direction, there was a passenger train stopped on an immediately adjacent track. It had been stopped at a station to discharge its passengers. At the other end of this train, there was a diesel unit, which makes a considerable amount of noise.
>
> A man who was twenty-three years old, a passenger on that train, stepped out from that unit without looking in my direction. He obviously did not hear either the horn or the bell, which were being sounded by me at that time.
>
> The man stepped between my running rails; when my engine was approximately fifteen feet away, he looked up and was

startled. Within a fraction of a second after I witnessed the expression on the man's face, the engine struck him. He was killed instantly.

The railroad management were apathetic. Their principal concern was the amount of liability that would ensue as a result of the accident. The employee and his or her feelings are secondary, tertiary, or perhaps not even a factor.

Similarly, students sometimes encounter cold indifference from teachers when they request leave time to recover. One student who accidentally hit a pedestrian with her car remembers the response of a professor whom she asked for extra time to make up work she had missed because of the accident: "He acted like he didn't care a bit and just emphasized the importance of keeping up with my assignments."

Official Disapproval

Some accidental killers are verbally attacked by authorities at or near the accident scene. Criticism from police, physicians, and other professionals can have a significant impact. Author Kurt Vonnegut, Jr., describes the traumatic reprimand of a twelve-year-old accidental killer in his novel *Dead Eye Dick*:

> So the ordinary cop drove me home. He kept his eye on the road, but his thoughts were all on me. He said that I would have to think about Mrs. Metzger, lying cold in the ground, for the rest of my life, and that if he were me, he would probably commit suicide. He said that he expected some relatives of Mrs. Metzger would get me sooner or later, when I least expected it, maybe the very next day, or maybe when I was a man, full of hopes and good prospects and with a family of my own. Whoever did it, he said, would probably want me to suffer some.
>
> I would have been too addled, too close to death, to get his name, if he hadn't insisted that I commit it to memory, since I would undoubtedly want to make a complaint about him, since policemen were expected to speak politely at all times.[5]

Unfortunately, the experience of official castigation is not confined to fiction. In some cases, ambiguities surrounding the accident's circumstances encourage authority figures to take a "guilty until proven innocent" stance. A rural youth remembers such condemnation immediately after an accident in which his best friend was killed:

> There were no legal proceedings. The doctor at the hospital gave a test for alcohol, but there was none in my blood. Before he saw the results, the doctor was upset. He saw the mud on the wheels and said, "Look what you've done. You've gone and killed your friend." He said I would be charged with involuntary manslaughter. He was really ashamed when the results came back negative.

The Courts

It would be difficult to exaggerate an accidental killer's dread of court proceedings. The judicial process can greatly exacerbate the accidental killer's suffering. The thought of going to court is terrifying, and a potential criminal conviction or loss in a civil court generates intense anxiety. The thought of being cross-examined by a shrewd prosecutor before a dispassionate jury also is frightening. In addition, the prospect of delivering emotionally sensitive testimony in the courtroom is daunting. Finally, the trial undoubtedly will disrupt the accidental killer's life, especially if it drags on.

According to Rabbi Earl Grollman, author of *What Helped Me When My Loved One Died* and many other books on grieving, going to court can have a negative effect on the healing process. He notes, "Legal procedures interrupt the process of going through anger, grief, and tears because the accidental killers are having to justify themselves."[6] Sometimes bereaved families press charges in hopes that punishing the person "responsible" for their loss will make them feel better. But psychologist Ann Kaiser Stearns reports that legal proceedings rarely ease the family's pain.[7]

From the accidental killer's standpoint, the trial magnifies the pain she is suffering. A woman who was in college at the time of her accident remembers that she received little support in the face of the legal maneuvers of the victim's family:

The day of the accident, the hospital staff sent me to the chapel with the Episcopalian (my denomination) priest. He just sat there; he didn't even try to talk to me. As we sat there, I asked him why he became a priest. He said it was because his mother wanted him to. I wanted *any* kind of reassurance, comfort, religious mumbo-jumbo—*anything,* but that was all the response I got from him.

The victim's parents were gone to Europe. Somebody notified her aunt and uncle, but the priest made me go with him to her grandmother's house so that I could tell this old woman (whom I had never met and who had recently lost her husband) that her favorite, her *only,* granddaughter had died and how it had happened. I had to do this within an hour of the death.

Later at school some people asked me to describe the accident. My father came across the country for the funeral, but all he did was get mad at me because I was unable to cry.

[The victim's] parents called me and asked me if I wanted anything of hers to remember her by. Then they got abusive. They found out that my father had established a trust fund for me the year before. They first tried to have me tried for murder, then manslaughter, then negligent homicide. They wanted, finally, the amount of the trust fund. Two and a half years after the accident, I met with their attorney and my attorney, and I was asked to diagram the accident. I did, and a month or so later, my lawyer informed me that [the victim's] parents weren't going to try to sue me anymore. They decided to sue the state highway department for not closing off a dangerous old roadway.

About a year after the accident I started to have trouble with my relationships with all my friends. I was sullen, combative, rude, aggressive, defensive—obnoxious. It seemed as though people were avoiding me. I met the boy who later became my husband, and we were having a terrible time arguing. I finally went to the campus student counselor. I told him about the accident, but he didn't seem to think my problems had anything to do with it.

When I wanted to talk about the accident with my closest friends, they didn't want to talk about it. Almost everybody had dismissed my fears as foolish. Nobody has ever told me it wasn't my fault. Even my husband, whenever I bring it up, goes into a long psychological explanation of why I feel guilty.

One of the most upsetting aspects of a trial is the start-and-stop nature of the judicial process. One accidental killer reports:

> Just about the time I was getting to where I could concentrate on work for an hour without thinking about the accident, I received a letter from an attorney saying that he was representing a relative of the deceased with regard to the damages. My own attorney's assurances that the matter would be handled were of no comfort. For years I kept getting panic feelings.

A woman who was involved in a fatal accident while driving across the country remembers her resentment of the numerous postponements of her case. The trial kept her household in an uproar for two years. She says:

> I have five children, and all of them were afraid for me to go to trial. It was a civil suit and was tried across the state from our home. Every time the date came up, I had to leave them with my mother. It was rescheduled three times. I just had to psyche myself up mentally because I was fearful I would break down under questioning and that the jury would interpret this as a sign of guilt. The suspense and fear of going through a courtroom session really haunted me.

To their fear about giving legitimate testimony, some accidental killers add the guilt of perjury. A seventeen-year-old who disregarded a yield sign at high speed and sideswiped a car, killing one of its occupants, says:

> The amount sought was huge—$50,000 above the amount of my insurance coverage. I felt worse after the lawsuit was over because I knew I was at fault and they should have won. I was scared. My insurance company hired accident reconstruction experts and the best lawyers available. I was coached on exactly what to say. The other side didn't have a chance. I wanted

just to tell the family how sorry I was and how I felt, but we were in an adversary relationship by the lawsuit, and I just couldn't do it.

Sometimes accidental killers feel persecuted by the judge:

> I had five hearings with the DMV [Department of Motor Vehicles]. [The judge] couldn't see how I hadn't seen the man run over the two lanes of traffic. The judge had the attitude that I had done something wrong and it was his mission to prove it. At one point, he had a policeman testify, and he said it looked like an accident. But nothing mattered to the judge. It's punishment enough to live to go through it. I wanted the judge to have to go through it and see how mean he was being.

Justice is not always rendered, as the threat of wrongful conviction is real. One accidental killer nearly served a prison sentence because of faulty lab tests:

> I ran over a drunk man lying in the road who had already been hit once by a hit-and-run driver. The hit-and-run driver could not be found, and the man died hours later. So I was listed as the cause of death. Two friends with me at the time agreed that it was very difficult to see the man on the road.
>
> Initially, the police knew that I had not broken the law in any way and therefore did not arrest me. They knew that I had not been drinking, so we all agreed that it would be best to have the positive proof for my protection. I had a blood test done by a doctor, and it was sent to the state toxicology lab. The results came back over a month later and showed that I was driving almost under the influence.
>
> The police had no choice but to arrest me for negligent homicide. One month later, I had to appear before a coroner's inquest. He felt that there was now a reasonable cause to send [the case] to court.
>
> Six months later, I went on trial before a jury; the trial lasted seven days. Because I had been in close contact with the police and a doctor just after the accident, I had eight police officers and a well-known doctor stake their occupations on the line

that I had not been drinking. My lawyer got the representative from the state toxicology lab to admit that they were very understaffed and overloaded with work. He admitted that because of this, there was a good chance that they could have made a mistake. The jury found me innocent.

Because the news media printed false statements about the accident—that I was drunk, hit-and-run, driving without a license, and resisted arrest—there was a tendency for rumors to spread very quickly. Those who knew me helped to tell my side of the story. I had the support of the entire police department. . . .

Because the man I killed was a member of an ethnic group different from my own, that group of people in town were very angry. They said the hearing was a sham. My family and I received threatening phone calls for years after. . . . I still feel uncomfortable in the presence of people of that ethnic group.

All lives are not valued equally in the United States. It is clear that the social status of the accidental killer relative to that of the deceased in large part determines the court's attitude. Punishment varies wildly. An aged, nearly illiterate woman never recovered from the judicial consequences of her accident:

I was driving by myself in the afternoon when I had a mild epileptic seizure. Until then, I didn't know I had epilepsy. I blacked out, and I hit two little children. They were brother and sister, little blond children, aged four and six. They were on bicycles.

When the police searched the car, they found a bottle in the glove compartment that had my migraine headache pills mixed in with my husband's pills for his gran mal epilepsy. The newspaper headlines said it was a drug-related accident.

The day I pleaded guilty, my husband died of a heart attack. I spent six months in jail. I can never drive again. I live a ways out from town. The only time I go to town is if friends come and get me.

Judicial proceedings also can cast suspicion on accidental killers among friends and family. A man who spent time in jail for accidentally killing his stepdaughter remembers:

The baby was blonde, blue-eyed, petite. She was my wife's by her first marriage, and we were expecting our own. She was two years old. . . . It was not yet her third birthday, and she could sit down and write out words.

It was a Sunday. We were working on a rental house we were getting ready to move into. We were getting ready to move out of our apartment. We had been doing yard work at the new house. My wife was making grilled cheese sandwiches, and I was in the bathroom shaving. The baby had been picking her nose and making it bleed. I had told her to stop twice, and then I saw she was picking her nose again. I reached down and swatted her hand, not hard, but it made her fall back and hit her head on the toilet bowl. I was looking in the mirror, and I miscalculated.

She didn't black out at first. She was crying, and I patted her head against my cheek. A half hour later, I put her pajamas on her for bed. I went out and looked at TV—I remember I was watching that singer, Englebert Humperdink. And then I saw the baby just didn't seem normal, and I said, "Something's wrong. Let's get this baby to the hospital." We took her in, and they were going to do surgery, but then they canceled the surgery. I couldn't understand why. I tried to find out, but I couldn't get an answer out of them. She had a cerebral hemorrhage from a cervical vertebra. After 6:00 or 7:00 A.M., they told us she had died.

When the police came, they just knew I had slapped her and hit her hard. When I had patted her cheek on my shoulder, her nosebleed got my shirt bloody. I had left the shirt on the bathtub when we went to the hospital, and that was the first thing the cops saw. They turned the house inside out looking for a murder weapon. They wouldn't believe she'd had fallen. They said I'd hit her with something. . . . They thought we considered the baby a nuisance and that we did it to get her out of the way.

I should explain. There was a big child abuse program on television, a six-week special on the news, and this happened in the middle of it. Why did I feel guilty in court when I knew I was innocent? They try to misconstrue events to make you feel guiltier than you really are. You don't get over it.

I found out from the district attorney's that a grand jury had indicted me for murder. They thought I had done it on purpose. They issued a warrant for my arrest, and the DA asked if I wanted them to come get me or turn myself in. I went down to the county jail. They read me my rights. I had to stay in the jail. I had as cellmates two robbers. One had hit three banks in an hour. I had watched the story on the evening news.

A blood test showed there were barbiturates in [the baby's] blood, and a doctor said it couldn't have happened that way. My attorney ordered an autopsy, which showed there were none. Later it was found there was a dirty test tube. It took seven or eight years to straighten that out.

While I was in jail waiting for my trial, a front-page story came out in the paper—"Stepfather Beats Child to Death." I thought the guy who did it should be hung. Then at the bottom I saw my own name. I couldn't believe the story was about me. It was not even close. I just came apart. I said, "No, it can't be." At the trial I insisted that my lawyer bar the press. In my opinion, they'd already done enough damage. Nobody believed my story about it being an accident. One night I tried to hang myself with a sheet from the bed, but one of the guys in the cell saw me and stopped me.

There was a detective on the case, and he would go every day in the afternoon and try to get a confession out of my wife. . . . He told her that the baby wasn't my kid and I wanted her out of the way. . . . My attorney got a restraining order to keep him from bothering my wife. I felt like she wouldn't have stuck by me if I'd done it on purpose.

At the trial, the issue was how hard I had hit [the baby]. It seemed like I only hit her hand, but apparently I hit her hard enough to knock her backward. The prosecutor asked me, "Did you or did you not strike a blow that killed a child?" I said, "Yes, of course I did. But not intentionally."

The judge asked me if I wanted a jury trial; they were making a big deal about the grand jury investigation. I told the judge, "I'm getting fed up with this. I don't need a jury. I'll just tell you what happened, and you decide what you want to do about it. I've been sitting in the county jail three months, and I'm fed up with the whole works." He went into his quarters and then came out. He said, "What would you do if I called this off and said you were free to go here and now? If I let you walk out of this courtroom right now, what will you do?"

I said, "I'm not ready. I've been in jail for three months. My little girl is dead. I need supervision. I need help before I walk back on the streets."

So he sentenced me to a work release camp. I could walk away, but I spent nights and weekends there. Then my wife was due to have our first baby, and I asked the judge if I could go home to be with her. The release came the next day.

I've had a lot of sleepless nights and tears. I wake up in the middle of the night; I still dream about it. But the roughest part of all was after I got out. You don't know if your friends are going to accept you. They look at you like they don't really know what to think. But those who didn't stick by me didn't mean anything to me anyway. I saw my best friend in the supermarket, and he said, "I don't know you, and I don't want to know you."

Family Stress

My wife kept bringing it up whenever she would get mad: "You killed my baby." After our baby came and if I was playing with her, my wife would grab her and say something like, "That's not your baby; that's my baby. You killed my baby."

One time she threw a butcher knife at me—it stuck into the wall three inches above my head. Another time I was walking up the stairs behind her. She stood at the top and turned around and kicked me in the chest and knocked me back down—totally unprovoked.

In the most fundamental way, accidental death brings up issues of trust, forgiveness, and unconditional love. All the members of an accidental killer's family are taxed by the tragedy. While the stress may not always erupt as strikingly as in the family episode just described, for many accidental killers, the crisis may strain the family to the point of breaking their most important bonds at a time when they most need support. Here is how some describe their family situations:

"Two days after the accident, my husband lost patience; he was tired of hearing my story."

"She went elsewhere seeking the affection I was denying her. I realized she was seeing another man, and we separated. The separation made me more lonely."

"We argue a lot more. He doesn't know how to help, and he gets angry when I can't tell him what will help, what to do, or what I need. I don't even know the answers to these questions myself."

Families in Crisis

Virginia Satir[1] and other family therapists have documented that families operate as units. What happens to one member affects the others. The systems model of the family looks at behavioral feedback loops, which maintain its homeostasis.[2] This means that members react to one another in automatic patterns, and their behavior maintains the dynamic balance of forces within the family.[3]

People are shaped by their relationships with others. Almost like elements that change their electron configuration in response to contact with other atoms, they become new people as the result of their interactions with other people. Families have the power to shape their members, and members also affect the family, which changes and adapts in response to what the members do and say.

Healthy families have clear boundaries and communication. Requests for clarification are encouraged, and unresolved issues are not allowed to build up. The marital pair share equally supportive power, and independence is valued. Hurts and losses are discussed, and grieving as well as joy is permissible. Healthy families negotiate problems, hearing what each has to say and incorporating everyone's input into the solution. The family also "has a sense of itself as a unit in which all members feel they have a special or meaningful relationship with each other. There is inherent knowledge that the whole is more than the sum of its parts. Others may be welcomed but not treated as if they were truly family members."[4]

Stress results from any demand that threatens the members' accomplishment of goals or the family's equilibrium. Families tend to react to trauma in their own characteristic patterns.[5] When the family's normal problem-solving skills are insufficient to deal with the trauma[6] or its adaptive mechanisms are overloaded,[7] it goes into crisis. If initial attempts at dealing with the problem are not successful, the family may intensify its efforts according to its initial patterns until either the system breaks down or the family can establish a new set of patterns.[8]

If the accidental killer becomes depressed, the entire family may be caught in a downward spiral. Depression has been conceptualized as a lower level of functioning, which can create a negative reinforcing feedback loop that provides fewer opportunities for interaction, thus causing more depression.[9] The accidental killer may make less eye contact; talk less; take longer to respond to others; and speak monotonously, slowly, and softly about self-centered topics, helplessness, and sadness. The family may try to help by relieving the depressed person of responsibilities. This approach can make an accidental killer feel useless. Alternatively, family members may try to give advice and feel frustrated when the accidental killer does not accept it. The depressed person, being sensitive to the family members' anger, may become more depressed, which makes the other family members feel as though they have failed. The negative cycle continues until something interrupts it.[10]

This is the family's chance to change. But recognition of this opportunity is necessary for change to be possible. Often the family is so distressed that the members may not recognize this chance for growth. A time of instability typically follows a tragedy while members negotiate the process of adjustment.[11] When changes do occur, frightened members often struggle to regain the group's familiar structure. They do not even want to consider new options that would introduce the possibility of even more drastic change.

Many families of accidental killers flounder. Since no widely accepted norm exists for responding to one member's involvement in an accidental death, the other members often react out of their own reading of cultural assumptions about the nature of the accident. These are highly subjective interpretations of the accident based on the members' personal histories. As one might expect, both strengths and weaknesses of individuals and family systems are magnified by this process.

Family therapist Irma Gottesfeld explains:

> I would look at what this death did to the way the family operates. Generally they have a preset pattern of dealing with stress, and they use that pattern, whatever it is. That could be reaching out to agencies; it could be alcohol; it could be to become a workaholic; or it could be one of the kids acting out. If you don't look at the family as a system, you might try to treat the father who is drinking or treat the child who is failing school and ignore the fact that the effects of the death hit the whole family. You have to be attentive to whatever the family pattern is. Constructive family patterns tend to repeat themselves, and destructive ones do, too.[12]

When family ties are supportive, they create a wonderful haven. They provide a shelter for the accidental killer from the accident's negative repercussions. Family empathy and concern may extend even to anticipating a tragedy. A railroad wife provides some insight into this situation: "I wonder how many ever think of the helplessness an engineer feels when confronted with an impending tragedy over which he has no control. It is a traumatic experience from which he never completely recovers. Each day I pray for my husband's safe return and that he won't have to live some tragic nightmare which can never be erased from his mind."

But loved ones may fall short of providing whatever the accidental killer needs to recover. Often the accidental killer's needs exceed the capacity of a spouse or other family member to respond. One accidental killer notes:

I was driving to work at night when a boy stepped out in front of my car. He was with a group of friends on one side of the highway. I found out that he and his friends had argued and that he had decided to walk home. I thought he saw my car lights in time to avoid being hit. I did not have time to avoid him. I then lost control of my car but was able to stop it. I was hysterical when I got out of the car. One of his friends kept telling me it was not my fault and that he was acting crazy. I could smell beer on their breath. I flagged a passing car and sent for my husband and the highway patrol.

We found the boy in the dark. Someone asked if anyone at the accident scene was a nurse or doctor. I told them I was a nurse, and they asked me if I could check him to see if he was alive. I really didn't feel I was in control enough to administer first aid. But after seeing him, everything I knew about emergency came to me. I was able to stay with him until he was transferred to a nearby hospital. He died three days later.

When the accident occurred, I was involved in intensive training as a nurse anesthetist at a medical center. I was obligated to twelve to fourteen hours a day at work which is mentally exhausting. The accident drained my ability to cope with home, family, and work.

At first I thought people were staring at me unnecessarily—

at work and in the grocery store, for example. I had to divert my attention at the time to school if I was to complete the course. I had one year left in school, and this served to take my attention off the accident. Also, only a limited number of people knew of the accident because we were living away from our hometown.

After graduation, I had a new set of circumstances to deal with. I also found I had extra time to go back over the accident, which was a year old. But I had never really had enough time to dwell on it. It was as if I was cushioned.

I had a delayed depression. No one knew I had been involved in a tragic accident, since we had moved to a new city. I felt the need for people to know, but I never told anyone. I had the desire to talk about it often but found I had no one to talk to. My husband, who was very considerate if I needed to express my feelings before . . . felt I had no need to talk about an accident which was a year old.

Sometimes family members have unrealistic expectations about their loved one's recovery rate. They may call the accidental killer selfish for being self-absorbed without realizing that this inward focus is essential to the healing process. Some spouses and family members are astoundingly insensitive in comparison to neighbors and friends. One woman recalls:

I backed my car over and killed a child who was riding a skateboard on his stomach. . . . My children, nine and seven years old, were extremely understanding and attentive to me for several days. My husband was wonderful to me for exactly two days, and then he had had enough of my upset and wanted me to do things I always did without talking about the accident.

Initially, neighbors and relatives took over the care of my family, doing the things that I normally did. But I felt that I had no right to go on living normally. I felt this so greatly that it actually made me unable to do these things. The neighbors provided me with that time to think and cry as I needed to do. I not only needed time alone to cry and think, but I also needed to talk. My neighbors, relatives, and coworkers were so patient to listen to my story over and over again. I needed to talk and talk to help justify my actions at the time of the accident, and I needed those present at the accident to tell me everything they saw happen. . . .

Two days after the accident when my husband lost all patience with me, he did not understand that I knew, even then, that time would heal my wounds but that I needed time to mourn for what had happened. I still feel that it was my responsibility to mourn, and I wanted to do it. If I had been miserable for weeks, I would have appreciated friends encouraging me to get back into things, but not three days after the accident had happened—in fact the day of the funeral. The boy had been my son's best friend.

Some spouses react from their own needs only. A woman who was hospitalized in an accident that happened out of state recalls her husband's accusation of infidelity upon her return home. "If he could only have seen me—I was in no condition to have an affair," she says.

Accidental killers can strain their families' coping abilities. People who go through an extreme trauma may regress into a passive, dependent state, feeling safer knowing someone else is in charge. They may avoid experiences they know cause excitation, including interpersonal involvement. They may lose interest in sex and follow a policy of "peace at any price."[13] They often show a compulsive need to tell the story of the tragedy again and again, bringing it up out of the blue, each time describing it with identical details and emphasis. But the most common complaint among families of accidental killers is neglect. Entirely absorbed by the accident, accidental killers sometimes shut out all their surroundings, including their loved ones.

A woman voices dismay at her husband's withdrawal following his involvement in a fatal accident: "I felt like I was living in a crystal house that could shatter at any moment. I felt useless. I had no way of knowing how he felt. I couldn't comfort him or give him advice, only listen. I felt neglected but accepted it for about a month. Then I told him I needed some attention because I was hurting just as badly as he was due to my inability to help him."

The husband explains:

At home I acted like a little boy who had his favorite toy just beaten to smithereens by the other neighborhood boys. I would brood and sit around with a glum look on my face. My wife would ask me what was wrong with me, and I didn't know. I'm not a person who drinks, but I got to where I didn't mind fixing myself a drink some evenings—not very often, but there were just some evenings when it became unbearable to even live with myself. I did anything I could to keep my mind off the accident. It took a long time, I guess, to settle back down to earth.

Sometimes the accident catalyzes problems that break up a relationship. One man says:

We met in our high school drama department. Our relationship was better than that of anyone else we knew, but still it was very shallow. In my first year of college, she got pregnant, so I came home from school one weekend and we got married. Three months later, she was diagnosed with a malignant tumor. I quit school, and we moved into a cabin her parents owned in the woods. We were broke in those days. . . . Our medical bills were huge. She had to have chemotherapy. Her hair was falling out, so she started wearing a wig. She went into remission, though, and the American Cancer Society paid for half the medical bill.

When the accident happened, we were still pretty immature. Neither of us was any good at communication except for the indirect way of acting things out. I really needed her, but I wasn't communicating that or anything else. There were lots of needs of hers that I wasn't meeting at all. Usually I will stay in a situation until it hurts and not express my pain. I might express it by making a small suggestion, but I will be really laid-back and gentle until I just can't stand it anymore. Then I just cut out.

She resented my sitting and staring at the walls all night. And we had always kept the right to go out with our friends. I didn't even notice she was gone so much. It wasn't until she left me stranded somewhere all night that I realized she must be seeing someone else. She was trying to make me jealous, which in her family was a way of showing love. To me, either you respected the relationship or you didn't. To me it had already ceased to exist. I moved out a few months later and left her everything we had.

Feeling a need for protection, some partners issue secret ultimatums to themselves. A woman reports:

My husband was involved in a car accident in which he was driving and the passenger was killed. The police, an investigator, and my husband cannot determine why the rear end of the car swerved out, causing the car to go out of control on a slight curve at a speed of only forty-five miles per hour.

While my husband's brother and I were en route to pick him up after the accident, he tried to commit suicide by throwing himself under an eighteen-wheel truck. Fortunately, his life was spared. He has been in a state of deep depression with no desire to live ever since the accident. Because his depression severely affected me, I made the decision to separate so I would be better able to handle the responsibilities of our twelve- and two-year-old sons and my full-time job. My husband has recently moved back with us because of financial reasons. He and I both sought the help of a noted professor of psychiatry at the university where I work. Not only were we not helped, but we came away feeling even more confused. Now my husband feels there is no one who can help and refuses to seek any other help. His method of coping—or not coping—with the problem is to bury himself in his work. He works from early in the morning to after midnight seven days a week at his aeronautical engineering job.

I have made the decision to wait two years from the date of the accident, and if after that time I see no hope for improvement, I will file for divorce. At the same time, I refuse to believe there isn't an individual or organization that could help him. The problem is locating that person or organization. I will do everything I possibly can to prevent a thirty-four-year-old man from wasting the rest of his life.

Sometimes the accident precipitates a breach of faith that cannot be overcome. A young woman who drove over a pedestrian lying in a dark street recalls:

> My fiancé just disappeared at the accident. He was among the onlookers—obviously not a source of a great deal of strength. As we left the accident that night, he said, "See, baby, I told you not to drive so fast." I was not speeding; I was driving twenty-five to thirty miles per hour. He wouldn't go to the hospital with me. I remember how hurt I was; I really needed him. On the day the victim died, my folks came to work to tell me. I went to their house, but my fiancé wouldn't come over. He said he couldn't handle it. So he spent the week after the accident drunk. If I sound bitter, I am. I thought love meant being there when someone needed you. The engagement was broken as a result of his behavior around the accident.

Some accidental killers find their family to be the source of the harshest reproofs and the deepest wounds. One woman says:

> The person who made it hardest on me was my own husband. He went to see about my car the day after the accident. He told me it was in extremely bad shape, that there was a huge dent in the dashboard where Gina [my passenger] had impacted, and that I must have been going at least fifty miles per hour when the accident happened. He seemed to enjoy my distress and wanted to add to it. His father later examined the car, and I did, too. It then became apparent that my husband was lying to me—there was no "huge dent" in the dashboard. The reason the car was totaled was that the engine had been damaged, and it was an eight-year-old car anyway.
>
> At the time the accident occurred, I was separated from my husband and was working as a legal secretary at a large law firm. When I say "separated," we had been living apart for a number of months and had just effected a semireconciliation the day before the accident, which occurred the day after Thanksgiving and the day before my birthday. . . .
>
> My marriage was dissolved, and I have subsequently remar-

ried. I believe that the accident contributed to the ultimate dissolution of my marriage and had a deleterious effect upon my life during that period of time.

Parents of adults often feel that they have the prerogative to judge their children's behavior. The family of origin can deliver savage denunciations of the accidental killer, as these criticisms hurt more than those from outsiders. An accidental killer whose mother called her "stupid girl" comes to mind. Since this disapproval usually comes out of an already established dynamic, the accidental killer's previously undermined self-esteem offers little defense. A young woman notes that her parents' response to her accident was "Well, we never thought you'd be involved in anything like this." She notes, "Consequently, I have no desire to confide in them about any subject."

A middle-aged woman with grown children remembers her mother's punishing attitude: "Knowing how my mother would react, it was ten days before I called her. At first she tried to understand. But within a week, she was screaming about how ashamed she was of me. And to this day, if I mention it around her, she always asks if I am 'proud of it.' Otherwise, she implies, why would I mention it."

Why are so many people hurt by their loved ones when they need comfort? Why is the home so often a combat zone when it should be a refuge? What makes accidental killing so devastating to the ties between those who care deeply for one another? According to Irma Gottesfeld, the answers to these questions lie in the family's sense of responsibility for its members: "One of the things that makes it so stressful is the enormous guilt, the faultfinding. We all need to assign the blame—Why did that happen?—to understand it. Families also construct a story because they feel somehow responsible— much more so than friends."[14]

Families Torn by Death

A family's feeling of outrage at a member's involvement in an accidental death cannot be compared to its devastation when the person who dies is one of its own. The lethal accident can result in great confusion and doubt, especially if it occurs in a context of struggle—for example, a child's assertion of independence or a sibling rivalry. No wonder accidentally killing a family member has been called "the final taboo."[15]

Surviving family members experience complex dynamics, which include feelings of ambivalence toward the accidental killer, since that person is at once the primary source of their grief and the object of their compassion. Poet Gregory Orr describes these mixed feelings in his autobiographical poem "The Mother," in which he runs crying from his fourteenth birthday party to his room, knowing his mother will follow and ask what is wrong:

> And I would say my brother's name, he whom, two years before, I had killed, by accident. And somehow I would have tricked her into forgiving me. But when I spoke his name, she sat awhile in silence, stroking my forehead, and then she rose and left.
>
> So for me nothing was changed. It was as if somehow my brother and I existed inside one of those thick glass globes that enclose a wintery pastoral—two children, bundled against cold, building a snowman while around them white flakes swirled. . . . At first you think the coldness stands for his mother who cannot comfort him, but you must realize that she is also the mother of the dead boy—her son taken so violently from her.[16]

Gottesfeld describes the family's role as protector and the problems it faces when violated by one of its own members:

> Suicide, accident, really any kind of death poses a problem. Even if somebody got killed in a plane crash, the person might think, "I told him his father would never forgive him if he didn't come home for Thanksgiving. He got on the plane, and he got killed."
>
> There is a lot of family breakup, a lot of divorce after accidents—especially where children die. Numerous parents split because they think it is not a good family, not a safe family. Whose fault is it? They don't want to talk about it. When someone gets sick, someone gets hurt, whose fault is it? In an accidental death, it is even worse. There is always the underlying question of whether it was suicide, whether it is verbalized or not. And it's worse when it isn't verbal. Car crashes, drownings, boats capsizing—whenever I hear of an accident, I think suicide. I don't think accident. People think suicide. People think motive. They don't say it, but they think it.
>
> I saw a family in which there were twin boys, three and a half, and

one drowned. And the remaining members of the family came to see me fourteen years later. It was apparently all quieted down, but the brother had a serious breakdown. At that point, the father and mother started talking about how the father really felt the mother was negligent and the kid had died as a result.

Certainly, murder and suicide are the extremes. But negligence, irresponsibility, and an attitude of "You didn't do what you should have been doing" play a big part. There is always this feeling that somehow chance isn't really chance. And the family is stuck much more with that—because the family looks for reasons, feels responsible. Because it's the family that's responsible for protecting its members. Why does your mother tell you to wear your sweater? Because if you get a cold, it's her fault.[17]

Beyond issues of blame and responsibility, the family has to grieve. It will never be whole again. There will be other causes for joy—holidays, birthdays, wedding celebrations, and births—but the loss of the dead member will always be tangible. For the accidental killer, the experience combines the two most important causes of depression—sadness over the loss of a loved one and a strong blow to the self-esteem for not having been able to prevent the death.

These issues are so fundamental that even among extended families, fatal accidents can be so bitter that they are never resolved. One accidental killer says, "I can't even put into words the anguish I have suffered or the guilt I have sustained for the last fifteen years." She continues:

I drove my sister-in-law's car to the doctor. I offered to drive my sister-in-law's mother to her home about thirty minutes away for an ophthalmologist's appointment. It was necessary to take all her children and three of mine as no one was home to care for them. My sister-in-law was also with us. She had a nine-passenger station wagon, so it was no problem. She sat next to me holding two babies [hers]—a 1½-year-old girl and a 2½-year-old boy. We were on our way home, and I was traveling the service road since the expressway was backed up.

As we approached an intersection, I saw the light was green. The car in front of me proceeded through. As I went through, a car came from my left and ran a red light. She hit me in the driver's door.

The next thing I remember was screaming for everyone to get out of the car, as I thought it was going to catch fire. Mitchell, the 2½-year-old, didn't move. He was next to me and his mother. She asked me to help her.

When I went to help her, I saw the shift on the wheel was stuck through his head. I pulled and pulled until I freed him. The next thing I remember is Mitchell lying on the sidewalk vomiting. His mother was screaming, "He's still alive," but the voice inside me was saying, "No, he's dead." I wanted to shake her.

We were all taken to the hospital for treatment and then released. My sister-in-law's car was totaled, and her baby was dead. My husband (a city policeman) handled all the affairs. He arranged for a lawyer from the city. Papers were drawn up, and it was decided by them that I be charged with negligent vehicular homicide.

I don't think I've ever forgiven my husband for this, but I've learned to live with it. The papers stated I willfully took the life of Mitchell. When the papers were mailed to my sister-in-law, she came over to my house and told me her baby didn't die. He was killed, and I killed him, she said.

The papers went to court and so did I, my husband, and my brother-in-law. I was charged and dismissed because of a witness who was in another car behind the car that hit me. She clearly stated the light was red, red, red. The reason given for the case to be handled like this was money. A baby has no worth in a settlement of this kind, or at least very little. They wanted the parents to receive something. The settlement was awarded, but to this day we do not know how much, only that it sits in a bank, collects interest, and is referred to as blood money. The younger children don't know that they ever had a brother named Mitchell.

Two months ago, while my husband was going through rehabilitation for alcoholism for the second time in the past two years, this accident was brought out as we were both being counseled together. The reason I was driving was because he could not do it, as he was going to court for his cousin on a drunk-driving charge. That was more important to him than driving or minding the kids.

Even now, fifteen years later, it seems like such a short time ago. To say I remember everything would be a lie. I've blocked out many of the sordid details. When the accident first happened, I was absolutely numb. I was grateful it was not one of my children but horrified to know a death of a 2½-year-old had occurred. I cried incessantly for months. After the funeral, I withdrew into myself. I tried to talk to my husband but felt rejected and shunned. I can honestly say I felt he hated me, and the closeness we once had was gone.

I desperately wanted to move away, as it was horrible living across the street from my sister-in-law whose child I had killed. . . . My sister-in-law and I had had a wonderful relationship up until this point. We had been friends for many, many years, since we were sixteen years old. Our children were inseparable—her four and my four. Mitchell (the 2½-year-old) idolized my husband. They were inseparable. I often felt he loved him more than our own.

After the accident, my sister-in-law turned on me. She wouldn't speak to me. The children were not allowed to play with each other. If I was outside, they were called away. This went on for two years until one Christmas I went over there and created a scene as to what was going on and ruined Christmas and left crying. On New Year's Eve the next year, my husband brought my sister-in-law and her husband over for a drink. To this day, I don't know what my husband said.

We tolerate each other now. Our kids are friends once again. We never mention the accident to each other. Her thoughts are hers, and mine are mine. I still feel guilty and feel fate has dealt me an awful blow. When things get bad or I'm hurting, it's as if I deserve it for what I caused. I worry that I'm doomed to hell and ask God's forgiveness quite often. I still hurt and can't forget, but I'm grateful that I don't think about it as often as I did.

My family was good in helping me care for my children at this time. Through it all, love and understanding from them was there. But I wanted it from my husband, and it wasn't there. I needed to be close to him, but he wouldn't let me. He shut me out. When the accident came up at the rehab center, it was the first time it was discussed in length. . . .

I still feel his problem with alcohol began at this time because that was when he drank for one solid month every day until he's finally reached a point now where he's an alcoholic. I also blame myself for this; I feel guilty all the time. Even though there was a witness, I still question the color of the light. I don't think I'll ever be free from guilt.

It is difficult to imagine anything more damaging to a still developing child than accidentally killing a parent. In addition to feelings of guilt, pain, and sadness, the child may feel abandoned. Other family members may blame her. A young woman remembers the shattering effect of the accident that took her mother's life:

Mother and I were very close. Until I was seven, I was the only child. We enjoyed just sitting together in a room reading or taking the bus into town shopping. We were both quiet people.

My grandmother, on the other hand, couldn't stand to be in the same room with my father. They couldn't be together without yelling. I had come down with mononucleosis, and my gram had come to see about me. My mother and I and my little brother and sister took her to the bus station to see her off because my father didn't want to come.

Mom asked me if I wanted to drive home and I said no. It made me nervous. It was at night and raining hard. I was fifteen and was just learning to drive on a permit at the time. Looking back, I can see I was really trying to avoid being put into a situation I wasn't ready for. Mom said, "Come on, come on." So I said I'd drive, even though it was at night.

As I was driving, Mom said to slow down because I was getting near forty miles per hour in a thirty-five zone. I looked at the speedometer, and at that instant, the car skidded off the road to the right. Mom reached over and grabbed the wheel. I grabbed it back. Some evidence of mechanical problems with the steering wheel was uncovered, but anyway we veered across the road into oncoming traffic. The skid seemed like slow motion. It took forever, kind of like a trance. We hit an oncoming car.

I woke up covered with blood. My little brother and sister, who were five and six at the time, were screaming in the back.

But they were okay. I could see Mom. I could tell she was dead. Her neck was at a very unusual angle. Her two front teeth were stuck into the dash. Our dog got decapitated and bled every-where. People were crowding all around, staring at the casual-ties, saying how awful it was. The paramedics tried to give my mom artificial resuscitation, but then they gave up. All this time, I kept fading in and out of consciousness.

I managed to get up and go sit in the car with the other family. It was a couple with a six-week-old baby and another child. The mother was extremely worried about the baby. She kept screaming—it seemed like forever—"My baby, my baby, my baby." They ended up with the driver spending one week in the hospital, the mother broke her jaw and still walks with a limp, the child had minor injuries, and the baby was retarded.

My pelvis was broken, my stomach was pierced by part of the motor, and some of my other organs were damaged. While I was in the hospital, the nurses kept coming in and telling me my mother was okay. I knew she was dead. But they kept say-ing she'd be in to visit me tomorrow, and I tried to believe them because I wanted to. Then two days later, they came in and said she'd already been buried. They were trying to protect me as much as possible. I hated them for it.

After I got out of the hospital, I was very depressed. Our insurance company asked a lot of painful questions. The other people got $100,000. We got nothing. We had no insurance on ourselves or our mother. After the accident, it was basically a three-member family trying to stay afloat and nothing else. My grandma tried to move in, but she fought too much with Dad. The simple logistics of living and going to school and cooking and running the house took most of my time.

My father accused me of killing his wife. He would keep all the lights on in the house all night and blast the radio so loud you couldn't stand it. He didn't let me drive. One time I was watching the children swimming, and he said I'd better watch them carefully or else he'd kill me if one of them drowned.

I started shoplifting. Shopping with mother had been so spe-cial. One day a friend and I cut school and went downtown. We got caught and had to spend time in detention.

One night Dad and I got into a fight, and he got so mad at

me he tried to strangle me. I scratched his neck and drew blood. That made him madder. He got the car and drove me to the other side of town and said to get out—he never wanted to see me again. I got an apartment and left but felt guilty for leaving my siblings.

To lose a child is one of life's biggest tragedies. It is out of sync with the life cycle. With the child's death, the family loses some of its reason for being.

Steps toward recovery from such a deep sorrow are not easily taken. All the issues of guilt and blame are intensified when the accidental killer is the one responsible for the child's security. It is amazing that any family thus affected manages to survive. A mother remembers the death of her daughter:

Joni was small for her age, very pretty, and had blue eyes. She had pale white skin and very long black eyelashes. Her hair was black. The time she did have in life was happy, and I feel good about that. She had wanted a kitten. Just six weeks before she died my husband said it was okay, so we got her a little kitten. She was the only one who could make my headache go away. She would just come and rub my neck.

There were things that she wanted to do that she got to do, like riding the bus to school. We lived too close to school for her to ride it normally, so we made a special appointment with the school bus company where I dropped her off at a stop, and she rode by herself. But she was so excited about the ride she couldn't sleep the night before, and in the morning she fell asleep in the bus and slept the whole way.

The day of the accident after lunch we drove over to the post office where I was to meet the sitter. I went around the back and saw her waiting by the building. I pulled in and stopped, put the truck into park, and my foot on the brake. I reached over, gave Joni a kiss, and helped her get her things together. She opened the door and slid down on the passenger side, got her things, and closed the door. The accident happened within the next ten to twenty seconds. There were no witnesses, and I don't remember exactly what happened. What I think happened is that when Joni closed the door, I turned to wave to the sitter, turned back and looked down, pulled the truck into drive, and looked up. I did not see anything in front of me and did not immediately see Joni. I put my foot from the brake onto the gas and started to go forward. I glanced toward the sitter to see if Joni had gotten there. The truck met some resistance, and I pushed the gas pedal down. I rolled over Joni.

I put the truck into park, got out, and ran around the front to see what had happened. I saw Joni on the ground, ran back around, turned the truck off, and ran back. I was screaming all the time. People started coming to help. I was screaming to get a doctor. My husband arrived just after the doctor and paramedics. They put me inside the truck with someone. There was nothing they could do for Joni.

Joni's father recalls the accident:

It was a high truck, and the tires were wide, and Joni had gotten out and run over across in front of it. What we can gather is she must have dropped something and run back to pick it up because her face was toward the wheel, and she was lying facedown. There was a little basket with something in it. She was smaller than the height of the vehicle anyway, so if she'd stood up in front of it, you would've never seen her. From the time of initial impact to actual cease-to-live situation was probably ten seconds or less. She didn't suffer. If she'd been hit any other way, it would have probably been worse for my wife and everybody.

I got to the scene in about ten minutes—as long as it took somebody to run to get me a block and a half away. I got there before the cops, and they were right across the street.

I saw a pool of blood, my daughter on the ground, and my wife curled up in a ball against the side of my truck. People around were staring in amazement. When I first got there, I got my wife away from the scene because she was out of it. I got her around to the other side of the truck from where it happened. Somebody else was there, and they stayed with her. I went over to the doctor. They tried to revive my daughter, but she was dead before they ever got there. My first reaction was that I realized she was gone when I got to the scene. There was not anything that they could do. Her head was smashed. You could tell it was a person, but you couldn't tell it was Joni. I know the doctor felt helpless at the scene just like I did, but he went through the motions to revive her—which was totally useless. They would have done a lot more to revive her if I hadn't told them to just stop. I've taken first aid, and I've been around accidents before—they wanted to put in a wind tube, but there was no need for something like that.

Nobody punished my wife, but she wanted to be. Everybody accepted it for what it was, an accident. If it had been somebody else, she could have been mad at the person and gotten over it. But nobody got mad at her. The only person she could get mad at was herself. She didn't really want to accept it as an accident. She felt that she had done something wrong. It was difficult for her. Nobody else called her any bad names or said, "You did something really stupid," or anything like that. It was all herself doing these things to herself.

The mother recounts a difficult visit with her in-laws:

Three months later, we visited my husband's parents for Christmas. I've never really gotten along with them, so it wasn't real comfortable being there, and there was the added strain of Joni's death. . . . I was already depressed when I got there, and they had photographs of Joni when she had visited my in-laws and stayed a couple of weeks. They were new to me, and they just set me off. It really depressed me quite a bit, and I didn't want to be around anyone at all.

My husband's sister had a little girl whose birthday was right after Christmas. We went over to her house for a birthday party, and there were other children with their parents there. Just being around little kids was real uncomfortable. I felt at a loss—like I ought to have one running around. I didn't feel like talking to the other parents there. They didn't know what to say to me. My husband wanted me to help out and join in with the game playing. I just didn't feel like being there at all.

My husband was talking to friends and family, and he didn't understand what was upsetting me and why I was insisting that we leave. He was upset about it and thought I should have been able to stick it out. He said, "Why are you doing this?" We had quite an argument about it after we left, and he couldn't understand. He thought that I should have had better control—because after all, it had been three months. That bothered me; that was the biggest thing. It *was* only three months, and they were expecting a lot out of somebody who had shared the life of somebody else for almost six years.

For the mother to keep working took some adjustment. She continues:

> I do know that my concentration at work was gone. I was the only woman in the office. None of the guys was real open, and they didn't know what to do. I was not at the same efficiency level as I was prior to the accident. . . . One time I did talk to my supervisor and said, "I've been having problems, and I hope you'll bear with me. It's been pretty rough." My boss was understanding because he'd lost his wife three years before, so he was familiar with what I was going through, I think. He was still reserved.
>
> I tried my best not to bring it into the office so they wouldn't have to be put on the spot about what to do, but the feeling was there. Sometimes I would go into the back room and cry for a while and then wash my face and come back to work. I'd ask the other person in the office to watch my desk for a while. They knew what was going on, and it wasn't embarrassing to come back after I'd been crying. I'd just say, "Thank you, I'm okay now." It didn't happen every day, but sometimes it would happen several times a day—it would go in spurts. The people in my office had no idea how to deal with me or what to say.

This woman also felt misunderstood at home. She reports:

> My husband had the ability to talk about what had happened with the guys he worked with but not with me. He never completely came around to understanding how I felt. We handled it in two different ways, I think. I was real open about it, and he sort of closed it off and wouldn't talk about it or think about

it except on his own. But I was real transparent. I couldn't put up a front. If I was down, I was down. If I cried, I cried. I didn't feel like it was my place to hide that, but I had a greater problem dealing with the grief and the guilt that I was going through. But he never understood.

Around the house I would get listless, and although I didn't realize it at the time, my husband said I just kind of stared off endlessly, looking out the window, having a blank look on my face. He thought that I should snap out of it and would say, "Why are you doing this? When you feel this way, why don't you go do something?" But I didn't feel like doing anything. I wanted to stare off if that's what I was doing. He didn't understand why I didn't get up and go do something because that's what he would do. This difference in our ways of handling our grief caused several arguments. . . .

On a day-to-day basis, it was real slow. Then months would pass, and I would say, "Gee, I can't believe it's been four months already." When I was doing it, the day passed real slow, but then all of a sudden, my husband would be there saying, "What about dinner, what are we going to do?" And it would seem that time had gone so fast. He probably thought I got lost in it, but I didn't think so at the time. It was what I needed. So I did it to take care of myself. Basically I thought about things we did, good memories, and then I realized she wasn't there and why she wasn't there, and then things would start hurting again and I would sit and cry. I guess that's when I'd get upset or something . . . then come back and start all over.

We talked about separating and trying to figure out ourselves alone. I would bring it up one time, or he would another. It was a mutual thing, just trying to figure out what would be the best thing, although we never really did it. We just hung in there.

My mom was the only one I could call and talk to, and she would say, "What you are going through is normal. It's going to take you five years to get over it; that's how long you had her." And when I needed someone to talk to, I would call her regardless of the hour, at one or two o'clock in the morning, and she would call and talk to my husband and try to make him see what I was going through. I think he thought that she was trying to help in her way. I didn't get any anger from him over that.

As far as lashing out and blaming me, he never did that. He never really came out and said, "This is your fault, you did this, and I hate you for it." I think he implied it once, but it was not really direct. It would have helped my guilt if someone had done that. I wanted to be blamed, and I wanted to be punished. And if nobody was going to do that, I was going to do it myself. It would have helped me if I could have been punished for the crime I committed. Whether society did it or the community or my husband or whatever, it would have relieved me from some of the guilt that I'm being put through, blaming myself for the accident.

The mother also had trouble being intimate with her husband after Joni's death. She explains:

I wanted him to be close, but I just wanted to be held like a little child who was afraid. Just held and rocked. Of course, at that point he was physically starved, and I wasn't responding to him in that theater at all. Then he would try everything he could—like if I wanted to be held, sure he would, but then he would try to turn it into something else.

I was talking to a woman friend about the problem we were having being intimate. I just said something that I had not made conscious to myself before—that no matter what happened, I was never going to let myself get hurt like that again, and the way to do that was to distance myself from my husband. . . . I think acknowledging that has helped me come a long way in getting over [the accident] and being able to work it out.

Because sex is so intimate, you get so close—you are one for a brief period of time—and I was afraid of that. I didn't want that because if he was that close, he meant more to me. Then the thought of losing him was even worse, and I didn't want to have to go through that. I wasn't conscious of this for three and a half years. . . . And it still scares me that I will be hurt.

The father voices his views of his wife's and his own recovery:

You just have to accept it—the fact that it's happened, it's over, and there's nothing you can do to change it. If you could, you would. But you know it's done, and you have to make the best of it. You can't bring her back, but you still have the memories and that's about all you can do. Just go on—that's about it.

I knew that no matter what I said or did it wouldn't change anything. I could be there to comfort her if she wanted me to, but she would have to ask me. I felt she dwelt upon the problem and the situation to the point where she wanted somebody to blame her, and nobody would. You have to get over it. It didn't change one thing, even in the little town we lived in, and the world didn't care one way or another. . . .

Since the accident, I have found myself sitting and thinking about the past a lot, about how things would have been if the accident had not happened. I find myself pushing myself on those who care for me and expecting them to understand me when I don't understand myself—wanting affection from those close and resenting it when they do not express it toward me. . . . I would expect my wife to come to me for more help. She didn't want to come to me because I was the person she supposedly had hurt, and I felt rejected when she didn't come to me. Something was wrong, I thought. It's no wonder. To her she just took the most precious thing I had away from me, and I'm going to love her for that? She couldn't understand how I felt. It happened, and that's that.

The mother concludes:

I still have an overall feeling that the whole thing is not real, that she will be coming back. It seems that just yesterday she was running around playing and into everything. I get very depressed at the smallest things. I start crying for no apparent reason and get a tight, dull pain in my chest. I don't seem to have any emotions. I don't feel happy, sad, love, or hate. People I know just don't seem to mean anything to me. . . . I will start to have a good time and then realize I am having a good time without my daughter and will get very depressed.

Families can be amazingly resilient. The man and woman described in the preceding paragraphs managed to stay together and have more children. Weathering the tragedy seems to depend on faith, the ability to trust again, and hope. These qualities were of great help to a man who was fourteen years old when he accidentally shot his brother:

I can remember the day and how white the snow looked. And how green the haystack was—the outside is brown, but when you pull it apart, the leaves inside are really green and full of chlorophyll. And the next image I remember is that it was night and we were home, and then we went to the funeral parlor where they had his body. It seemed cold and windy and dreary.

And then I just didn't notice colors after that. In the summertime when the colors would come, for the next two years I just remember feeling dark and dreary, and not remembering anything except shades of gray. It seemed like the greens had a gray, pale-green kind of color. They didn't have vividness to them. I remember buying a paisley shirt when that style was very popular, and I remember how bright those colors seemed to me. And it was like that was one of the first times I saw color.

It was December 27. We were out of school. Mother was working in a potato-processing warehouse on the midnight shift. She told my older brother to get the cattle fed while she slept. There had been a fight about her going to work because of the value that the man should provide and the woman should stay in the home. So she felt some guilt about working outside the home, but they needed the money. They had also lost a potato crop about four years before, in 1962, so these were financially difficult times. Dad was working at a cheese factory at pretty close to minimum wage, and he didn't like that kind of work. He wanted to be a farmer. We had the eighty acres, so he ran that in the summer. My older brother was sixteen, I was fourteen, and Joe was twelve. We milked thirteen cows, and we had milk and cheese. . . .

A lot of people in the area at that time hunted, and guns were common. So we had several small-caliber rifles around that we hunted rabbits with and things like that. The hay stack was about three-quarters of a mile down the field. There was a path the cows had walked in, and so it was a path that only one person could walk on. We walked single file down there. Mom was sleeping because she had to go to work. My older brother didn't want to feed the cows. So we talked him into letting us take an old pistol that never had worked as long as we'd had it and a rifle, an old .22 rifle with a hexagonal barrel that had poor compression. It was real loose; you could fire it, and it would hardly make any sound. We just didn't believe it was really capable of killing anything. But we didn't stand in front of it. We knew we could kill magpies with it, but it wasn't like a brand new rifle.

So it was like these were toys, even though Dad had taught all three of us a lot about gun safety. I tended to be impulsive then, doing things without thinking. But I don't think it was outside the range of what's normal for a teenager. So we went down to the field, fed the cows, and then played around the haystack a while with this rifle and pistol. . . .

I loaded the rifle but don't remember putting a .22 bullet in the chamber. I know when I went down into the field, I had it in my pocket. It was empty when we went down and when we played, or we might have had bullets in there in case we saw a rabbit or something on the way. But I know that when we were playing, I thought that I took them all out. Now part of this was playing quick draw. We started to head home, and my brother was by the haystack. There was barely any snow there; it had all been trampled down. I was some twenty feet behind him, and I could swear to this day I heard a voice say, "Draw." And it didn't sound like my voice or my brother's voice but like a man's heavier, deeper tone. All I know is that I turned around and pulled the trigger, and Joe looked like I'd knocked the wind out of him.

He looked startled. I remember that vividly because he looked happy. Then as soon as the pain hit him, he looked sad. That was the lingering impression that even now saddens me because the feeling is he never looked happy again. He didn't look happy in the casket, obviously. The freshness and exuberance that was my brother seemed to go away that second, and the rest of it was a process of all of him dying.

And so for me there are degrees of death—that kind of feeling where parts of personalities slip away. I think in those terms intellectually now, but at the time it was just an emotional reaction that, "Oh, something terrible has happened." And the next emotion that I remember was, "Fix this. Make this not really happen." Like when I would break a glass jar in the house, and I would feel that instant shock of "Uh-oh, I'm in trouble." And this was like "Uh-oh, this is bad. This is something that can't be fixed."

Then I ran over to him. I still couldn't believe that the bullet could have actually hit him and done that kind of damage. I opened up his shirt, and right below his sternum, that last bone in the chest, there was a little tiny hole, about the size of a .22 bullet. There was blood right in the opening of that hole. And I remember thinking, "Oh, it didn't go in very far." I think that I was hoping.

Then he said something like, "It hurts so bad." And I said, "I'm sorry, I'm sorry"—I know I was saying that all the time—and "I didn't mean to." But he wasn't responding to anything I was saying. He was in such pain that he was just talking about the pain. [Today] that kind of experience can really set me off—when I'm talking to someone and they're not hearing me. I think it creates an incredible echo back to that moment.

And then he was almost speechless with the pain. I thought, "I've got to take him home. I've got to hurry and get help." I went to pick him up, but I was only maybe thirty or forty pounds heavier than he, and I couldn't pick him up. When I did, he gasped. It was obvious on his face that it hurt, and I remember his face whitened when I did that. I said, "I'll go get help." He appeared almost to have passed out at that point.

The next feeling was one of rehearsing all experiences that had been frightening but from which I had always extricated myself, like losing animals, getting lost in a crowd, etc. This experience just couldn't be undone; the finality was overwhelming.

I ran that three-quarters of a mile. It was on snow-packed ground, but it was still slippery. I was crying and thinking, "Please, God, make him live. Please, God, make him live," and "What have I done? I've done something so bad this time, so awful, so wrong." When I got to the house, to the back door, I yelled, "I've shot Joe—get help." I felt ashamed and ran back down the field. My older brother grabbed his coat and also went running down the field.

I can remember Mom in the back door, but I don't remember if she hugged me. It was almost like she held me against her and sobbed, "Oh, no, oh, no, I've got to call your father. I've got to call the ambulance."

I don't remember her calling or anything. I just remember running out in the road, not thinking about going down to the field but just out in the road. It was the feeling like, "I've been bad, I've got to be punished, and I'm not going to run away from this. I'm going to stand here and wait for Dad to come and punish me." And there were instances when I was younger when I had tried to run down into the field when I knew I was going to get whipped for something, and this time it was like I was going to stay there and face it.

It was two days after that big celebration of Christmas. So there was this nice celebration and all those emotions and then this sudden tragedy. I don't know if that deepened the depression of the family.

We were a religious family, a rather conservative religion, so it was real easy for us to believe in the hereafter. After the accident, we all believed that our brother who had died was in another place and we had to live very good lives to ever get to be with him again. So in a certain emotional and spiritual sense, he has always been with us since the death.

Accidental killers can heal, no matter how devastating their loss. Somehow, once they have mourned, most are able to step forward into life. They feel they have no choice.

8

Healing

The path of healing consists of facing the thing most feared, of confronting what has been denied, of strengthening the member most wounded. The man whose story of shooting his brother ended the last chapter describes his painful recovery, which took many years:

> I was standing in the road waiting for Dad and the ambulance when I suddenly saw yellow light. It was like my vision—my whole visual range—was filled with this warm, serene yellow light. It was like lying in the summer sun and having your eyes closed; your eyes see yellow, and it feels warm. And then it was like a little Teletype at the bottom of my visual range that said, "This is your father in Heaven. Jesus Christ is your Savior, and your brother is with God."
>
> It was like God was saying, "He's with me; don't worry about it." I don't know whether that was a stress-related hallucination that I had conjured up to help myself through that point, but from a religious standpoint, I had had a revelation. I can look at it from all sides of my mind, as a therapist and a psychologist and from the religious part of me. All I know is that it has comforted me and given me a sense of tranquility whenever I have thought about it.
>
> As soon as Dad and the ambulance arrived, that feeling went away, . . . and I didn't feel those same feelings for probably nine years. . . .

We walked down to the field, and when we got there, the ambulance attendants verified that my brother was dead. They put him on a stretcher. And then there was the bitterness. I remember being sick and throwing up—and that kind of stomach acid, how sour that is in your mouth and throat, that's how I remember feeling about myself for four years. . . .

With all those religious beliefs, of course, I just knew I was going to hell. It was hard to get rid of that belief. But, the moments of reprieve were those testimony experiences. So I look back and see black and whites in my life—the black, acidic, awful repulsion in myself or the white, wondrous God-is-beautiful-and-can-make-you-feel-completely-holy-if-you-live-totally-righteously. So I'd feel guilty about anything that wasn't quite a perfect action. And being a normal human being, I had plenty to feel guilty about.

The most annoying emotion was realizing that when a person takes another's life, accidentally or purposefully, there is no awful physical pain, no ESP connection to express that other person's physical pain—at least not between my brother and me. I then understood how people can take life indiscriminately. This led to a curiosity for the macabre, and I wonder whether my present involvement in counseling people in constant crisis is not the extension of this curiosity.

After Joe's death, there were a lot of times when I would go into the house and see Mom. She would see me and then start to cry and leave the room. I thought she was crying because she hated me for having shot her son. Now I think it was just that she didn't know how to relate to her feelings. She hadn't been taught in her family of origin, so she just felt the pain suddenly, saw the pain on my face, reacted to it, not knowing how to help me. After the death, Mom and Dad's pain seemed so great and so enduring and always there that our pain didn't count. . . . I don't think [my father] ever knowingly directed any of his anger at me. It was like he couldn't deal with it; he couldn't talk about it directly, so it came out in hidden, covert, or backdoor kinds of ways—like being angry at me about something specific on the farm. . . .

I tended to push my father to get angry with me. When I felt a lot of pain about my brother's death, I'd go out and do contrary things. If I pushed hard enough, Dad would get mad and slap me or whip me or knock me around. I'd forget to do chores, forget to get the cattle fed, waste time playing or goofing off. At the time, it just seemed like I was the kid in the family who did wrong things, didn't seem to know how to obey, kind of like I was dumb or something.

Now I look back and realize I was in the midst of a chronic, fairly moderate depression all those years. But it was normal to me at the time. I think that the violence with Dad was almost like electroshock. I would push him hard enough, then he'd get crazy and get me out of that depressed state. I think it was almost healing to have him stimulate me with an adrenaline rush that a whipping gives. . . .

Fourteen and fifteen remained dark years. I could do lots of positive things but always still see myself as a failure. I was leader of the marching band, the drum major. The teacher put me in charge, and I did just fine. But I decided that he had me do it because I couldn't play the trumpet well and because I was tall—and that was the only reason he had me do it. I couldn't believe the band would follow me, either. It was like he had made a secret agreement with them, that he'd put me there and so they had to follow me. I had this feeling of not being important. But I was in the uniform and they couldn't really tell any better so they followed the uniform. I had a convenient way of throwing away anything positive I did.

Then as I became a therapist, I couldn't keep doing that because the clients felt like I had something worth listening to. If I tried to throw it away, then they wouldn't start feeling better about themselves. I think I had to start feeling better about me.

And then I went on a mission. Before going, I went and talked to the state president of the missions. I opened up my feelings and talked about the things I had done wrong. I felt a great relief, a sense of serenity, which was like that yellow light I'd seen. . . .

I guess it was obvious to a lot of people that I was somehow trying to live two lives. I was trying to do what I was doing, but all the good stuff was going to my brother because he was a saintly person. And if anything didn't go perfect, that was me, the bad part. I didn't feel separated. It wasn't like distinct parts as much as compartmentalization. I could put my bad feelings in one part of me, so it was like all of me didn't enjoy all the fun. It was like I couldn't laugh, but the former Joe part of me could.

After I was married, sometimes the "me" part of me would yell and scream at my wife, while the former "Joe" part of me would comfort her and make her feel better. My uncle confronted me with this and planted the idea in my mind that I had to quit doing that.

Teachers in college made me face the fact that I tried to get my father's approval. No matter what he wanted I would do it. I was in college, but I'd spend every weekend at home working on the farm. I couldn't go to social functions if I needed to be home helping out. And my logical excuse was that I had four sisters who shouldn't be doing farm work, so I had to go home and do it to protect them. But I think underneath was a sense that I shouldn't enjoy myself. It was all part of that incredible need for approval and doing things right. . . .

[Now] I work for a nonprofit agency that specializes in drug and alcohol abuse counseling. I speak to several church groups a month about drug and alcohol abuse, and I tend to share my experiences fairly regularly. Even though it's in the context of drug and alcohol abuse, I tend to share how you can become addicted to something negative. For example, I became addicted to depression. . . .

Dad had a real strong value that his son should date and not go steady, but date lots of girls. My brother and I both dated a lot, and I tended for about three years to tell every one of those dates the whole gruesome story of the day Joe died. I cried and became very open and vulnerable. I don't know if that's why I didn't get a lot of second dates—I think I was pretty overpowering. I think this helped me get over it.

I realized in my death and dying group that just having people tell their story helps them to realize that they're not strange or different. I don't think that Mom and Dad . . . ever repeated this story to anybody outside of each other. And so I think they perpetuated their own myths with each other, and they didn't have any kind of outside reference. I just kept talking about it and used church principles. One of those was getting up and talking about our feelings. That's a great way to vent things and to get them out in the open. So, once a month I'd be right up there talking about my pain and the next lesson God had taught me. I really opened up and translated my hurting into a religious language. People would tell me it was marvelous and made them feel good. I found out that by being open and vulnerable I could help people to express their emotions.

After Joe died, when someone was interested enough to help me a little, I made sure they helped me as much as they could. I look back and say, "Why didn't I have a therapist? Why didn't I get one?" If a person had any kind of love in them at all, I demanded they help me. I would do it in a gentle way, but I would push them to help me get better for that day.

"On the wings of time, grief flies away," wrote Jean de la Fontaine.[1] But accidental killers know that although time helps, healing requires conscious attention and the working through of anger, guilt, and despair. "People are given to believe that time heals all," explains one accidental killer. "Sure—but at what price? A broken bone will heal, but if set improperly or not set at all, it may forever be deformed."

Accidental killers have many obstacles to overcome, different aspects of "coming to terms with a world in which bad things can and do happen to oneself."[2] The world is drastically different from the way they thought it was. They themselves are not who they thought they were. They must revamp their own identity and their explanation of how they fit into the world as they have reconceptualized it. This includes accepting their capability to do incredible harm. To go forward with their lives, accidental killers must struggle to transcend fears and phobias and to recover from self-destructive compulsions and addictions. They must work to convince themselves that others are not constantly judging them by the accident. They must find ways to believe in themselves once again.

One of the initial problems accidental killers face is sorting out the onslaught of emotional reactions that the accident evokes. Not only do they need to look at their own emotions, but they also need to draw boundaries, to see where their emotional responsibility ends and that of others begins. But even within themselves, emotions can be confusing. They are responding to many kinds of loss at once. Often one emotional response triggers another, as when anger causes guilt, guilt brings on depression, or depression invites rejection. It may not be possible to separate and understand each emotional response by itself or to determine its origin.[3] One accidental killer recalls her trouble sorting out her feelings: "I couldn't figure out if I felt so bad because I helped to cause her death or if it was just from watching someone die." Others describe feeling sad, agitated, anxious, and guilty all at the same time.

Grieving

Grieving is essential to the healing process, but it is not pleasant. Many accidental killers may have expected grief to be something one experiences only after the death of a loved one, but they find themselves grieving deeply regardless of their relationship to the deceased. Accepting the pain of grief is an important part of the resolution process. One author has put forth the idea that suffering is a healing agent in human life because it unites the being and creates a basis for lasting happiness that does not depend on outside circumstances.[4]

Psychologist Leo Buscaglia goes so far as to encourage people to welcome the pain:

> There's nothing wrong with pain. I've learned so many wonderful things over the years in painful situations. In fact, sometimes it takes misery to teach us about joy. So embrace it when it comes. Say it's a part of life. Put your arms around it. Don't deny it. Experience it! Learn to feel it again. Maybe it does hurt. Say it's okay to hurt. Scream, yell, gnash . . . cry. Bang on the table. Be angry! Let it come out and then *forget it*. Otherwise you are going to store it up forever. And you know what happens when you store up pain? It takes its toll from *you*. You're the one who gets ulcers and the migraine headaches.[5]

Grief is the price we pay for love. Thornton Wilder describes this connection in the closing lines of *The Bridge of San Luis Rey:* "There is a land of the living and a land of the dead, and the bridge is love, the only survival, the only meaning."[6]

Grieving something sad is natural, but during the time people are grieving, they are not in what could be called a normal state. Some lose their appetite or overeat, some are not able to sleep, and some have sexual difficulties. Many grieving people describe a feeling of tightness in the chest.[7]

Separation from a loved one is one of the greatest stresses of life. Those who lose a loved one in an accident experience grief in an entirely different dimension than do those whose victims are strangers. As much as the bereaved accidental killer may want to start life anew, accepting the loss and going on, part of him wants to linger and preserve all that was valuable and important from the past.

The hardest part of the grieving process seems to come about two weeks after the accident, when everything is expected to slip back into its usual routine. Then comes the moment of truth—when the accidental killer must face all the small holes the death has left in the fabric of her life. According to associate pastor Bob Johns of Waco, Texas, "Often the full impact of a loss is felt when one starts to say something to someone who is not there, or longs for a companionship that has been taken for granted for so long, or comes to decide on a lonely vacation or go to a concert alone."[8]

For those who accidentally kill someone they love, the ultimate goal of the grieving process is the withdrawal of their emotional investment in the deceased by abstracting the fundamentally important features about that person and incorporating them into their own personality. Then they can face the new reality, retrieving that energy so it can be reinvested someplace where it can enrich their lives.

Although attending the funeral service may be difficult, doing so can help the accidental killer to accept the fact that the loved one is dead. Even when the deceased was a stranger, an accidental killer can benefit from attending the funeral, although the deceased's family should be consulted first. Usually, the more significant and elaborate the funeral ritual is, the more intense the accidental killer's emotions and the more quickly grief is resolved.[9]

Saying good-bye to a dead friend is important. A woman who was at the wheel when her car was broadsided says, "I needed to go through the saying good-bye stage before I could cope with the reality of her loss, which was my loss. I went through the rooms of my house where she had walked. I talked to her and said good-bye."

Tears are an essential part of grief. Shakespeare wrote, "To weep is to make less the depth of grief."[10] According to Dr. William H.

Frey of the Psychiatry Research Laboratories at St. Paul–Ramsey Medical Center, shedding tears is even beneficial to our health. Tears of sorrow carry away potentially harmful proteins that do not exist in tears shed from eye irritation.[11] People with ulcers and other stress-related illnesses cry much less than healthy people.

Accidental killers must take as much time as they need to grieve. But once the grieving process has been played out, it is time to re-enter life.

Picking up the Pieces

Once their psychological wounds have mended sufficiently to withstand the pressure of the resumption of a normal life, most accidental killers are eager to put the accident behind them. Many see it as a choice between life and slow death. "It takes a lot of determination not to let [the accident] destroy you," one accidental killer says. "It would be very easy for me to hit the bottle and never leave it." Other people may influence the decision to try to get on with things, but the accidental killer basically must come to this decision herself. "I don't even recall a specific time for this, but there was a time when I said to myself, 'You're okay. You're stronger than you've ever been, and it's time to quit feeling sorry for yourself and get on with things,'" one accidental killer notes. Another says, "I just realized the accident cannot be undone."

The motivation for embarking on a conscious adjustment process is often the realization that the accidental killer does not deserve to suffer anymore. "The fact that I killed someone doesn't cancel out my life," one accidental killer explains. "I still have a right to the kind of life that's meaningful to me. I must still get what I need out of this existence."

The Tasks of Healing

According to stress researcher Dr. Mardi Jon Horowitz, recovery requires nothing less than a whole new way of looking at the world:

> Serious life events, such as the loss of a loved one or a personal injury, can shatter a person's reality. Inner models of the world that have sustained the person must now be changed to accord with the new situation. It is necessary to revise memory, attitude and belief systems

to accommodate the new life development. Faced with resistance to trusting the human order, [one] needs a new identification, sense of connection, and significance in life to come to terms with a past disaster.[12]

Shock can damage the accidental killer's nervous system, and the neurological gap between the preaccident self and the postaccident self needs to be bridged. At the time of the accident, important survival mechanisms proved ineffective. The brain interpreted this failure as its own faulty processing, tagged the responses involved as malfunctioning and deleted them. As a result, the vital reflexes of orientation and escape became frozen in the instant of impact. Only by renegotiating the accident through hypnosis or a new technique known as Somatic Experiencing can the subconscious regain control by eliminating the "delete" code. The mind needs to become aware of the positive resources at hand just prior to the accident so that it can see itself as successfully negotiating the crisis. Until that happens, the accidental killer is likely to suffer from free-floating anxiety, for the vital instincts required to cope with an emergency are repressed, and the person senses this impairment on some level.[13]

Traumatic shock aside, accidental killers can encourage healing by changing what they tell themselves about the tragedy. A key step seems to be reframing the accident in impersonal terms—to look at it and judge it as if it happened to someone else. One woman describes her reframing process:

> The way I deal with it is thinking that I am a good person, and accidentally killing someone doesn't change this. Thinking that if there were any way I could have saved her or brought her back to life, I would have done it. But I can't, so I've got to stop dwelling on what might have been and take care of the here and now—which is my own life. Feeling that there is no way I wanted the role that I had, that in having to go through this ordeal and having the memories for the rest of my life, I was the other victim of a terrible tragedy. And I certainly don't deserve to be punished for that.

The rhythmic nature of recovery reflects the accidental killer's own dynamic balance. The focus usually shifts from aspect to aspect, like a rose that unfolds its petals in sequence. On one side are realizations of one's capacity to do great harm, the threat to oneself, and the horrors of death and injury.[14] On the other side are the accidental killer's desire for personal integrity, the image she once held of herself, and her previous roles.

Healing means recognizing and reversing subconscious mechanisms of defense and temporary coping. The key is to examine the most troublesome aspects of the accident and translate vague representations of it into words, images, and actions. The more conscious and effective the thought processes are, the longer they take. With each step of this adaptation process, the mind is able to revise the patterns used in unproductive subconscious reactions. By unlearning the automatic responses of the past, the accidental killer can resolve the conflict between subconscious reactions and conscious ways of being.

This adjustment requires constant alertness to what is happening now without relying on old habits of interpretation. "They are looking at me because they know about the accident" needs to become "They may or may not be looking at me, and if they are, it could be for any one of a thousand reasons."

This process requires an attitude of detachment. It means holding back an emotional impulse to read a situation the old way and being able to insert a new behavior aimed at producing the desired result. Adjustment is not passive, although it is a receptive form of activity based on understanding and appreciating.[15] It cannot occur without identifying destructive patterns. The predominant pattern is fear of repeating the accident. Many accidental killers fight to overcome panic reactions springing from the accident trauma. One describes the battle he faced to overcome his anxiety over his family's safety: "I would panic if my wife was twenty minutes late or if the kids went around the block. I would see their bodies in the road and the blood. Finally I put it on a stopwatch. I told myself, 'How long do you want to feel miserable? An hour? Two hours? Fifteen minutes? Thirty seconds? No!'"

As this man found, beginning a new pattern can mean consciously suppressing thoughts about the accident. Psychologist Stanley Rustin explains:

> There are some things you really can't do much about. You can't bring back the dead. Dwelling on it excessively only keeps the mourn-

ing going, the self-recrimination going. I think there is some positive value to suppression. Repression is more an unconscious defense mechanism. But with suppression, we literally try to push things out of consciousness because it's counterproductive to dwell on them. It's not going to bring the deceased back. And this is why I think in a very healthy way people say after the loss of the loved one, "Hey, you've got to pick up your life. You have to go back to work. You have to do what you have to do."[16]

Devising an Explanation

It is natural for accidental killers to search for a reason why the accident occurred. But descriptions of cause and effect do not answer fundamental questions such as the following: Does fate exist? Is there an unseen divine intelligence that directs what happens? Did the laws of nature combine to produce such a directive force, or is randomness itself the only thing of which one can be sure? The world does not, however, necessarily operate according to the constructs of the mind. Whether events are directed by some force beyond human knowledge is irrelevant to the events themselves. Yet people often need to experience the transcendent to derive meaning for their lives. Rustin notes:

> I think there are some things that defy understanding—no rhyme or reason. Accidents sometimes defy reason. We don't know why somebody is walking down the street and the scaffold falls and crushes the person's head, leaving the family with a tragic loss. And what is the family to do with that? I don't think you can make sense out of certain situations. And what you're left with is to accept something that has no solution. I think part of psychology, psychoanalysis, has forced the notion of solutions. That somehow if we dig enough, if we understand enough, we can resolve something. I don't think so. I don't have a solution to everything, particularly when it comes to the human condition.[17]

Acceptance is vital to recovery. An accidental killer describes circumstances that could have given rise to endless questioning:

> The accident happened in 1964, in Germany. It was nine o'clock at night. It was raining. I was working for the American newspaper. We lived in an American ghetto, many of us

civilians working for the army living in base housing. I was driving a VW bug. In Germany, they have bike trails that are completely separated from the cars so the bikes don't have to go in the traffic. However, at one point, the trail crossed the highway. One minute there was nothing, and the next there was this bike five feet in front of my car. It wasn't a matter of being able to swerve at all. He was too close. He was just there. I don't know what was on his mind. My lights were on.

He smashed up on the windshield; you know how the front of VWs are built. And I knew that it was fatal. It was an awful feeling. Then the car catapulted his body forward, and he and the bike slid along the pavement about fifty feet. He lived about four days, but it was always clear he was going to die. If he had lived, there would have been severe brain damage. It was a seventeen-year-old boy, the mother's sole surviving son. The Berlin Wall had gone up in '62, and people were still trying to go over it. That's where his brother was killed, on the wall. The mother and this son had crossed into West Germany, and now her second son was killed this way. . . .

I went to meet his mother and to the funeral. She freaked out when she saw me there at the funeral, but I had to go. It was something I had to do. The police ruled that it was unavoidable. I thought so, too. . . .

It was an accident as much as it could be except that there are no accidents. Why was I on that road at that time, and what drew him there? I see it as based on a lot of facts that come from outside of my experience, and since I was in the middle of it, if I tried to figure it out, I would be doing that on the basis of incomplete information. The other thing is it doesn't make any difference whether it was an accident or not. It's what happened—anything else is fantasy. This was not a rational conclusion, not at all. It was more an act of faith.

Part of the difficulty in dealing with accidental death is U.S. society's lack of acceptance of death in general. "Earthquakes may cause great misfortune," writes Dr. Edgar Jackson, "but without them there would be no new mountains, no new valleys. People who cry out against death are seeing the small picture."[18] Some accidental killers are able to view their accident as neither punishment nor reward but as part of a larger process that must be accepted so that one can feel at home in the universe. Looking back, the initially compelling impulse to take the accident personally seems egocentric.

A teenager who was the driver in a car wreck that killed her mother says, "Everything bad that happens just makes you stronger. I feel like you get each lesson when you are just strong enough to take it, and then you're given something harder. Maybe it's a rationalization, but it's the only way I've been able to live with the accident."

Healing with Religion

Religious beliefs provide the basis for the recovery of many accidental killers. One notes, "My religious background was an anchor that proved effective." Another reports, "Had not God been with me every minute, I could not have pulled through."

Some accidental killers turn to religion when they feel they have run out of their own resources. One says, "First I went over and over the accident, picturing it all over again, trying to explain away my responsibility. Finally I had to turn it all over to the Lord because I couldn't handle it."

Although it upsets some, the idea that the accident was part of a divine plan comforts other accidental killers. One explains, "My belief in the ultimate will of God overriding our measly mortal will pulled me through." Another reports, "I believe the only way to handle something like this is to turn it all over to God and to realize that no death occurs unless it's part of His plan." And a third says, "There was someone greater than I who planned this accident. It could not have been foreseen by me or the child. It was no one's fault. I know the Lord planned this and had a reason for the child, me, his parents, and my family."

The importance of religion to many accidental killers' recovery cannot be overemphasized. Stanley Rustin affirms the comfort that religion can provide:

> People who are deeply religious, I think, have an easier time dealing with death on all levels. And somehow one deals with it by saying, "Behind this accident there is some meaning. We have to learn or try

to understand what this meaning is. This is my trial, my test of faith."
And I think that gives the person who caused the accident a different
handle on it. Maybe the handle would have to be understanding why
the Lord used me in that way.[19]

Some accidental killers take comfort in the belief that the deceased's spirit continues to live on. One explains:

I know that my religion allowed me to believe that [my
brother] is alive as a spirit and that his essence can visit me—
visits which, in my opinion, I have had many times. I've been
asked to speak at five funerals in the past six years, and I'm
very sure I have felt his presence there. This is a guardian angel
concept compatible with my religious beliefs.

Others experience a religious conversion as the direct result of
trying to cope with the accident:

My initial reaction was one of disbelief. Afterward I was so
shook up about the whole thing that I couldn't study in college.
So I dropped out and went to work. For quite a while, I
bounced around from job to job, not really being satisfied with
what I was doing and not really knowing what I wanted to do.
    I got involved in my church after some discussion with my
pastor. The reassurance he gave me eased the guilty feeling I
had unknowingly developed. The assurance of [God's] love, regardless of whether I am right or wrong, the fact that Christ
died for all my sins, and knowing that, as the Bible says, "The
Lord will not let you be tempted more than you have the ability
to resist," have all helped me to see that what happened was
God's will and that the other person has surely found what I
have as a goal in my life—eternal rest, love, and peace with
God.

But religious belief is not always blissful. It also can generate guilt,
as this accidental killer explains:

The accident was a truck and car wreck. I was in a large
truck—truck driving is my occupation. This man came from a

side road into my path without looking, and I couldn't stop, as I was too close to him. His friend, who was following me in a log truck, said he had been drunk since Saturday, and this was Monday afternoon about four o'clock. He came off the side road on the wrong side of the road. He was really traveling. He never knew what hit him.

My pastor was very helpful following the accident. He was raised in that area and went with me to visit the victim's family and friends at the funeral home. The people where I go to church were helpful in many ways by praying for me and having kind words when most needed. Some of them made remarks that hurt even though they meant well, like "It was God's will for that to happen that way," or "You did the community a favor because he was a strain on his family and community," or "It was not your fault, why worry? The law can't do a thing." They seemed so unthoughtful and uncaring of another's feelings, especially those of the victim's family.

It strengthened my faith by causing me to rely more on God's leadership and to study the Bible more clearly and more prayerfully. I felt guilty because I always asked for God's guidance each morning on rising, and I was warned to stop just before the accident occurred. I always went off by myself and prayed for strength to live with these feelings and also to ask God for forgiveness for my disobedience to His warning to stop.

The relative validity of a religion's principles does not seem to affect its effectiveness in healing, which seems more to depend on the strength with which it is believed. One accidental killer reports:

Prior to this accident, I probably had a real eternal optimism. Being a pretty good guy, I thought that not too many things would ever go wrong. I thought that I could go out and whip the world if the world would just stand still and let me have a chance. After the accident, I guess I suddenly realized that I probably wasn't Boy Wonder, that the world wasn't going to stand still and let me whip it, and that there were things that could happen that I couldn't have any direct control over. . . .

The two men were changing a tire by the side of the road. The jack fell, and it pushed the car in their direction, so they both stepped back directly into my path. . . . The whole accident took place in a matter of twenty seconds. I saw something that looked like it flew across the front of the truck, and the truck jumped. . . . I had assumed I had hit a spare tire. The only thing I could think of was where that spare tire was or whom it would have bounced off of. In the meantime, my problem was getting my truck under control so that I could get off to the side of the road.

When I got out of the truck and looked back, I saw two bodies. At first I thought that the next person behind me had killed them. Well, I didn't know that they had been killed. Of course, running up the interstate, it became very apparent that I had hit them. By looking at the front of the truck, as dented as it was, it was very apparent that I had hit them and had also run over the spare tire at the same time. Evidently one of the bodies had bounced back and forth between the car and the truck. . . .

I think I learned a lot about myself [after the accident]. I learned how much I could take [and] probably a lot about how much I could give. I wouldn't go so far as to say that I would be glad that it happened because it made me a better human being. I don't think anytime you put your body through that much stress that it makes you a better human being.

I always had the idea that if you are good, go to church, believe in God, then everything is hunky-dory. God blows up a plastic bubble, sticks you inside of it, and you never fall down—you just roll along. Nobody ever can get to you; you just roll. And then all of a sudden, I was in my early twenties, and I'd had an accident, and I was trying to blame God for it . . . trying to blame anybody I could.

It eventually got to where my mind just did not want to think about it anymore. . . . I had to just say, "Okay, God, you take care of it." People can scoff at that; they can say that's a bunch of bull. It might be to some people, but it's not to me. Just knowing that He could take care of it let me go on and get my life structure back so that I could function again.

One critical function of religion is to allow the accidental killer to find a sense of forgiveness. Psychologist Joseph Nicolosi explains why this essential component of healing is often found in religion:

> Personally, I think that forgiveness by God is the strongest and most effective way to get over the guilt of an accidental killing. For people who don't believe in God, my immediate answer is that God works through us whether we believe in Him or not. But on a more practical plane, we find forgiveness or peace through another relationship—if it's a meaningful relationship—because I think that God works through people anyway.[20]

Healing Guilt

The biggest obstacle to healing is guilt. The obvious solution is self-forgiveness. But many accidental killers have no idea how to forgive themselves. As one accidental killer puts it, "I tried to put the guilt out of my mind. But it was and still is impossible. I tried to overlook it, but I will never forget the guilt feelings involved."

In an attempt to assuage their guilt, some accidental killers adopt elevated standards of behavior. A woman whose coworker died the day before the accidental killer's twenty-eighth birthday speaks to this point:

> It's important for people to realize that you reap what you sow, and the key to pulling oneself out of a tragedy like this psychologically sound is to know in your heart that you're responsible and that you're not paying for some misdeed from your past. That means living the kind of life that in the future when something like this happens you're not consumed by guilt.

Overcoming guilt feelings often means letting go of a rigid attitude with regard to oneself. Dr. Rustin explains:

> Part of people becoming more adult is recognizing that most of life is not black and white, there are shades of gray. I had a patient who accidentally killed someone in a car accident, and because of fear, he gave up his driver's license. It was a way to avoid doing it again. But

it was also saying, "If I deprive myself of ever driving again, in some way this will expiate my guilt."[21]

Unresolved guilt almost inevitably leads to depression. Dr. Nicolosi describes his approach to helping people break out of the guilt-depression cycle:

> What you're trying to do is to turn over this negative affect and let the accidental killers see what the dynamic is beneath it, and the dynamic might be guilt. They might be punishing themselves, and you want them to look at this process. You make it conscious, and then you have to work it through. It won't clear itself up just by making it conscious. You have to use judgment and make the person really reflect on the difference between justified guilt and unjustified guilt. That takes conscious thinking out.
>
> To work it through means to consolidate the two split parts of the self. One part of the self did produce the negative reaction, and the other part finds it guilty of not meeting the ideal. So one is punishing the other. We have a split in the person between the behaving self and the observing self. In the therapeutic process, what you are calling "working it through" means coming to a consolidation between the behaving self and the observing self. You don't have to lower your standards to forgive yourself. You just have to be more accepting of the behaving self. You have to expand. The observing self has to become more sophisticated and more refined in its acceptance.
>
> The process of atonement is a suggestive process that has to do with one's relationship with oneself. The word *atonement* means at-one-ment.[22]

The Healing Power of Relationships

Besides making space for the vital flow of words that enables accidental killers to flush out their agony, personal relationships provide a basis for acceptance that helps to reestablish the accidental killer's dignity. Dr. Nicolosi points out that relationships have great potential as avenues to forgiveness:

> I think that way down deep, we don't forgive ourselves. I think we have to find forgiveness either philosophically or religiously. I think that people can't do it on their own. I think that people are not capable of granting themselves forgiveness. . . . Forgiveness and guilt

are such primary and such fundamental issues that people cannot do it on their own. And the assistance has to be a context greater than themselves.[23]

For many accidental killers, a loving relationship is the primary route to regaining self-esteem. A man whose first marriage broke down after his involvement in his stepdaughter's accidental death praises his new mate:

We had known each other since we were fifteen, but we hadn't seen each other for twenty years. We've been together since the day we met again. She understands. She doesn't have an enemy in the world. It's just her personality. She's intelligent and very understanding. I consider her not only my wife but my very best friend. It took a lot of years of love from a good woman for me to get over this accident.

A Sense of Purpose

Whether they think of it as indirect penance, revalidation, or guilt expiation, many accidental killers feel the need to think about their values and rearrange their priorities. They want to make sure they spend their time well. This period of reflection and rescheduling is not unlike what people experience after other major tragedies.[24] One accidental killer advises, "For whatever reason, the 'powers that be' let you live through the accident. Prove that you're worthy, especially to yourself." Another recommends, "Set yourself a goal and go for it."

This earnest necessity to make every moment count may be a way of handling guilt. A teenager who urged the driver of the car he was in to pass a bicyclist, starting an impromptu race that resulted in the cyclist's death, reports:

Initially I experienced a great sense of shock and disbelief as to what had actually happened. The person who was killed also happened to be a good friend of mine. The accident occurred when we were both seventeen years of age, and we had at- tended school together since the age of nine, although not always in the same class. I guess at that age not too many people think about death very much.

After about four years had elapsed, a maturing attitude, greater knowledge, and acceptance of life (reality) began to help me put the experience into perspective. I have determined that it was an accident and that I would do anything to prevent anything like this from happening again.

I have thus developed a sense of safety consciousness in trying to justify my continued life in society. I strive to do what is right and best. I give to charities and have studied first aid techniques to further my justification. There are still difficult times when I regress into the past and remember the incident and damn myself and pray for forgiveness.

The only way I know of to cope is to accept what has happened and to concentrate on the here and now, believing I can be of some beneficial use to society.

Often when an accidental killer starts the new initiatives that come out of this inner work, her self-esteem grows. One accidental killer advises, "Each must push for ego-reinforcing experiences." Another explains his approach of mindful labor:

I put on a good front—like painting my house and going out with this girl I knew from work before my accident. (I didn't even develop feelings for her until two months afterward.) I even tried taking a summer course in sociology. Actually, all my actions and involvements weren't intentionally done as a front, but I was just trying to piece things together—trying to understand what life is all about.

Many accidental killers get involved with community service. A father who accidentally killed his three-year-old tells why he started a group home:

It was for teenage girls who were hard to place in the community. Foster families wouldn't accept them. They were too off the wall. At the same time, they weren't sociopathic or crazy enough to be put in institutions, so they just ran the street. I wanted to provide a place for kids who were being rejected by the community in one way or another. I saw too many in school get into a whole bunch of personal trouble and ruin their lives because there weren't good homes for them in the city.

He and his wife also adopted a little girl one year after the death of their son. He says, "As soon as she could understand, we told her we were not her real parents and that we loved her even more for that."

Physical activity is a powerful mood elevator. Psychologist William James has written that mood or emotion follows behavior. James notes that one cannot count on moods to dictate what one should do.[25] A seventeen-year-old who accidentally drove into a pedestrian on a dark street says, "I knew it wasn't my fault. When I feel guilty I go golfing and pray a lot." Another accidental killer took up a rigorous aerobics regimen after her suicide attempt. "It settles me down," she explains, "and gives me something to strive for."

But not just any activity will do. It has to make sense to the accidental killer. A woman who accidentally ran her car over a child notes, "When I get depressed, I go and do something physical, like cleaning out the garage. People say, 'Go on a shopping spree,' but that wouldn't help me a bit." The more an activity ensures that something valuable will result from the tragedy, the more it satisfies the accidental killer's needs. A man whose best friend was killed when their car was sideswiped continues to work off his guilt:

All along I knew that it was in no way intentional, but I had to make myself understand that I could not have avoided it. I feel that I have pretty much accomplished this, but in an accidental killing, there will always be that small element of doubt. I spend a great deal of time coaching high school kids in soccer. It's a year-round thing, and it puts me in a position that when I know teenagers who are about to get their driver's license, I can relate my story to them and explain the responsibilities of driving a car. I feel it makes a difference when it comes from someone like myself and not from their parents. I know I have reached some of them and hope that I may have helped them to avoid the same thing I went through.

Some accidental killers are able to contribute through their jobs. A newspaper reporter whose car fatally struck a child included accidental death in a series she wrote about the local mental health crisis center.

Many accidental killers are very aware of the self-healing effects of their service to others. The man whose story opens this chapter constantly creates opportunities to share his experience with others. He says, "Without the healing I gain from trying to help others, I believe the craziness and complexity of my past would grow like a tumor into self-centeredness and eventual self-destruction."

Healing Social Tension

Many accidental killers find themselves unable to heal some of their social relationships, but this is something they cannot completely control. They can only learn whom to trust. As one accidental killer puts it, "After the immediate period is over, normal life resumes with its contacts with people. These people tend to react as the people they are—good people will be good; bastards [will be] bastards. I don't know how you can change their basic nature."

Some accidental killers learn through experience the danger of volunteering information—no matter how much they may need to talk. Rabbi Earl Grollman advises, "Don't share your feelings with those who aren't insightful enough to help. You don't always have to wear your feelings on your sleeve. You must know when to handle them yourself. People can hurt you with clichés and boggle up your mind."[26]

Most accidental killers feel the need to apologize to the victim's family. (This is discussed in detail in chapter 10.) One accidental killer notes, "I couldn't have left town without speaking to the mother of those kids."

Since accidental killers tend to have a strong sense of their own vulnerability to other's reactions, most keep up their guard. In some cases, they feel they can depend only on themselves. Dr. Stanley Rustin lays out some prerequisites for overcoming the rejection of others:

Clearly we're talking about how resilient the person is in the face of rejection. Some people are not very resilient. They get very hurt, withdraw, become depressed, or respond by being very angry. It takes all sorts of different forms. I think the ability to reject the negative evaluation of others has to do with your own sense of yourself prior to the experience and what kind of support you're able to gather when one group has rejected you.[27]

An accidental killer who became the subject of gossip after a man jumped out in front of his van describes how he maintained his self-esteem: "Believe in yourself. If you know it wasn't your fault, don't let what other people say make you feel guilty."

A widely known community figure whose two sons were killed in her accident explains her social strategy: "Perhaps having been in the public eye as I had always been (both my father and my husband were school administrators), what people thought of me was important to me. It was hard to get out, but I did so almost immediately. . . . I feel people are far more sympathetic when they see you getting out and trying to make a comeback as soon as possible."

Concentrating on a Positive Aspect

Some accidental killers adapt by developing hypothetical scenarios that are worse than what actually happened. Sometimes this is impossible, as in the case of a father whose daughter's mutilated remains were buried in a closed casket. He says, "I haven't thought about how it could have been worse, and frankly I don't want to."

But in circumstances that do allow it, imagining how the situation could have been worse seems to help. A mother managed to conceive of a possible outcome worse than the deaths of her two sons. She says, "I do think it would have been harder to lose them at an older age. Two of the other women had children, and I thought, 'At least those children weren't with us.' If it had to be somebody's children, at least it was mine so long as I was doing the driving."

This tendency is so strong that sometimes members of the victim's family extend themselves to the accidental killer. A woman whose car hit an elderly man responds that the family "told me they had been expecting to hear something like this for a long time, except they expected him to be mangled—which he wasn't. The accident happened seventeen years ago, and we're still friends to this day."

Professional Help

Relatively few accidental killers seek psychotherapeutic help after the accident. For one accidental killer, it took a failed suicide attempt before her physician could convince her that she needed therapy. She says, "He just asked me, 'Do you want to be crippled all your life, or do you want to live?'" At the time of her attempted suicide, her mother had just died and she had just retired from a career in the Navy. She continues, "My therapist and I were really in tune. I had just lost my Navy mommy and my real mommy, and my psychiatrist was my psychological mommy for a while. He let me grow up. He saved me." (This subject is discussed in more detail in chapter 10.)

A Healing Dream

Sometimes self-healing resources surface in the dream realm. The mother whose sons were killed in her accident describes how her own unconscious mind conjured up the experience she needed:

> After the accident, I missed the older boy more because he could talk. When I left the car and went out into the storm, I had to leave him behind. I carried the baby in my arms, and I had such an inward desire to hold that older boy. And I thought, "Well, that's silly. He was taken care of." It was like I didn't take as good care of him because I left him on the backseat. But I couldn't carry both of them.
>
> One night I had a dream that I was at my dad's office up at the courthouse, and we were coming out and down the steps. And here came Bobby about halfway down the walk. I knelt down, and I put out my arms and held him. And I remember I thought at the time, "I know I can't keep him, but I get to hold him." And that feeling of wanting to hold him left. It was just such a strong desire that I had a dream about it. I haven't tried to analyze it, but it did the job for me.

The Aftermath

A fatal accident eight years ago played a role in Ira Attebury's random rifle attack on a street full of parade watchers in San Antonio, relatives say. . . .

Attebury directed a withering fusillade of sniper fire on police and spectators at the Battle of the Flowers parade Friday in San Antonio. Two women died and fifty-five others were injured by gun fire or the panic that ensued as Attebury fired into a crowd of 5,000.

Attebury, who would have been sixty-five on Sunday, took his own life after firing at the crowd and a ninety-minute battle with police.

His family said Saturday that Attebury was never the same after his semi-trailer truck rammed a car that ran a red light in front of him eight years ago in Ohio. Both occupants of the car were killed. Attebury's two brothers said he was not at fault in the crash. But they said the accident left him with a disabling injury and emotionally scarred. Attebury injured his neck and back in the crash and had to retire from truck driving, his primary occupation since leaving the Coast Guard at the end of World War II.

"He thought the police were after him all the time after that," said his older brother W.H. Attebury, 66, of Poplar Bluff, Missouri.

—Associated Press

Fortunately, destructive rampages like that of Ira Attebury are rare. In most cases, accidental killers show an incredible amount of resilience. Through struggle, most manage to overcome the tragedy and to incorporate it and the lessons it brings into a new self.

By doing the work required to go on with life after a tragedy, many accidental killers grow in significant ways. They see the importance of their connection with other people and make efforts to extend themselves, especially to others in similar situations. They gain perspective on what does and does not represent a crisis. They learn to love and respect themselves without gauging their worth by external standards. One accidental killer notes, "Small things used to get on my nerves. Now I say, 'What is this compared to the accident?' I learned that I am strong."

Transformation of the self is the only solution to the problems that follow a fatal accident. This transformation comes primarily through talking about the accident, looking for help from others, reaching out for spiritual strength, and service to others. The only way for survivors to go on with their lives is to grow into individuals who can handle even accidental killing. The fact that so many people took the time to relate their stories for the benefit of others who read this book shows more than mere survival. It shows empathy rising out of tragedy, caring coming from inexplicable sorrow, and the integration of the experience into their once fragmented lives. It shows an attempt to redeem agony through helping others by people who easily could have remained self-absorbed.

Two* famous twentieth-century men were accidental killers, but the circumstances of their accidents and the subsequent effects differ greatly. Future senator Adlai Stevenson was twelve years old when he accidentally shot an acquaintance in an in-home accident that was covered up and became a lifelong drain on his confidence. In contrast, when writer William Burroughs accidentally shot his wife, the incident received national publicity. For him it became an impetus for his lifework.

Author John Bartlow Martin wrote a book about Stevenson in which he describes how, on December 30, 1912, Adlai Stevenson shot and killed Ruth Merwin.[1] That day his older sister, Buffie, had a birthday party at home. A guest wanted to demonstrate how to use a rifle, so Adlai brought out a .22 rifle. When the boy was finished, he handed it back to Adlai, who, presuming it to be empty, pointed it at Ruth, whom he barely knew, and pulled the trigger. The bullet struck her in the forehead, and she fell dead on the library floor.

Afterward Adlai went upstairs to his room alone. The day of the funeral, his mother took him out of town. A week later, then again a while after that, he wrote to his father, casually mentioning the Merwins twice, as if nothing had happened.

---

*Were it not for lack of information and possible drunk driving, Senator Ted Kennedy's 1969 involvement in the death of Mary Jo Kopechne at Chappaquiddick Island might have been included here.

These letters give an impression of an extraordinarily self-contained boy so soon after so terrible an accident—or one who was heavily repressed by his parents—or of one almost frighteningly unfeeling—or of one blocking, unable to face it. Except for two notes in his sister's diary, so far as can be learned, the accident was never mentioned in the Stevenson family.[2]

Stevenson never told anyone, not even his closest friends. Years later, he was shocked to hear that his wife knew of it.

Perhaps the most important imprint this accident left on Stevenson was his remarkable capacity to doubt and to derogate himself. Though a prominent statesman, he turned triumphs into disasters, honors into burdens. At the 1952 Democratic National Convention, he told the Illinois delegation that he was not fit for the presidential nomination and that he would have preferred to have heard the acceptance uttered by "a stronger, a wiser, and a better man than myself." He dismissed his honors as tarnished and worthless. He referred to his gubernatorial office as a "hideous ordeal." Of his campaign in 1948 for the governorship he wrote, "I wonder what the hell I'm doing and why . . . so why do I want to win and get into that hideous mess for four years of solitary agony and heartbreak. I must be nuts."[3]

Though Stevenson was silent regarding his accident, he seemingly served a secret penance. Forty-three years after the accidental killing, he wrote a letter to a woman whose son had had a similar experience. "Tell him that he must live for two," Stevenson said.[4]

When William Burroughs accidentally shot and killed his wife, the story ran in several different versions in newspapers across the country. He describes the tragedy in the documentary film *Burroughs:*

That day something awful had happened. I was walking down the street, and tears started streaming down my face. If that happens to you—watch out. I had always thought myself to be controlled at sometime by this completely malevolent force, which Byron described as the Ugly Spirit. But my walking down the street and tears streaming down my face meant that I knew that the Ugly Spirit, which is always the worst part of everyone's character, would take over and that something awful would happen. And I took a knife that I'd bought in Ecuador and left it at a knife sharpener to be sharpened.

I went back to the apartment where we were all living with a terrible sense of depression and, foolishly of course, in order to relieve this depression, I started tossing down drinks. Then I said to Joan, "It's about time for our William Tell act," and she put a glass on her head, and I had this piece of .30 junk. I fired the shot. The glass hadn't been touched; Joan started sliding down toward the floor. Then Marcus stood, walked over, and took one look at her, and he said, "Bill, your bullet has hit her forehead. Oh, my God!"[5]

Burroughs later described the accident this way: "Just an absolute piece of insanity. Absolutely hell to live with it day and night. My entire life has been a fight against the Ugly Spirit."[6]

The death marked a turning point in Burroughs's life. According to his friend, poet Allen Ginsburg, "It opened him up quite a bit. It was then that he began writing. Bill got very serious. He began looking around for something to do to lift himself. It grounded him a bit. From then on, as I remember, writing became a grounding objective."[7]

A Wide Range of Responses

The impact of the crisis can send people in any of a thousand directions depending on the nature of the accident and the landscape into which it falls. This chapter is a compendium of possible effects that involvement in a fatal accident can have on a person's life.

A man who remembers his infant daughter's accidental death says: "When you look down at a person, and you know you stopped that person from breathing, it totally changes your life."

It is almost impossible to kill someone, even accidentally, without undergoing dramatic change. Some accidental killers are mildly debilitated by their accidents in ways that only someone who knows them well would notice. Others experience more obvious changes. Some feel that their personality is strengthened by the things they learn in the process of getting over the tragedy; others do not. Some sense slight shifts, while others see the entire course of their lives change. Some emerge more afraid of the world than before the accident, while others grow more tolerant. Some become shy, lose their desire to participate in any activity they associate with the death, or switch careers. Others deepen their religious faith, feel they have lost their innocence, see their families as changed, or demand more of themselves as a result of guilt. Almost all find that certain things trigger their memory of the accident. The coping mechanisms that develop in response to the accident are as diverse as the accidental killers themselves.

One woman describes her daily penance to the child she accidentally killed: "Since he was only six years old and had not had much of a chance to make a mark on the world, I feel it is my duty to remember him every day. I feel a terrible responsibility to remember the child."

The accident's impact on the lives of many survivors is subtle enough for them to be able to keep it to themselves. One notes:

> The world looks on me as a happy, well-adjusted woman. This view is a satisfaction to me, although it may not always be true. I was living with a family as a mother's helper in another part of the state from my home. I was sixteen at the time. In the evening, I was asked to deliver papers to a home in another town on a dark, lonely road. There were no houses, no lights, and a woman walked across the road dressed all in black. Only my employers and my parents knew about the accident and then later my husband. Only as an older adult do I realize the effects on my life. But I have been able to cope.

Another accidental killer says, "Sometimes at night I see dark shadows fly up in front of my car. It is still very hard to drive on that particular road. And whenever I hear the victim's last name, it all comes back. I'm happy now, but I think there is always that spot of unhappiness that I'll never forget."

Fear becomes a major part of some accidental killers' lives. Physical injuries incurred in the accident serve as ever-present reminders of the accident. One woman notes, "My feet must have been frostbitten that night while waiting for help because the ends of my toes peeled afterwards and are still very sensitive when the weather is cold. I still have trouble with my back. Hardly a day goes by that it doesn't hurt, but I rarely mention it to anyone. No one wants to hear of a sore back."

Some accidental killers find it necessary to practice a daily meditation of self-forgiveness. One says, "My method of keeping control over the memories is by firmly telling myself almost in a verbal way, 'It was an accident and it was not my fault.'"

Others find driving or riding in a car frightening. One reports,

"I've never really felt safe in a car since the accident—especially if the car skids, or seems to be skidding, off the road. After the accident . . . I was terrified; my heart would race if ever I had to drive on a highway and exceed thirty-five miles per hour."

Some are never able to process their guilt. One notes, "The memories of the accident do not surface as often as they once did. But they are still very clear, and the feelings of sadness and remorse are still there. I have never really forgiven myself completely. When the memory does come back, I find myself going through the whole sequence of events thinking, 'If only I had. . . .' "

Accidental killing can deepen a person's awareness. Some survivors shape their lives around their philosophical analysis of the accident experience. One reports:

It looks like the karma involved in this situation is still at work. Your letter reached me just one day after I gave a deposition regarding the pending case. Phil (the deceased) and I worked together at a restaurant. Phil's parents are trying to find the owner of the restaurant guilty or liable for the accident. So everything is still very much a part of my life.

I have come to conclude things happen for a reason. Even if we can't see that reason right away, I believe the events of our lives all fit together as if in some large-scale cosmic plan. I believe that Phil's death was in some way part of my plan. It has taught me that there is more and that I must go on with my life and try to be the best person I can be while I'm here on this earth. I try not to ask why but to accept events, good or bad, and gain understanding from them.

When I say I know, I don't mean I know with my head; I mean I know with my heart. Maybe one should call this faith. So I guess you could say I have gained a great deal of faith over the years since 1980—both in myself and in my life and, I guess, in life in general.

Let me close with this as an example. . . . Phil's and my desire [was] to live on a farm in northern New England. Well, I am writing this letter from my house that sits on the top of a mountain on 150 acres of land in the backwoods. It's a very rural area. I take great pleasure in being here, planting my garden, cutting firewood, putting some venison in the freezer in the fall, and just wandering the woods and fields with a large dog named Bliss.

Phil may have died physically, but I know his spirit is here, and I'll bet he's smiling, too.

In contrast, some accidental killers do not seem to incorporate lessons from their accident into their lives:

> My life has been a roller coaster of good and bad experiences— the recurrence of helplessness and sorrow for Angie, the girl who died. . . . The new love of my life was involved in depression and drugs. I broke down and cried, begging her to stop and not die like Angie did. . . . I saw Angie's face in her at that moment. I am married to my new love, and we have two children from her previous marriage. My driving has not improved; I am classified as a persistent violator of traffic laws. I have been arrested for driving under the influence. I am under five years, probation for stealing. I am in business for myself doing landscaping. I am also seeing a doctor for mental problems.

The trauma of an accident has resulted in a slow, painful death for some accidental killers. The widow of a police officer who shot and killed a would-be escapee writes:

> My husband died on February 26, 1985, of colon cancer. . . . Bill thought of this killing every day in one form or another. When he was down and out, he would get the scrapbook out that I had made and read and reread it. . . . There would be a long period of silence, then he would talk about it and say how sorry he was for it. He also would drink heavily after this. Bill was very ill for thirteen months before he died. He said it was his punishment for the shooting. Bill chose to die at home. And on his deathbed, he was still asking for forgiveness. . . .
>
> My feelings are that I would still have my husband of many years had this not happened.
>
> My youngest son is trying to get into police work; he has his application in. I asked him for his comments; he replied, "You're never sure when the mother of George [the deceased]

is going to stab you in the back." I am always looking over my shoulder.

The next to the youngest says that our family and especially his father has been through too much, and we should get royalties for this story. See the bitterness, after all these years? I hope I have been of some help to you.

In rare cases, the accidental killer is not aware that the accident has had any effect at all. A man who hit an aged pedestrian when he was a teenager working as a bicycle messenger says, "Not until I received this letter have I even given the accident any thought. I have never felt any effects on my life because of the accident."

Some accidental killers are unable to separate the effects of the accident from their own character defects. A man who accidentally shot his brother when he was a boy reports, "Having spent almost thirty years wrestling with inner problems [and] seeking psychiatric help, all to no avail, [and having had] one failed marriage and another doomed to failure, I am not sure that I am an ideal candidate for your study."

One obstacle to the accident's healing is long-term amnesia. One accidental killer explains:

> I still don't remember the accident, but now I believe that God hasn't brought my memory back because He feels I wouldn't be able to cope with the reality.
>
> I often think about the deceased's family and friends, how they are doing and how they are coping. The man that died was a minister. Somehow I feel this is all connected.
>
> I've come to the conclusion that I may never know in this life why this happened, maybe in the next. I still have a very strong guilt feeling. If I could remember, just maybe there would have been something I could have done to prevent this terrible tragedy.

Nor is everyone able to talk about the accident and find relief. It takes some accidental killers years before they can discuss the accident with anyone. A man who was involved in an accident while driving under the influence of codeine says, "Since participating in your study, I have been able to talk to many people in the school system about the horror of drug/alcohol abuse and my involvement with this awful accident. Sometimes it is very difficult and emotional, but that's okay. I need to talk about it. For ten years I could not and would not discuss it with anyone, not even God."

Another accidental killer reports:

Probably any professional advice would be that a person should talk about such a painful incident in one's life, but I cannot. In the six years following the accident, I have coped by keeping my feelings to myself. I know this is probably wrong, but each time I begin to talk to loved ones, the words literally stick in my throat. I have not talked to anyone at all regarding my feelings.

The hurt is still there, but I feel it is a cross I must bear. Time has lessened the amount of time I am preoccupied with thoughts of the accident, and I honestly feel that it has been easier keeping the hurt to myself. I would welcome the opportunity to read your book and see how others may have successfully handled the guilt.

Sometimes accidental killers gain some sense of satisfaction from knowing that the accident resulted in a positive change. A railroad engineer's accident led to one such change. He said, "The railroad finally recognized the problem. They agreed to have the tracks in this area elevated off road level."

A Changed Attitude toward the World

Seeing the stark reality of life and death causes many accidental killers to feel as though they have lost their innocence. One remembers:

I was very immature for twenty-seven years old, probably not as mature as most eighteen-year-olds. I was the youngest of the family. I knew I was very immature. After the accident, the saying dawned on me, "You grow old overnight." I felt different and had a more mature outlook on life. I felt too old to do things like get out and roller-skate—young people things.

Some accidental killers become fearful of the world and hesitate to take risks of any kind. A Kenyan who was a soldier in Her Majesty's Regiment at the time of his accident describes his generalized apprehension afterward:

> I was going to visit an aunt who was to be in the country for only a couple of days. She was back liquidating her possessions and selling her properties because her husband had died and she wanted to move home with her sisters in Nigeria. It was afternoon, and I was in the mountains, driving a jeep. I looked out over the land and saw the chocolate-brown treetops and the golden grass shining in the sun. I came to a place they called Dead Man's Curve, and there I came upon another car. It was a couple driving to their prom dance. The boy was frightened of the curve, and he went onto my side of the road. We hit head-on.
>
> Having been in action before and having seen fallen men, I felt the agony when the car hit. As a soldier, I knew that death could come at any time. In a split second, I realized this was something different, not war. It was civilian. If it had been war, I would have been prepared. But this was something different.
>
> When I woke up in the hospital, I knew fully where I was and what had happened. I felt sad about the accident. Reading about accidents makes me feel sad since then. After a while, I started to be afraid. At that time, I was supposed to return to Sandhurst, England, for further training, but there was a psychological evaluation because of my accident. It concluded that the return to England would do me harm. So I did not get the promotion.
>
> I decided then never to marry so that I would not have children. I am too afraid of losing them gradually through the years.

Fear of Recurrence

Many accidental killers stop taking their security for granted after the accident. In this sense, they resemble sailors who have trouble returning to a ship that has collided with another vessel. Having been trained to believe in the invulnerability of their ship, the catastrophe casts doubt on everything the sailors had previously trusted.[8]

Researcher Martha Wolfenstien describes this lingering wariness: "One of the most common reactions of people who have undergone a disaster is the fear that it will happen again . . . it would seem that for the disaster victim the world had been transformed from the secure one in which he believed such things could not happen into one where catastrophe becomes a regular order."[9]

Rabbi Earl Grollman notes, "They will always be a little insecure. They will never really gain security."[10]

Having been on the dealing end of death, some accidental killers are struck by the fear that the tables will be turned and they or someone they love will someday be the victim. Dr. Elisabeth Kübler-Ross has noticed this phenomenon among accident survivors. She theorizes that it results from an unconscious fear of dying a pathetic death in payment.[11]

Some accidental killers fear for their family's safety. One says, "I have an almost paranoid fear when I know my loved ones are driving for long distances. When they are absent and the phone rings, for a brief moment I feel very frightened. Another notes, "I am often complimented on 'having it all together.' I put on a real good front. I am afraid for others in my family that something will happen. It's not hard to be overprotective—not only for the fear of losing someone but not wanting them to be the cause of an accident."

This fear is common among those who face death in any form. According to scientists who have studied widows whose husbands died unexpectedly, death becomes an ever-present force that could return and take another life at any time. Some widows whose husbands were shot at night are afraid to go out at night and rarely venture from the house after dark. Other widows are so afraid of another unexpected death that they become phobic toward marriage.[12]

A mother who accidentally killed her child explains:

Several times a night I'll be sleeping soundly and the girls will make noise turning in bed or rolling over or coughing or bumping each other or whatever. At the very moment that I become conscious, the first thing in my mind is that they're dead. Then I don't hear anything, and I hear regular breathing. At first I used to get up and check them, but I don't do that anymore. But at least every other night, several times a week, that thought occurs.

Many fear becoming a perpetrator a second time and avoid the accident scene and settings similar to it. They are often unwilling to carry out actions similar to those they carried out right before the accident.

The heightened sensitivity experienced by accidental killers can change the way they operate in the world. A woman who suffered one continuous headache for thirteen years following her accident says, "Almost every trace of emotion is gone now except if a child along the street almost darts out in front of my car. I just use good judgment and pull over to the side and sit there until I am sure I am calm, then go on." She describes how she was upset by a minor incident twenty-two years after her accident:

> I ran over an opossum on the highway, and it upset me that night, but I pulled myself together and went on to a play. But the next day I had to call my doctor, who was a close friend, because I had a pain in my head as I had never known before. He left his office, came over and gave me a shot, and stayed until my husband could get there. I slept, and when I awoke, it was gone. The doctor came by the house and said, "I have the feeling something happened that brought that headache on." I told him about the animal. He said, "Say no more; that was the cause."

A man whose accident happened when the victim's car jack slipped describes how he reacts to similar circumstances:

> Even today when somebody gets out of a car, I swing over to the left-hand lane if I can. I get directly out of their way. If I see someone changing a tire in a very inappropriate place, I catch myself wanting to pull off to the side of the road and go back and tell them what a fool they are. If they only knew what jeopardy they are putting themselves in, as well as their family and the people driving by.

For some accidental killers, taking precautions means behaving in what many would consider a commonly acceptable fashion. One man relates, "Before the accident, I used to be quite a barroom scrapper. But now that I see how little it takes to kill somebody, I am more careful. Before, if somebody bothered me, I wouldn't think anything about getting into a fight. Now I stay away. If people want to fight me, they are going to have to catch me in the parking lot first."

While not becoming phobic, many accidental killers develop a strong dislike for things associated with the accident. A man whose accident victim was riding a motorcycle says, "Over the years, I have noticed within myself an almost intense dislike for motorcycles on the road and a great deal of distrust of cycle drivers."

A few react to their fears by taking precautionary measures to help ensure that they will have a clear conscience in the future. A farm boy who watched his friend die of a heart attack, for example, later took a class in cardiopulmonary resuscitation.

Work and Accidents

In cases where a fatal accident happened on the job, the accidental killer may be forced to reenact the accident time after time. This is enough to make some accidental killers quit their jobs. A policeman who shot a fleeing suspect left the police force for this reason: "I don't want to hurt anybody anymore. I don't want that to happen twice. As long as I was carrying a gun, it was likely it could happen. I was glad to get out. I worry about a cop shooting somebody; he's the one who is going to suffer. The one killed is through suffering."

One man's father sold the family business for a similar reason:

Everybody knew Dad. He had been in business fifteen years at the time. The business was sold as a direct result of my accident. My father lost the desire to remain in business due to the fact that he didn't ever want to have trucks on the road again. Since we were a small company—we had one other fellow to drive—Dad just didn't want to be in a position to put me through that again, nor did he want to go through it himself. I lost the desire to even drive the truck.

To this day I still see the truck because the people who bought it from us still use it. But it won't hurt me any when that truck is completely out of this neighborhood and I never see it again.

The change can be striking. Instead of continuing his premedical studies, one teenager entered mortician school. For the duration of his training, he took a job that required he live at the mortuary.

Railroad engineers are particularly susceptible to work-related tragedies. These people average one fatality every three years, according to Joe Cassidy, chairman of the Brotherhood of Locomotive Engineers of Long Island. He notes that there are 150 crossings in a typical stretch of track 250 miles long, offering that many chances of hitting someone disregarding the warning signs and trying to beat the train.

One engineer explains to a potential victim:

A train is not a motor vehicle; it cannot be steered, nor can it chase anyone down the street. The weight of our largest diesel unit plus five cars and a power unit is 440 tons of rolling stock moving at up to sixty-five miles per hour. This amount of weight cannot be stopped on a dime.

Young man, death embraced you, and you escaped. Both the brakeman and I could see the expression of stark terror on your face. But we wonder if you have any idea of the anguish we on the engine felt when we knew that you were about to die on such a beautiful morning and there was nothing we could do about it. You not only endangered your life but also the lives of the four men on the crew, as the train brakes were in emergency when you crossed in front of us. Please, son, the next time you approach a railroad crossing, slow down, be alert, and thank God for a miracle that you are alive today. We did.

Another engineer says, "When you hit a car, you can see the people in there. You see their faces when you are right on top of them, and there is nothing you can do. You relive this scene many times."

An engineer describes his feelings when passing the site of his accident:

I was running an electric motor train as my normal tour of duty. As I came upon a railroad grade crossing doing about forty-five miles per hour, the legal speed limit, and was blowing my horn, a young adult leaped out from behind a gate control box, onto my track, directly in front of my train, approximately one car length away. Immediately I placed the train in emergency. Just as I was about to hit, the young man turned his head around to look at me and smiled. The train hit him, and we moved approximately another one and a half car lengths before we stopped. We stayed there until the coroner pronounced him dead and his father identified him.

I have torment sometimes when I pass the site of the accident. I wonder what would bring a young adult to take his life. Also I feel anguish at the drug dealers and law in this country in regard to drugs and knowing that teenagers and young adults will not confide in their parents more than they do.

Joe Cassidy describes what it is like to get back into the cab after an accident:

Once you are on the road, as a result of being required to think about your job and the responsibility for the people you are transporting, it tends to push out of your mind those traumatic things that you've experienced. But if there is a lull in the operation and you're going along a stretch of track where for about three or four miles there are no signals and you're just ambling along, your mind may tend to wander for a few minutes, and more often than I would care to remember, my thoughts turned to my kids and their being on the tracks as the train is moving down. I thought I was weird, but I talked to other people, and they thought the same way. It's a complete visualization because you've seen bodies ripped apart before and you start to envision your own kids. And that rips right through your entire body. . . .

We had an engineer who killed about twelve people in two years, and he wanted to quit the job. That man had over twenty years on the railroad. It seemed like every other month he was killing people. Once every sixty days—that's a staggering figure. We have engineers on this railroad who've killed upwards of twenty-five to thirty people over the course of a career. Most of us are married; we have families.

And we have a good job, regardless of what kind of trauma we have experienced. First things first, we know we have to climb back up into that cab. And when it's looked at philosophically, I think there's a certain rationalization of saying, "Hey, I was doing what the railroad expects me to do. You simply cannot stop a train on a dime like you can a car."[13]

Many health care professionals also find themselves immobilized by accidents. "I literally froze and could not perform my duties," says a pediatric nurse. "I needed to know I could save people, but it wasn't until about two years later that I could finally face children without turning away." An anesthetist who used a mislabeled tank of gas was unable to continue working in her field. She says, "Any little snag would absolutely tear me apart."

Phobias and Other Difficulties

Some accidental killers have to overcome phobias related to their accidents. A common problem is the inability to drive a car or to drive the stretch of road where the accident occurred. An accidental killer says:

When the shock wore off, I had great difficulty driving the car. The thought of getting into the car was the worst. It is forty miles each way to work, and I have to be 100 percent alert every foot of the way. After arriving at my destination, I am always tense and tired. The first few years, my hands used to shake, and now eight years later, I have made a conscious effort to steady my hand when I sign in.

After accidentally killing someone in a recreational setting, most survivors find it difficult to enjoy that activity again. One notes, "My best friend and I were out hunting, and he bent over to pull apart a barbed wire fence for me. As he did, his gun went off. The bullet went through his heart, and he just slumped over. I feel like I am responsible because he was helping me at the time. Needless to say, I didn't enjoy hunting much anymore and finally gave it up." Social awkwardness also is common. A woman who ran over her daughter describes her discomfort in responding to new acquaintances who ask how many children she has: "Depending on the situation, I say either exactly what happened, or I say my firstborn daughter was killed in a car accident and leave it at that."

Some bereaved members of the victim's family may seek revenge, which can wreak havoc with the accidental killer's life. One recalls:

> The brother of the youngest victim harassed my sister and mom and tried to hit them with his car every time he would see them. This went on for about a year. I got so mad I called him up and said to him that if he had anything to settle, it was with me and to name the time and place—that I was ready. He said he didn't want any trouble, and I haven't heard anything from him again.

Some accidental killers feel distrustful toward loved ones. One says, "When I need to talk to someone, I turn to my wife, but not in this. I cannot trust her not to use my wounds against me."

Some experience other family-related problems. One reports:

> Time has played the major role in easing my guts about killing my mother in a car accident. The feeling I get about the wreck is kind of melancholy. The worst times—which are not by any means debilitating—are when the subject comes up in conversation, such as when a family member is introducing me to someone who knew my mother and the introduced person will ask, "Is he the one in the wreck?" It's not a sad or hurt feeling as much as an awkward feeling I have at these times. When I go to visit my family, I find that most of these people will not talk with me about the accident. And two of them will not ride in a car that I am driving because of that accident.

A woman who feels responsible for her three-year-old daughter's death observes, "One of the things I find of interest in talking to others in my situation is that all of us went through a stage where we didn't want our other children out of our sight, but we didn't want them near us. . . . The other common thing is we do not discuss our deepest feelings with our spouse for fear of hurting them more."

Not all accidental killers are able to reconcile with their families:

My life is going well. However, a few things are not rosy. I don't believe my father has ever accepted my mother's death and my role in it. He has gone from accusing me directly of having killed her to just not communicating with me at all. He is stiffly polite in my presence. I know this is more than just something with me; he is basically an unhappy person and has trouble with all his relationships. This has been the hardest thing to get over, but I think I am about ready to give up on ever having a good relationship with him. I am concentrating on the other people in my life, sister and brother, etc., with whom I do have a mutually supportive and loving relationship.

Some accidental killers have a hard time resolving the issue within themselves, especially if they were in some way at fault. This accidental killer still suffers from his largely unresolved feelings toward the accident:

We took a walk in the woods and got high. Then I started back because I wanted to be home for the basketball game. On the way home, I just faded out while I was driving and hit another car head-on. I was the one who crossed over the centerline. Then a third car crashed into us; a father and his four-year-old son were killed. The mother and baby were injured. Because the blood test didn't show that I had anything in my bloodstream at the time of the accident, the grand jury refused to convict me. But I felt pretty bad anyway.

First off, I had tremendous guilt, and I lacked self-respect. I wasn't as emotionally stable as I once was. I look back comparing myself then and now. Of course, I'm much better off now. Then I was a student, and now I've got a decent job and nice apartment. But I'm not at all satisfied with myself. I lack emotional stability, aggressiveness, and drive.

The death by fire of her unattended baby and the subsequent murder trial caused a young mother to regress dramatically. Speaking in confidence, a therapist who tried unsuccessfully to counsel her explains, "She was very young, but already she had spent years in and out of abusive relationships. She had never had a good relationship with her parents. After she was acquitted, she got divorced. She basically became a kid again."

In some cases, accidental killers do not resolve their feelings because they are unable to talk about them. Another psychoanalyst speaking in confidence tells of a highway patrolman who hit a drunk man but was never able to discuss his feelings:

> In therapy, he would discuss details of the accident in terms of the trajectory of the body after it smashed his windshield, but he couldn't begin to talk about how he felt. He had a macho facade that kept him visibly rigid, and he was obviously uncomfortable with himself. He wore heavy personal armor at all times. He may have been stiff before the accident, but he must have intensified the guard he placed around his protective zones.

Accidental killers may experience a range of emotions that arise unpredictably. One reports:

> I don't know that all of this is related to my son's death, but crying happens to me at inconvenient times. It's been the case for a long time now. It's an area of my functioning that I have to look into. I know that my son triggers it now, memories of him and that kind of thing. But I just wish I could control the timing of it so that I could enjoy it. I'll be sitting at the dinner table and hear some song on the radio and burst into tears.

Dr. Stanley Rustin explains the unpredictability of emotions this way: "I think there are some losses that we will never get over. We can forget. We can push aside. We go on with our lives. But deep down somewhere in us if somebody presses the right button, we end up crying. Even understanding it doesn't make it go away."[14]

One accidental killer found himself curiously detached from the problems of others after his girlfriend was killed in an accident in which he fell asleep at the wheel. He says, "I have noticed that I am highly unaffected by another person's ill-fated occurrences. I can understand the feelings the person must be suffering, but I have an attitude that the person will endure and life will go on."

Another notices a bizarre tendency revolving around her accident:

> When people are crossing the road, I play a game where I say, "Get out of the road. I've done it before, I can do it again." I don't think it's weird, but my friend cringes. It's a way of releasing anger.

Repercussions of a fatal accident also can affect others present at the scene. One accidental killer says:

> My daughter to this day says she can't remember any of it, though she was with me and she was old enough—four or five, that age where she was learning how to ride a bike. She refused for two years to even get on a bike. She was old enough to know something pretty bad had happened. But to this day when we talk about it, she remembers nothing. My son asks a lot of questions about it; he knows he was in the car when it happened. But my daughter won't even discuss it.

A mother who was at the wheel when she was broadsided reports, "I think it scared my children—one in particular, a son who was five when he saw the baby vomit as his last reflex. Even though he is seventeen now, he has a terrible fear of vomiting if he should get sick. He is a poor student, has nightmares, and sucks his thumb at night."

Overachievement and Personal Motivation

Often accidental killers raise their personal expectations after the accident. One says, "I am living for two people. You have to prove that you are worthy of life, especially to yourself." He describes the accident's contradictory effects, at once spurring him toward greater achievements and making him feel bad about himself:

> It was Christmas vacation of 1952, my sophomore year at college, a car wreck. I was driving my mother's car along an abandoned highway, following another car, speeding slightly, had a

couple of drinks before, two couples in my car. I looked down to change the radio and then looked up and saw a sharp left curve. I was not able to make it. I remember tumbling over and over down a hill into a pond . . . coming to, upside down in water . . . comforting my date, flashing the lights on and off to attract attention.

I remember being told by the guy in the backseat that Sonia was unconscious and moaning . . . finally being rescued, doors pried open, people helping us up the hill . . . bitter cold, ambulance to the hospital, lying tucked under a sheet on a gurney in the emergency room . . . hearing Sonia screaming in the operating room . . . waking up the next morning in a hospital room . . . being told Sonia was dead. The other three of us were released that day.

I had guilt, self-blame, repressed feelings of pain, anger, and hurt. I went over and over in my mind the circumstances of the accident: hearing her scream on the operating table; the aftermath of numbness and confusion; being afraid to say her name or hear it; feeling bad and worthless, careless and hurtful, mostly careless; feeling stared at, pitied, different; being scared to drive sometimes; feeling all the old stuff come up again when I've been inattentive, had a near-accident, got caught speeding, actually had an accident (a minor one twenty-five years ago).

I also think I overcompensated (beneficially) by trying to prove that I wasn't worthless. I have had many achievements— not terribly satisfying then, but now, as I look back on life, the bad and the good, I have done a tremendous number of things of which I am proud. . . .

If I had been more careful, Sonia wouldn't have been killed. I've had to accept the fact that it's so, that I feel guilt for the reason given, and that the reason is true—but also that it's done and nothing can change it.

A woman tells how her accident pushed her to try bigger things:

I got depressed after the accident. Then I got out of it and started taking chances, not being afraid of doing things. I made it a point in my life to try to be more involved, to take advantage of all these opportunities, because I am probably more of a loner naturally. I look at everything as a learning experience.

The accident became a potential liability when the accidental killer entered public life, especially when she gave up her school board seat to run for county commissioner:

> I found it really difficult during the campaign to be in the fish bowl position you're in when you seek higher office. I was really worried that something would be brought up about that accident, even though I wasn't ticketed. I hadn't done anything wrong, but I was so afraid. Children are so helpless. I mean, accidents do happen all the time, but there is a certain element of people who could just never understand how you could be driving down a street and hit a child. You've got to be more alert, more careful. You know, it just shouldn't happen.
>
> I was nervous simply because I didn't want to have to go through it again. One of my opponents got into dirty politics trying to drag up everything, but luckily the accident didn't come up. It's a small community, and a lot of people knew about it. If they had wanted to pass that on and try to hurt me, they could have. I was just very thankful. You can always say that it happened years ago, it was a tragic accident, or I was never found liable, but that still doesn't erase it. A certain part of society thinks somehow you had to be at fault.

Changes in Religious Belief or Philosophy

Involvement in a fatal accident often intensifies whatever religious beliefs the accidental killer held before the accident. Those who believed in God find their faiths validated, while those who did not feel more certain than ever that there is no God. One accidental killer notes, "I had been taught that God would be with me no matter how deep the trouble. I believed this because my Bible and my parents told me. But I now know what it truly means. Had God not been with me every minute, I would have lost my mind." Another reports, "I wasn't much of a believer to begin with, and this just weakened my belief."

In other cases, religious beliefs seem to be quite malleable under the accident's force. One accidental killer says:

My religious faith was temporarily strengthened. Beginning a week or so after the accident, I became born again and then active in the Campus Crusade for Christ [CCC]. That lasted about six months. Since then I have quit CCC, and my religious faith has become more generalized to accept all religions. At the time of the accident, I expected God to save my friend. For a week, I was an atheist—how could he have ignored my prayers? Then I decided the fault was mine, and I resolved to be a better Christian.

A woman whose father died in her accident changed her view of God. She says:

I no longer believe in the providence of God. How could one be so selfish as to believe that any good could come to himself from a situation that has robbed another of the precious gift of life? This realization has caused me to look again and examine my religious beliefs. I can no longer apply "In all things giving thanks" or "All things work for good to those that love the Lord." God must not be responsible if He indeed is love.

Another accidental killer offers this explanation of her religious views:

I don't blame God. The most concrete feeling about God that I've had is that I'm not in charge of my life, that God must be, that there is a higher power, and I'm going to choose to follow God. He intercedes in my life in ways that I can't predict or control, and my son's death is one of those intercessions. I respect that power in ways that I never did respect it before. And not just negative ways. I believe that God intercedes in positive ways, too, and has in my life. And they're easier for me to recognize and acknowledge and appreciate since my son died.

I'm still not real keen on organized religion and still not a regular churchgoer. But I have a real healthy respect for God and what He can do in my life, positively and negatively, and that is directly traceable back to my son's death.

Before that, I felt it was my ballgame entirely. And I don't know anymore. I feel like I could be gone tomorrow and there's not a lot I could do about it, . . . so I'd better make the most of now.

Many accidental killers think in philosophical terms about the meaning of their experience. One says, "I feel that I have learned very much about myself and how my life affects and does not affect the lives of people around me. I am constantly reminded of the temporary nature of most things in life, and I can only guess about the nature of things, if there are any things, in death."

Another reflects, "My feelings about the accident and life in general have changed a great deal. While I still think about it from time to time, I am now able to accept what happened for what it was—a tragedy." Says another, "The universe is perfect in its imperfection. Birth is not a beginning and death is not an end."

A fourth accidental killer reports:

My recovery from the accident and major hurdles since have been one day at a time. There are days I fall back two steps, some many more, but others I run ahead. Blowing my head off or choosing to hide for the rest of my life would not have given me the opportunity to fly and soar, to see just how far I can go. The most important thing I have learned since the accident is to cherish life itself. It is God's greatest gift to us. He promises He will be there not to protect us from life, but to give us the opportunity to live it.

I do not know what lies around the corner for me—maybe another disaster but maybe, just maybe, the greatest, most wonderful experience I have ever known. More important, I want—I deserve the right—to look, to run around the corner and take, with gusto, whatever I find.

Relationship and Family Changes

A fatal accident is sure to have an effect—positive or negative—on the accidental killer's relationships. A father reports, "I have become a more caring parent and more serious about my marriage. It's a miracle we are still together, and we are pretty solid. I appreciate that." Time and again, accidental killers say that this experience showed them who their real friends were.

At the outset, interpersonal readjustments are not always peaceful. As an outgrowth of her accident, a woman became angry for the first time in her life at her mother, whom she idolized. The change came about when the knee she had injured in the accident had to be rebroken because doctors had neglected to remove a pin. For a year before the pin was discovered, she was given psychotherapy for what was diagnosed as hysterical pain. The counseling enabled her to confront her mother with her anger over not being protected as a child from her stepfather's sexual abuse:

> The problem with my stepfather had colored everything in my life. When the accident happened, I never thought "Why me?" I just thought I had it coming. I always thought everyone else's job, their cars, their art projects, were better than mine. These were the main things I was dealing with in my life at the time of the accident. It fundamentally changed me.

An accident encourages some accidental killers to wed:

> Six months after the accident, I moved to California to complete college. This had been in the works prior to the accident. I met my present wife within one month after moving to California and never really dated anyone else. We were married two years after the accident. I am convinced that I became involved with her largely due to the rebound from my tragedy. She also thinks that I carry around my emotional scars. The last time she mentioned it was two weeks ago.

Some accidental killers immerse themselves in new relationships. A man who accidentally killed his girlfriend in a car wreck says:

> Two years following the accident, I was despondent and apathetic and had a deep sense of guilt. Since that time, I have met another person and have none of the above feelings. Time does cure wounds, both physical and emotional ones. The relation-

ship I am in at present is more developed and active than the one I had with the person who was killed in the accident. I am engrossed in this relationship with a person who needs my personality and level head to cope with daily situations in life. Also, she has a daughter from a previous marriage. We both care very deeply for her. This might be a reason why I don't consciously relive the accident or our past together—well, at least not very frequently.

Sometimes life brings surprises. A mother who accidentally killed her only child recalls:

It was crazy. I was on the pill, and I was regular with it—but I got pregnant. Then we found out I was having twins. I even considered terminating the pregnancy because I didn't know if our marriage would last or not. We really never came to a decision to keep the pregnancy; we just sort of ignored it, and it followed its course. The people in town believe it was their own private miracle, that I would get pregnant almost immediately while on the pill and then have twins. They think I was given a blessing back.

But even blessings can have their bittersweetness:

While I was pregnant, I had a recurring dream that I was talking with my children and they would ask me if they would have to die. I'd tell them, "No," and then the dream would fast forward and I was angry at them for some reason. They would say, "Are you going to kill us, too?" The dream was real hard to deal with. In the beginning it was almost every night. And I wasn't so sure I could go through with this because I would think, "What am I going to do when it comes up?" What was I going to tell the girls when they asked what happened to their sister, and what is going to happen to them at school? Kids can be downright mean.

When I went to the doctor, I told him that I had a severe emotional problem. So I had more prenatal visits than normal. They kept a real close watch on my emotional state. We would talk sometimes for an hour or so, and they would just take the time and talk to me about it. The dream went away eventually. But the same question always came at the end of the dream. I'd wake up crying, and I'd talk to Harry about what I was going to tell the babies about their sister. He'd say, "We'll have to deal with it when we get to it. There's no point worrying about it now."

Flashbacks, Flare-ups, and Anniversaries

Many accidental killers find that the accident has made them sensitive to bits of information that can trigger memories or vivid flashbacks. A woman whose two sons were killed in her accident says forty years later:

> I must admit that even now as I answer you, I am shedding tears. The loss of little children never leaves. Sometimes I just could not go to church because the music was hard to listen to. I am always touched by some music and still find that some Christmas music makes me emotional, especially "Away in a Manger," for it was sung at the funeral. So I identify with that kind of music. But I still like it. You wouldn't want not to have memories. Just don't dwell on them till you make yourself and others miserable.

A boy describes a recurring dream in which the friend who died in his car crash is still alive. "I always hope it is not a dream, so as to convince myself that he is really not gone," he says.

Some people experience vivid flashbacks long after the event:

> I have not forgotten the day the accident happened. I can still see the look on the face of one of the bystanders. I can, in a flash, recall the scene of the accident. If I could erase anything, it would be the darn flashbacks. For no apparent reason, I envision the whole ordeal as though it is a photograph. Less frequently, when I pass the location of the accident, I remember the day. But I cannot get over the flashbacks.

Another accidental killer says, "Having to live with memories of faces and bodies is most difficult at times. But I do realize it is something that will be with me forever and I must learn to ride the rough times out, so to speak. The accident doesn't flash into my mind a lot, but when it does, it is as clear as if it had just happened."

Sometimes details of the accident trigger emotional responses. A man whose car hit a mother on Mother's Day says, "Mother's Day—sounds of sirens—the song that was playing on the radio when it happened. Especially when a person runs across the street in front of a car, it brings it back." Another notes, "Whenever I see the deceased's surname, I wonder if that person is part of the dead person's family."

Sometimes the accident experience heightens the drama of a later situation:

> During the last eighteen months, another tragedy took place that had an effect on me indirectly—yet very profoundly. Two sons of very good friends of mine were involved in a car–train accident. Also, two young girlfriends were with them. Their sixteen-year-old son was killed instantly, as was one of the girls. Their nineteen-year-old son is still alive but was left brain damaged with virtually no hope of recovery. The other girl did survive after suffering physical injury, but apparently will totally recover.
>
> A trial took place during April of this year. I attended one day of the trial. I was in the audience the day the brakeman for the railroad testified. . . . I had an actual chill as he spoke of the frantic last seconds of being a part of a person's death. It left me very upset and feeling so very, very sorry, not only for my dear friends but also I felt such a sad and intense kinship with the brakeman. I have thought about him since that day and sometimes wish I could talk with him.
>
> I also had the uncanny feeling that during his testimony, he was looking directly at me. It was strange. One thing he remarked on was the look on the boy's face as their eyes met. I could identify with that horror, as the little girl I had hit with my car looked at me. And of course, to this day I see her face . . . her eyes.

Holiday celebrations can be particularly difficult for some accidental killers. A man who accidentally smashed his girlfriend's side of the car into a tree says:

Although Christmas is not normally an exceptionally emotional time for me, this year the death of my girlfriend hit me extremely hard. I vividly remember attending a New Year's Eve party, quite a ways down the coast, alone, crying most of the evening. I left suddenly, driving very fast up the freeway in an extremely dense fog, not really giving a damn if I made it or not.

Stress often activates feelings about a fatal accident. A man who had shown his friend an underwater trick that may have led to the friend's drowning says, "The accident happened when I was twelve. I am now forty-three. I did not think about it much until about ten years ago. Since that time, I have thought about it many times. But I do not dwell on it too much except during times of emotional stress caused by other circumstances."

Anniversaries of the death also are especially painful, particularly the first anniversary. A man whose wife accidentally killed their child reports:

The child's birthday was December 4, and the accident happened in November. Even now, five years later, my wife is just now getting over it in January. Every year this happens. Last year on the day of the death, I took my wife to the grave. She tried to put flowers on it, but she couldn't. She was crying too much, and she asked me to do it.

The Opportunity for Growth

One woman expresses an opinion held by many accidental killers: "Certainly how you handle yourself after such a tragedy has so much to do with your life later. I can't recommend that anyone go through such an ordeal, and yet it can be used as a stepping-stone, and you can benefit from it. You grow inside a great deal."

Saul Bellow writes, "Trouble, like physical pain, makes us actively aware that we are living." [15] Some accidental killers feel that the accident brought them a deeper meaning in life:

One thing I learned that day by the haystack holding my brother in my arms was never to put off saying how I felt about a person until later. Holding him in my arms there, I was able to tell him that I loved him and that I was sorry, and I'm glad he got to hear that before he died. Now I never wait for better opportunities to tell someone I love them. I make sure I do it right then before we say good-bye. I guess you could say that it resulted in a need to love people deeply while we are around each other. But I am also learning to extricate myself from assisting people when I realize that I personally cannot give any more energy. . . .

I still can't believe that someone could like me, even though I know I'm likable. I'll never forget what it was like to feel totally reprehensible. In a way, that's amazing, and in another way, it adds a spice to my life because it makes me appreciate trust in a profound way.

It's strange. I don't feel pain anymore when I talk about the accident except when I'm with one of my clients who's gone through a death very recently and they say, "Do you understand how I feel?" Then I go through my story. . . . But it has to be a special occasion, and they have to be in a lot of pain before I'll open up. It's still sensitive, and when I'm around someone who is feeling pain, it connects us. These people feel my sensitivity and open up, and the therapeutic process really speeds up.

One of the ways I dealt with my inability to laugh was to make sure I remembered jokes and to tell them and watch other people laugh. I think that was because I had a fascination with the release through laughter. I couldn't quite get that release myself, but I would do it vicariously by getting someone else to laugh and enjoy their laughter.

A father feels that his son's death taught him many things about himself:

When he died, I came up short. I lost it. I mean, that was a hell of an adventure if you look at your life in terms of adventure, which I do. That was one of the weird ones. I learned what I'm capable of doing and what I'm capable of enduring emotionally and psychologically—and that's a very real part of my definition of myself, something I wasn't aware of previously.

There's not much now that can shake me. I can feel bad, and

I can be shaken, but I'm not going to feel personally threatened by very much anymore. Prior to the accident, I led a charmed life. Things would always go well, I thought. That notion was blown apart. I emerged knowing that I was a powerful person—powerful enough to kill someone and powerful enough to get life together again. I feel a sense of power around others. I'm not threatened. There's no one who can intimidate me. Before I wondered how I would handle death. Now I know I can handle it. The fact that my son died, that I'm living with the fact and living quite successfully with it, makes me feel like I'm going to make it—not because I'm lucky but because I'm a strong person.

Increased Tolerance and Empathy

It is said that the amount of error people tolerate in others is proportional to that which they will allow themselves. Realizing that they are capable of killing by mistake, many accidental killers take on a less judgmental attitude and become more patient. One person says, "I know I've become more tolerant since the accident. I know that people react differently under different circumstances. I am quicker to give them the benefit of the doubt."

Another describes the empathy she feels with children she sees suffering: "One of the little boys I work with lost his father when he was very young. He is always talking about death and injury. I feel a lot of pain for him."

A third says, "While I am able to forgive my boyfriend for his actions the evening of the accident, it is hard for me to forget that I felt like he let me down when I needed his strength. Probably as a result of that disappointment, I feel like I'm more tuned in to people. I'm not uncomfortable being the shoulder someone needs."

Remembering their appreciation when another accidental killer talked with them, some make a point of contacting others as soon as they hear of a fatal accident. One woman says:

If I see a name in the paper, I write to the people—something brief. You don't know how they are reacting. So I just write that I've been there and back, I'm very sorry, and if they want to contact me, here's my number. It happened to a friend of mine. It was rough for me to get there as soon as I could. His wife said she knew I would come and that he couldn't wait for me to get there.

A Different View

The readjustment to life as a person who has taken a life means relating the accident to something meaningful and beneficial to the world, a redemption in bits and pieces. An accidental killer explains:

> I think I appreciate my friends more because of what I've been through. A girlfriend even told me she envied me and that she wished something awful would happen to her because she could see that I was so changed. At the time I was horrified, but now I understand what she meant. I know that death can come soon and it can come without warning. Everything I do has a purpose. I don't watch daytime television. I don't fiddle away my time.

Sometimes the accident can change the way life looks to a person, as if the illumination has shifted angles. One man recalls, "The accident just sort of brought everything to the surface. When I look back, I'm really grateful for having gone through that experience because there's hardly anything that scares me. I know that things will work out; even though they may seem to be bad for a while, they will improve vastly."

Some changes are unconventional. An accidental killer notes a desire to conserve that is reflected in his buying habits:

> I have to be economical. I have to conserve. I guess my mind is softening—the part that deals with the accident. I had wasted a life accidentally, and you should never waste anything. I have made arrangements with several grocery stores to go and get the vegetables that they're about to throw out; I use the parts that can be used. And I think it ties back to the death, one of those little neurotic behaviors that I have to conserve whatever is out there that I can conserve. I salvage wood for the fire

because it's cheap, close, and available. We shop at the Salvation Army or the Goodwill store. If we can't find it there, we'll go over to the other stores and get it. Once I found out about avoiding retail stores, it was like an addiction. I can't stop doing it.

Some accidental killers believe that the accident has allowed them to handle difficult situations better. One recounts how her accident experience helped her cope with the sudden death of her daughter:

Five years after the accident, my oldest daughter, then twenty-five, was killed in an accident. . . . The loss of my daughter was a far more painful and distressing crisis, although . . . there was none of the guilt that so incapacitated me with my accident. . . . Whoever coined the word *heartache* knew of what he spoke. The fact that I had undergone trauma before was an aid; I understood what to expect at various times through the healing process.

It has been fourteen years [since my accident], and I no longer think about it very often. The accident was simply something horrible that happened in another lifetime. I am a much tougher person now. I tend to think that I have been through just about as difficult a time as you can go through, and I have survived. At least I don't know anyone else who has accidentally killed a child and then lost one of their own. . . .

There is one lasting effect. God, how I hate the word *suffering,* but that is exactly what I did a lot of, and it has made me very finely attuned to the suffering of others—not the whining of the individual who thinks that a very small obstacle is a mountain, but to the real suffering people. And animals—I couldn't begin to count the number of times that either my daughter or I have taken stray animals home and taken care of their medical needs at our own expense. I can't bear to see them suffer.

I try to help when I can. Sometimes it helps just to let a person know the time will come when they will be happy to see the dawn, when what has happened becomes a part of their life but not the focal point of it. Anyway, I am much tougher now, but not to those with broken hearts.

Eastern philosophers write of grief as creating an immobilizing moment when the future is able to enter a person. When the accidental killer becomes aware of life's recently demonstrated fragility, life becomes a more precious thing. Grief passes, and the new insight has entered the person's innermost being. One accidental killer says:

> I feel that I have faced death early and have come away with a knowledge and awareness that many people don't acquire until later in their lives—that this existence is temporary, that we are not in complete control of our lives, that what is important is what is happening now and how we handle the present.

Many accidental killers begin to appreciate their lives more, or at least in a different way. They sense that they have a mission to fulfill on Earth. The past and the future seem to become less important. Forced to mature a great deal at an early age, a woman whose accident claimed her mother's life lives today in a spirit of profound contemplation:

> It has been nineteen years since my mother's death. I am thirty-four, and I have lived longer without her than I knew her. Now I am almost as old as she was when she died.
>
> Because I live in the same area and the car wreck was on a major highway, I often drive by the site of the accident. Many things are different there—new stores, a wider road. But a fire hydrant remains just feet from the point of impact, and it has become my own private memorial, which I silently acknowledge when I drive by. I am not morbid about this; I just salute the memory of my mother.
>
> This is basically a compelling theme in my life—that my actions and accomplishments are dedicated to her, that my successes become her successes, that my growth becomes a tribute to her influence on me. In this way, I have transformed the adversity of her death into a motivating factor.
>
> I never forget her. I never try. In little ways, she is still with me—the curve of my palm, the color of my cheeks. But, of course, the person I knew, the one who I could talk to, is gone.
>
> Sometimes I miss her badly, and I am overwhelmed. I wonder if she could, would she tell me she is angry with me? But

finally, after all these years, I have done what my mother is unable to do, I have forgiven myself.

In Eastern philosophy, there is a concept called *tapasya,* straightening by fire. That is what living through a tragedy feels like. I think that it has given me an edge in coping with periods of discouragement because no matter what happens, I have learned the tools with which to deal with grief.

This doesn't mean that I don't expect to be sad. This doesn't mean that I don't expect to grieve. Perhaps that is the whole point—I do expect it. I know it will come, and I know I will live through it. But when I am with the people I love, I do not ignore their presence. I show them that I love them, and I do it often.

The sharpened self-awareness and the willingness to look within that so many accidental killers experience are built into them gradually. The words of one accidental killer echo the feelings of many others: "What a shame it would be if these things did not change our lives to some degree."

How to Help an Accidental Killer

Phil and I had been friends since high school. . . . We shared each other's views and ideas. In all the time we knew each other, I can't remember arguing about *anything*. We also shared the same goal—it was our hope that we could buy a piece of land in northern New England and start a self-sufficient farm where someday our children could grow up together and enjoy the same friendship and experiences we did.

In the last three years we were closer than ever. We had been working at a resort in a very well-to-do restaurant. It really seemed like things had started to fit together for us. We both had become independent of our parents in the last few years and begun to build a respectable reputation of our own.

I had a feeling all summer before the accident that by the end of the summer Phil and I wouldn't be friends. I thought it was my relationship with my girlfriend that was interfering with my friendship with Phil. So I broke up with her.

Phil died in my hands after an accident where I was driving. I say "in my hands" because that's literally what happened. Before the police arrived on the scene, I was holding his hands, crying for help, when he took his last breath.

At 7:00 A.M. on August 24, Phil, Ken, Paul and I were on our way to the beach after breakfast in town. I was driving the car with Phil in the front and Ken and Paul in the back. I passed a policeman in a parked car faster than I should have and looked in the rear view mirror to see if he was coming. When I looked back at the road, we were in the wrong lane. As I turned back to the right lane the front wheels went off the road into the sand causing the car to roll over. While the car was rolling, it took down a telephone pole.

I was hardly injured. Ken and Paul had major broken bones. The police came and had to cut the car open to get them out. The police were frantic because power lines were down, and the car was leaking gas. Phil's chest was crushed, but there was no blood. He'd been thrown from the car. Before the police got there, blood trickled out of the corner of his mouth and his hands went limp.

About four hours after the accident, my parents were there. They caught the first plane out. Phil's brother gave me a hug, and he wrote a letter to the court saying I would never have done anything to hurt Phil. His dad said that if anyone should have been there when Phil died, it was me. Phil's fiancé quit her job to come and be with me for three months.

I was charged with a number of motor vehicle violations and motor vehicle homicide. The staff where Phil and I worked closed down the restaurant to come and testify in court. All the charges except homicide were dropped. I was found guilty and put on probation for two years.

For a long while I felt very depressed. I couldn't get myself together to find work. I guess I could describe it as an aimless feeling. Often I would just begin to cry wherever I was.

Nobody ever accused me of killing Phil. Nobody treated me like it was my fault. My folks let me stay at home and not work or go to school for about a year. I spent a lot of time crying at Phil's grave. My father was concerned that I might become an alcoholic, but he never lectured me about it. I tried to be my own best friend instead of worst enemy. I got together with people as much as possible and tried to discuss the accident if they wanted to. I took a trip across the country.

As a result of the love of my family and friends, I managed to come through with a smile—not as bright as it once was, but it's still there.

After a crisis, an accidental killer grasping for help is particularly susceptible to outside forces. Support from those nearby can act as a vital buffer against stress and free the accidental killer to go about resolving his guilt. One study of drivers in fatal accidents concludes that "the support of family, friends, and significant others was by far the most important help reported by the drivers."[1]

This chapter is addressed to relatives, friends, coworkers, and partners of accidental killers; professional care givers; members of the victim's family; and especially accidental killers themselves. These guidelines are meant to help during the delicate time of recovery. Some of what is said here (especially in regard to reinterpreting death) is controversial, and we do not expect everything to apply or appeal to everyone.

If someone you care about kills a person accidentally, your responsibility is clear. The basis for all effective helping, no matter what the situation, is love and acceptance. This acceptance is not blind. Loving a person unconditionally does not mean approving of everything she does. Your responsibility is to seek your own truth and to express it if you are asked.

Practice good communication skills, especially active listening, which will ensure that you understand better what the accidental killer is trying to say. Unfortunately, accidental killing leaves a person so sensitive that many would-be aides end up hurting the accidental killer in spite of their goodwill. Remember that you are of much more use as a listener than as an adviser. What often separates the harmful imposition of your own judgment from a sensitive response is an invitation from the accidental killer for you to speak.

It is important to understand the needs of those who have taken a life unintentionally, including how to help the person rebuild self-esteem, how and how not to show concern, why listening to the story is so important, and how to encourage the person to break out of a depressive cycle. Encouraging a new concept of life and death also may be necessary. Friends must be sensitive to the hard truths of the situation, and family members must be open to the person's need to break old patterns. Accidental killers need to learn how to be gentle with themselves, as well as what to look for in professional and nonprofessional help.

Be Prepared to Listen Again and Again

Access to a sympathetic ear is extremely important to the accidental killer. One notes:

I want everyone to know that talking about the feelings with someone who was empathic and supportive, especially after some of the initial shock wore off, would have been wonderful. I want them to know that talking to someone about the gory details and the person's own feeling is very painful but brings an incredible and much-needed feeling of relief. I feel that having someone other than those involved with the accident helps you get a grip on the guilt and fear. One of the things which I only recently thought of, and which helps a great deal, is that my role in the accident doesn't mean I am a terrible person, and I realize I don't deserve punishment for it. I feel that having a supportive, objective person to talk to strengthens this idea. It did for me.

Rabbi Earl Grollman cautions, "Grief work comes back again and again. You don't just say it once and it's over. There's no magical incantation. It takes a long time."[2] An accidental killer echoes this thought: "I think that other people should know that there are times a person has to talk about the accident, even though it may become boring. The anxiety of keeping it to yourself can drive you crazy. Talking about it relieves tension."

A woman stresses the importance of checking in on the accidental killer periodically to give her a chance to talk about what has happened: "For God's sake, don't avoid them and don't tell them not to talk about it. Don't tell them not to think about it. The talking is necessary; the thinking is unavoidable. And don't stay away. Don't try to make us feel better. Accept our grief—allow us that grief—and stick around."

Failure to listen to an accidental killer may reflect one's own inability or unwillingness to deal with grief that continues for some time. It is important not to rush the process or to try to make the person see things in a different way right away.

Most people who have not had an experience similar to that of the accidental killer's have as a main issue trying to get the person to be who she used to be. They want the accidental killer to stop grieving because the helper cannot deal with this new person. Seeing someone go through so much pain can make one very aware of one's own vulnerability, which can be uncomfortable.

Let the Accidental Killer Determine When to Talk

"People should be sensitive to the person's feelings and grant them the privilege of talking about the incident or not," emphasizes one accidental killer. "It is a mistake to try to force a person to talk about it until some mental adjustments have been made. Some people do not understand that when the person they are with is silent, it is not necessarily unfriendly."

Another accidental killer warns against trying to set an agenda:

> Let the person talk about the accident when he wants to. Don't force a conversation about it. Don't bring up the subject. If the person wants to talk about it, other people should try to listen. After my accident, there were times when I wanted to talk about it; then there were times I wanted to forget, and I didn't want to discuss it. People assume you're okay in a fairly short period of time. They talk of the accident in my company, but I'm not over this yet. I am not prepared for conflict, even routine. People wonder if I'm using self-pity, and sometimes I wonder the same. People bring [the accident] up when I'm unprepared, yet it's not convenient when I wish to discuss it.

A third accidental killer expresses appreciation for his family's attitude toward his accident: "My wife and children have been wonderful. They have never initiated a conversation regarding this accident. Yet they give me the feeling that they are always ready to listen or discuss the subject should I want to."

Psychologist Ann Kaiser Stearns points out the need for sensitivity to the accidental killer's style of response.[3] Be aware of the accidental killer's voice. Is he abrupt? He probably doesn't want to talk. Slow and soft? He probably wants to. Also, be careful not to ask questions in public where you could cause embarrassment. Don't say I'm sorry because that focuses on your feelings rather than on the accidental killer's. To respond empathically, you have to know the situation and the accidental killer's feelings about it. You may need to gather that information by giving the person an open invitation to talk about the accident.

Do Not Feel Compelled to Say Anything

Speaking at length about the accident to an accidental killer can create awkwardness. One person notes, "They wanted to make me feel not so bad, but they weren't using the right words." Others stress that words are not always needed. Creating a climate in which the accidental killer can share her feelings is much more effective. You might say something like "It must really hurt." This may open the person up and allow her to speak if she feels like it.

It is important to let the person know that you still love him even though he may feel unlovable. Encourage him to talk about his anger and to record his feelings in a diary. The person may even wish to draw pictures or act out his feelings in a role play, as if he were talking to the deceased.

One accidental killer describes the importance of her husband's effort to be close by when she needed him: "My husband rushed hundreds of miles to be by my side. No need for words—just love."

Another advises, "Let the person involved talk about it without giving advice or making soothing little noises. My main observation is that people generally do not know how to listen and are usually eager to assert themselves."

Words are noticeably lacking from the "medicine kit" that an accidental killer devised for those who wished to help: "a warm smile, a box of Kleenex, a cup of coffee, and a listening ear." Another gives this advice: "There isn't anything that can be said that will help, so don't worry about that. Just be there. The very presence of a friend or relative is what matters. Words are meaningless."

Learn to Listen Actively

Summarize and restate the accidental killer's narrative every few sentences so that the person knows you understand. Ask if your summary is correct. If the accidental killer looks confused, ask where you went wrong in your understanding. Keep in contact with your own feelings. Do not fear silence.

Accept the Accidental Killer's Tears

One man says that he appreciated the fact that his friends prayed and cried with him when the accident happened. He notes, "Tears are the best way of letting the pain go." Indeed, crying provides an emotional cleansing that allows accidental killers to withdraw their emotional investment in the victim, the accident, or both with as little self-injury as possible.

Sometimes accidental killers or those around them are tempted to circumvent the grieving process by using drugs. It is important to remember that stress is a natural by-product of confronting an imperfect world. The person needs to work through that reality, not bypass it. Emotional strain requires emotional therapy, not medication. One accidental killer says:

> Above all, I think it is wrong to give a sedative unless there is a real danger of [the accidental killer] doing some harm. How dare anyone deprive them of their grief while it is fresh in their minds. How like our society to take the easy way out and give a pill so it will go away. The pill or shot does more for those giving it than the one receiving it. I believe that if I had been put to sleep for hours after the accident, I would have taken longer to get over it.

Another adds, "People kept trying to pressure me to take a sedative. I would have felt more guilty if I had gone to sleep. I did not want to be robbed of my tears at that time. I needed them much more than a sedative."

Another way of artificially smoothing things over is to come up with a quick answer. This can make it much harder for the accidental killers to deal with their grief. One person recalls:

> My parents made an arrangement for me to talk to our rabbi. I think I should have gone directly into psychotherapy. My parents seemed afraid to talk about their feelings and mine, and so they didn't. Whenever I brought up the confusion I felt about the accident, they would echo the rabbi's theme back to me: "Everything happens for the best." This occurred after I spoke to the rabbi. What he said confused and upset me, and I wanted them to negate or change what he said. I feel that the rabbi's talk with me aggravated my feelings. The gist of what he said was that everything happens for the best because it is God's will and that we couldn't question His actions because

it was beyond our understanding to comprehend His reasoning. I feel very strongly that this was one of the most frightening things to come out of the accident.

Do not provide the accidental killer with easy answers or trite clichés. Author Robert Kavanaugh describes the importance of rugged honesty:

> Easy answers only decorate the lips, cherishing the falsity in my own cheerfulness more than the truth and the profound sadness I wish to bury. I could no longer imagine a greater insult to a stricken friend than to send a phony letter to soften the heart. There is no shame in sharing my humanity. I can share my queasiness and reluctance, even consciously leaving out those usual bits of wisdom society seems to expect. Now it is only important to send the letter before I fashion it into another means of stepping back from the clumsiness and human warmth and mutual love all friends appreciate in tragedy. The eloquence in self means far more than the eloquence of fine writing.
>
> In retrospect, the only letter I still recall from memory after my own days in tragedy simply said, "I am your friend for good!" And it was signed with "love" I still feel.[4]

Make a Gesture to Show You Care

Many accidental killers remember small gestures that people made after the accident. Donating food is a common act of tangible kindness. One says, "I was really babied for about three weeks after the accident. I had a room full of pies, cakes, and all sorts of food." Another notes:

> To my surprise, neighbors were so kind and considerate. I thought they would blame and hate me. But so many people I had never met were bringing all kinds of food to my house for my family when I was trying to muster strength to take something down to the neighbor's house whose child had been killed. All this attention surprised me because I felt I was the guilty party and deserved nothing.

One accidental killer recalls a simple deed by a friend who "came to see me and brought me three or four bananas. This was during

World War II, and bananas were very scarce. I have never forgotten the bananas."

Friends do many other favors for accidental killers—helping with housework, baby-sitting, providing concert tickets, taking them out to eat, arranging the funeral, helping handle insurance processing, and answering the telephone. Many other gestures also are remembered fondly. One accidental killer recalls, "A farmer took me on a long walk in the woods. Then we went to his house, and his wife cooked a meal from organically grown vegetables. It was great. I fixed their record player while I was there."

Another reports:

> There was a friend of mine who would come and play music with me—guitar and piano. We would just get down and be sad and sing together. He shared with me that what had happened to me was the worst thing he could imagine happening to him ever—in the sense of causing my own son's death. We just shared a lot out of this recognition. I felt a lot of empathy from him.

Give a Hug

According to one accidental killer, "There is healing in touching and holding another person who has known grief." The benefit of hugging is well established scientifically. Hugging can help people who are depressed and tune up the body's immune system, breathing life into a tired body and making one feel younger and more vibrant. It can reduce tension. In *The Gift of Touch,* Helen Colton states that the blood's hemoglobin level (hemoglobin is the carrier of oxygen to the cells) increases significantly when a person is touched or hugged. She asserts, "If you want to be healthy, you must touch each other."[5]

Be Honest but Compassionate

Being involved in a fatal accident is a mean blow. It is very hard to look at the situation objectively. Dr. Joseph Nicolosi warns of the precarious position of someone speaking with an accidental killer: "Friends have to be honest with themselves, but at the same time they have to be compassionate. People have to maintain integrity but do so with sensitivity. Keep it to yourself, or if you think the person is able to hear it and asks for your opinion, give it. But you have to be very delicate."[6]

One thing many accidental killers resent is when the facts of the accident are hidden from them. One advises, "Don't hide the truth because of preconceived notions about the psychological impact. The mental anguish of *not* knowing is worse."

Some people feel the need to pretend they already know the facts about the situation because they are uncomfortable asking the accidental killer or are afraid of what they may find out. One accidental killer remembers, "People who didn't know anything about the accident were saying I wasn't guilty because they thought they had to, but it didn't help." By being honest, carefully examining their own feelings, and communicating those feelings without fear, the friends of another accidental killer aided his grieving process, as well as their own. He reports:

> Our circle of friends was extremely enchanted by Jacob. He was delightful. He was the first child. When he died at my doing, a lot of their heart left with him. They told me, "You've hurt us." They were honest about the impact but supportive and caring. I didn't have to assume anything.
>
> Later they expressed anger toward me for killing Jacob: "I know it was an accident, but I'm angry at you for taking him away. I had really enjoyed Jacob and loved him." They took the event and weighed it in their minds and helped in ways that were not neurotic. They made me feel meaningful. My relationship with all those people has grown strong because they supported me. They told me I was still a good person. Their openness was a loving thing to do, although it wasn't comforting. They shared out of caring.

Help the accidental killer see the situation clearly and gently dispel harmful illusions. A common misperception of people who have been through a crisis is the illusion of centrality, believing that the destructive forces of the world have been carefully aimed at them. This distortion leads to feelings of helplessness. A man tells of his friends' common-sense approach to this belief: "They tried very hard to comfort me and make me understand that it was an accident and that it could have happened just as easily to any one of them."

Encourage Accidental Killers to Face Their Fears

The most common phobia to develop from vehicular accidental deaths is a fear of driving. Many accidental killers recall how others encouraged them to drive again and how much that helped. A woman describes her husband's help: "He never said I had to drive. He just made an excuse for me to pick up his mother so that I would have to drive."

Help Build the Accidental Killer's Self-esteem

One way to help people rebuild self-esteem is to help them measure the crisis in terms of other problems they have solved. This approach helps them see themselves as capable people who have handled other difficult situations and can develop the skills needed to continue on with their lives.

Another technique is to give them legitimate compliments. Since every person's process of self-discovery depends to a large degree on how other people feel about him or her, it is important to build the accidental killer up at this time.

One of the best ways for accidental killers to overcome self-hatred or depression is to encourage them to fulfill outside obligations and thus stop focusing on themselves. The more accidental killers are able to work on constructive efforts, the better off they seem to be. On a long-term basis, do nothing for an accidental killer that she can do for herself. This conveys the attitude that she is capable and only temporarily overwhelmed by extreme stress. It is important not to let the accidental killer's crisis become a crisis for you. Make it clear that you do not have all the answers.

A young mother says, "My mother repeatedly told me that my life must go on, my children were depending on me. She presented this to me in such a way that she left me no choice. She was not tender or overly sympathetic; she was firm and unyielding. I needed that strength from her because I had none of my own."

There is no conflict between allowing accidental killers sufficient time to grieve and expecting them to fulfill their responsibilities. It is more a matter of letting them know you are there if they need you. Here is how one accidental killer explains it:

> Some people encouraged me to go right back to my job, to get in my car and drive it again a few days after the accident, just to jump back in and do things because all this would help me forget. How dare anyone suggest that I should forget! I knew that time would heal and that I would go back and do all these things, but I think I would have regretted it all my life if I had not taken time to mourn and think about the child and the accident.

Rabbi Earl Grollman suggests the pursuit of a new endeavor as a way to rebuild confidence. He notes, "Whatever they are capable of, the risks which they are willing and capable of taking . . . it's like giving them a pair of magic glasses and letting them see what they can see . . . whatever they like doing—crafts, gardening, jogging."[7]

Seek Professional Help

Outside help may be necessary depending on the gravity of the accident's psychological impact. By killing another person, the accidental killer psychologically has killed part of himself. According to sociologist Leonard Cottrell, human beings sense on some level both sides of any interaction into which they enter:

> In analyzing or treating personalities, it becomes necessary to assume that the reactive system includes not only those response patterns the person has manifested, but also the response pattern of his life situations. Thus, from this point of view the rebellious child is also in part the authoritarian parent; the saint is part sinner; the communist is part capitalist; the southern white is part Negro psychologically.[8]

In psychological terms, then, John Donne is correct in his assertion that no one is an island, everyone is part of the main, and anyone's death diminishes all who are involved with humankind.[9] To the extent that people are aware of their essence as part of the whole, they become more human.

The accidental killer often harbors a part of the self that identifies with the victim—an enraged self that seeks revenge. How can one mobilize one's defenses against this self? This is a difficult problem that may require outside guidance. But the nature of this guidance is very important.

Find someone experienced with grief and trauma counseling. Psychotherapy may be helpful to someone who has been unable to vocalize the accident's trauma. It offers the opportunity to speak to someone about the accident at a specific time, which can be a distinct advantage given the fast pace of modern life. Also, as Dr. Stanley Rustin explains, psychotherapy gives a person the opportunity to "examine the antecedents of the event. Were there things one could have done differently? And you can break it down in a microscopic way."[10] This may be especially helpful if there is a depression that has lasted more than two years. In these cases, the whole family probably should seek treatment.

Some accidental killers may find some models of psychotherapy lacking as an aid to healing. The problem lies in what some construe to be the limits of the client-therapist relationship. Social psychologist Richard Korn explains that the therapeutic situation can exacerbate the problem:

> By means of his responses as well as his silences, the therapist continually conveys the same essential message: "Deal only with yourself and your feelings. Do not concern yourself with me or my feelings as such, except as you think they may affect you. Only your thoughts and feelings are important."
>
> In the patient's relationship outside of the sphere of therapy such an attitude would be characterized as highly narcissistic—and its manifestation would certainly be cited as a symptom of psychopathology. What is curious, in the light of this certain diagnosis, is that the same kind of total self-preoccupation is virtually insisted upon during treatment as a matter of therapeutic protocol. Very likely, one of the principal reasons the patient is in therapy is that he was so inescapably imprisoned within his own concerns that he found himself unable or unwilling to grasp or respond to the concerns of others—with the result that his relations with them deteriorated to the

point where, in the deeper sense, he *was* alone and had little but his own loneliness and unhappiness to concern him.[11]

A person can know herself only through revealing herself to another person and knowing the other in return.[12] If the patient needs to know and be known, the therapist's withholding of emotionally authentic feedback would cut off the healing process. Korn explains, "The patient accepts the fact that he is, after all, an analytic patient—and that the analyst is, after all, not a parent, not a lover, but a stranger and an analyst. What has he learned? At the risk of appearing either obtuse or banal, it seems to us that what he has learned is the folly of giving love to indifferent strangers."[13]

This is no help in learning to give love in real relationships. As Korn puts it, "Anyone can talk to a neutral observer. The problem is some of the people in your life are trying to kill you."[14]

If the accidental killer finds a therapist who sees the client-therapist relationship as an emotionally valid one, much can be accomplished. Dr. Joseph Nicolosi explains:

> The role of any therapist is to be a person in the client's life who accepts them. This acceptance is the therapist's main tool to get the person beyond guilt. Not just a blind acceptance, but, having heard the story with sensitivity, telling them they deserve to go on with life.
>
> Eventually in the relationship the client takes in that message, internalizes it, and that's how healing happens. Analysis is only secondary—the great curative process is a kind of mystical thing that happens between client and therapist. Part of the early job of the therapist is to convince the accidental killer that they are worthy of such a relationship. This is all subconscious, you don't talk about it. The important stuff that happens in psychotherapy is the stuff that never gets talked about.[15]

Korn suggests a type of therapy that reproduces the trauma so that the person can come up with a better response and thus stop feeling retraumatized whenever the accident comes to mind. Perhaps the accidental killer can imagine an avoidance maneuver that enables him to escape injuring anyone. This idea echoes the Somatic Experiencing technique, which calls to mind resources available to the patient at the time of the trauma so that he feels capable of retracing his steps, thereby rebridging the neurological gap that separates the traumatized self from the earlier self.[16] Accidental killers can do this in a limited way by simply visualizing the accident with a different ending—not confusing this vision with reality but using it to heal.

Avoid "If Onlys"

"If onlys" are not what life is about. People can get into deep trouble if they can't get beyond the "if onlys." People who get stuck in "if onlys" can never really get over the crisis. To repeat, "if only it hadn't happened" is in many ways a lack of acceptance of the situation.

People who have caused an accident tend to go through long periods of feeling bad, and they try to get through it by saying, "I'm a horrible person. And I'll always be a horrible person because of what I did." They need to know they are choosing this feeling.

Many accidental killers send themselves into great depression by saying, "If things had only been different." People need to see that they did the best they could, and maybe it wasn't enough. But that was the best they could do at the time. The ultimate conclusion to guide the accidental killer to is this: "Yes, there was a horrible accident. But you do not need to let it ruin the rest of your life. How can you turn it around to make your life better?"[17]

Do Not Be Judgmental

Probably the most difficult situation for a friend of an accidental killer is feeling that he erred in some way. To be helpful, one needs to use judgment without becoming judgmental. That is a fine line to walk. Ask for the facts gently. When the full account is finished, put yourself in the accidental killer's place and see how you feel. If she asks you whether you think she made a mistake, you need to be honest. Unconditional love does not mean unconditional acceptance. Part of loving someone is to be truthful with that person when he is wrong. The key is to be detached enough to see the facts without letting what you already know about the accidental killer color them and at the same time to avoid blame. As difficult as it may be, this approach is much more healing than surface approval.

Be Patient

Shakespeare wrote, "Everyone can master grief but he that has it."[18] Realize that people tend to stop mourning and being upset when grief has accomplished its purpose for them. Their progress may be erratic. One accidental killer explains, "People do not improve day to day. You have good weeks; you have bad weeks. Sometimes you can rationalize that it was fate, that your life is back to normal. And then the next day you feel so depressed so as not to function."

Do not expect the accidental killer ever to be the same as before the accident. She has paid a price for the knowledge she has gained.

A List of Don'ts

- Don't make jokes about the accident.
- Don't stare at the person.
- Don't press for morbid details.
- Don't encourage the accidental killer to blame others. This just leads to more guilt.
- Don't doubt the person's innocence. You may be able to help the person investigate what he sees as his responsibility, but he does not need another judge. Your condemnation increases his guilt, which hinders coping. Silent judgment is the worst.
- Don't say you feel sorry. The accidental killer needs respect, not pity.
- Don't minimize the pain by comparing it with other pain.
- Don't visit because you think it is expected. An accidental killer explains how uneasy a perfunctory visit made her feel:

My husband and I were going about a hundred miles in the middle of the afternoon, and I was driving. I ate a sandwich and an apple. About five minutes later I fell asleep, woke up immediately, and realized that I was going down the side of the road on the dirt. I tried to get myself back on the road, but when I did, I hit a car. We spun around and landed on the dividing area of the freeway, but the other car overturned and the occupants were thrown out. (I was wearing a seat belt.) The other car contained a mother and a child. They were flown to the hospital by helicopter—the child was released that night, but the mother died. Neither my husband nor I was even slightly injured.

One of the horrors to me is that I could fall asleep so easily in the middle of the afternoon after having had a good night's sleep, after just eating, and without any warning as one usually has. I was not cited by the police.

The worst thing was when two people came to visit me representing the women's group in my church. They did not come when the accident occurred. They came several days later and were sort of very official—no feeling—and made some dumb remarks about how they had almost gone to sleep when driving and had driven late at night, and so on. I had not been driving late at night. In fact, some years ago, because of other accidents that had happened to friends, I had vowed that I would never drive too late.

I think that what I learned from this is that if you really have a feeling—empathy, love, or whatever—for a person, go and help. If you are doing this out of a sense of duty, just stay away.

• Don't assume that someone peripherally involved will not feel a great deal of responsibility for an accidental death. An accidental killer explains:

I felt bad because my family and friends didn't seem to comprehend what I was thinking and feeling. For instance, a woman at the scene approached me and asked me if I knew the girl and where she lived. This woman told me to take her there to notify the girl's parents. She drove me to Mary's house and rang the bell. After Mary's mother stepped out, I nodded and said, "That's her mother." She proceeded to tell the mother the news while I stood by. This woman never said anything to me about how I felt, and she left me on the landing of the staircase while Mary's mother became hysterical.

I think the primary issue which caused a great deal of difficulty for me was that I felt—and am very aware of feeling now—extremely guilty. Because people were not aware that I might feel guilty, these feelings were often aggravated. By this I mean that several people either unintentionally or with good intentions said or did things which really did a number on my head. Also, not saying or doing certain things hurt me, like not letting me acknowledge my feelings of guilt and terror, simply perpetuated these feelings.

Helping as a Professional

Coroners, doctors, police officers, social workers, and insurance agents are involved with accidental deaths on a routine basis. Although the completion of the task at hand (filling out forms, tending wounds, or taking statements) requires their attention, the attitudes they convey can have a profound effect on how accidental killers see themselves, and how effectively they cope with the experience.

Coroners

It is the coroner's job to determine the cause, manner, and means of death in circumstances legally deemed reportable. Although an autopsy may be hard on the victim's family, it can provide valuable information to the family and to the accidental killer, such as the presence of a fatal illness or a disease that could have caused erratic behavior. As the coroner, you might organize a group of counselors to whom those in need can be referred. You must, however, make a clear distinction between your work and that of the counselors.

Doctors

A compassionate attitude can be the best medicine for an accidental killer. A woman who talked to her family doctor the night of her accident reports, "After he checked me for broken bones, he just sat quietly by my bed, held my hand, and gently asked me if I'd like to talk about the accident. I cried when I told him about it. It was the first and last time I have cried to anyone about this." It is important not to make disparaging comments about or to the accidental killer, even if he appears to have been negligent in some way.

Police Officers

Because of their official status, the opinions of police officers are important to some accidental killers for legal and emotional reasons. If you are a law officer, be sensitive to this vulnerability and give the accidental killer the benefit of the doubt. A railroad engineer voices a complaint about the insensitive behavior of police officers in his experience: "The local police treat you like criminals. My grandfather was a locomotive engineer, and they handcuffed him to his steam engine when he had killed somebody. Very often, the police treat you like you're a suspect."

An accidental killer remembers: "One of the officers was very nice to me. But the other one caught me in the hallway of the hospital. He really let me have it verbally."

Social Workers

If you are a social worker, you must be sensitive to the fragility of accidental killers. This is not the time for snap judgments. While honoring the limits of the professional relationship, you should recognize that finding support can be a matter of life or death for an accidental killer. Perhaps you can refer the person to a support group. Flexibility also is important. A playwright and producer who was twelve years old and living in a foster home when he shot his best friend in a hunting accident explains his resentment at being cut off from the only available social support:

> It was bad enough to be the poorest kid in town, but to be thought of as the village idiot and have the guilt of killing another boy put on me was almost too much. The boy's parents (he was their only child) were the only ones who showed me love and understanding during the time between the death of their son and the burial. They later expressed the desire for me to come and live with them (they were an upper-middle-class family). I wanted to live with them, in part as a replacement and to better my situation and also because they loved me. The Children's Aid Society found the idea too strange, and I was ordered never to see them.

Insurance Agents

Claims adjustors see a lot of accidental killers. The question of liability is often an issue in these interactions. Many times the financial ramifications of a fatal accident demand that accidental killers avoid expressing guilt or remorse to the grieving family. Yet they usually have a tremendous need to express their regret. One accidental killer recalls, "The insurance company said, 'Don't you dare be nice and talk to the family,' and that cut me off from the people I had hurt. It bothered me as much as anything else about the accident. I told the adjustor, 'You mean I have taken the life of their child and I can't tell them I'm sorry?'"

There is no need to prevent accidental killers from experiencing this important aspect of recovery because of a possible lawsuit. Suggest an alternative way for them to express themselves. It is possible that they could show regret without self-incrimination. If the situation is sensitive, you may want to brief them on what they should and should not say. Agree on the form of communication to be used, be it face to face, by phone, in writing, or through flowers for the funeral.

Helping as a Journalist

Facts are facts, but the interpretation and organization of facts is the job of reporting. The way the media tell a story will have a powerful effect on the accidental killer. When a teenager accidentally killed his girlfriend by going off the road on an unmarked curve, the headline in a local paper read, "Freak Accident Kills High School Junior." The term *freak accident* helped the boy to regard himself and the accident more positively. Instead of blaming himself, he took the county to court over the lack of a curve sign.

Helping as a Member of the Victim's Family

As a member of the victim's family, you and your loved ones have plenty of your own healing to do. Just accepting the reality that the victim is dead is a lot of work. Only after you do this can you define new goals. During this time, your feeling of helplessness is likely to increase your vulnerability and sensitivity both psychologically and physically. The crisis may consume all your energy for some time, and your grief may be so deep that you cannot see beyond it. But as a surviving family member, you are in a powerful position to help or to hinder the accidental killer's recovery. An accidental killer explains:

> I have always been grateful that the husband of the friend who was killed was never vindictive. The first flowers we three survivors received in the hospital were from him. We knew the friend who was killed had terminal cancer, and her husband told us that the doctor had told him three months earlier she probably had only six months to live. She died instantly in the crash, and people tried to impress on me that she was spared the last suffering from cancer. I suppose it was this fact that made the whole ordeal at all bearable.

A man who was distraught over accidentally running his car over a little boy on a bicycle remembers the family's response:

> A strange car drove up. A big husky man got out, a total stranger to me. My heart sank; hurt and guilt returned. The man identified himself as Jason's uncle. He extended his hand to offer comfort. . . . He said the family of Jason felt no resentment toward me. . . . They felt it was truly an accident and wanted me to know the family understood and accepted me. Doug (the uncle) invited me to the funeral, saying the family would understand if I did not wish to attend. . . . I went to the funeral home with mixed emotions. As I walked up the stairs into the chapel, I was obviously a stranger in the midst of family and friends. Various relatives approached me and assured me that I was not at fault, that they didn't blame me. The boy's mother looked me straight in the eye and said, "Do not cry," and generally assured me that she didn't blame me for her son's death. The burden of guilt, depression, unacceptance, pain, and sorrow had been lifted from me.

Helping as a Friend

Being a friend to an accidental killer may be very time consuming. But accidental killers need friends who are patient, willing to hear the whole story, and willing to bear with their intense emotions. Lengthy discussions of the accident may be necessary to let their feelings run their course. An accidental killer's ability to resolve the trauma depends on this catharsis. By letting the accidental killer know you understand this aspect of recovery, you can generate a sense of security that allows the accidental killer to change.[19]

Be aware that if the accident occurs within a year or so of another crisis, the accidental killer may be overwhelmed. In such cases, it is probably a good idea to suggest that she receive professional help. You should continue to provide emotional support throughout this process. During this time of adjustment, individuals are more susceptible to illness.[20]

A useful tool is to role play, with you exchanging roles with the accidental killer so that you both can identify and change negative ways of interacting. But remember to go slowly.[21] Keep reaffirming and valuing the accidental killer. You may have to repeat yourself hundreds of times before you will be heard.

Be on the lookout for the accidental killer's seemingly contradictory needs, which may include companionship and privacy, independence and inclusion, to talk and then to be left alone for a while. In particular, honor your commitments. This is not the time to let the accidental killer down. Allow her to pinpoint her personal difficulties and let her know you are confident that she can overcome them.[22]

Anticipate difficult days for the accidental killer—for example, the one-year anniversary of the accident—and make a special gesture to let him know you care. Perhaps you could say, "Today must be very sad for you. I'm here to help if you need me."[23]

Helping When the Victim Was a Member of the Accidental Killer's Family

Whether you are friend or part of the family, the sadness of the accident is intense. This is a time for *being* rather than *doing*. Allow the accidental killer to relive and celebrate the good times. Let her know that no one can take away these experiences. Help her to understand the ongoing relationship between herself and the part of the victim she has internalized. Help her to accept the reality yet hold on to the memory so that she can be free as grief completes its task.[24]

The Wisdom of Ann Kaiser Stearns

Dr. Stearns's book *Living through Personal Crisis* suggests to the accidental killer that the accident was very unfair to both the one who died and to yourself as well. She outlines the different aspects of your being that were violated simultaneously—your sense of safety, natural protectiveness of life, perhaps your self-confidence in your physical actions and judgment, your faith in balance and fairness in the world. Writing a letter to the deceased explaining your choices may help to ease your guilt, she says, because putting the facts down on paper may give objectivity and you can compare your decisions with what you would expect from a responsible person.

Dr. Stearns recommends that the accidental killer seek empathic support. She points out that the empathic person has the following characteristics:

- Does not shock easily, but accepts your feelings as human feelings.
- Is not embarrassed by your tears.
- Does not regularly give unwanted advice.
- Is warm and affectionate with you.
- Reminds you of your strengths when you forget that you have these strengths within yourself.
- Recognizes that you are growing.
- Trusts you to be able to come through your difficult times.
- Treats you like an adult who can make your own decisions.
- Acknowledges that he or she is human, too, and shares this humanness.
- May sometimes become impatient or angry with you but does not attack your character.
- Is not afraid to question you directly concerning your feelings of loss.

- Respects your courage and sense of determination.
- Understands that grief is not a disease.
- Has been through troublesome times and can tell you this.
- May not feel comfortable with a certain feeling you are expressing, such as a hate feeling, or a particular sexual yearning, but tries to understand what the feeling means to you.
- Tells you honestly when he or she is unable to be with you because of problems or needs of his or her own.
- Is faithful to commitments and promises.[25]

Dr. Stearns also suggests that accidental killers try to fantasize about what life would have been like without the accident. She says that they should try to be specific and gives them permission to mourn these losses. Involvement in a fatal accident will never be a source of pride, but given that something horrible did happen, the accidental killer can take pride in having survived it. This event and its suffering have helped to shape the accidental killer, and the growth resulting from it is no less important because it emerged from tragedy. One can be stripped of everything except the attitude one chooses to have toward what has happened.

Helping as One
Who Has Been through It Oneself

"The main thing," says a heartbroken accidental killer, "is to know someone else who has gone through it and lived." The feeling of isolation resulting from a fatal accident is one of its most harmful effects. Very few people know others who have gone through something similar to this. Those who do find someone are very grateful. One person recalls:

These two friends lived about a hundred miles away. They called immediately after the account of my accident was in the newspaper. Then they came to see us and spend the night. The wife in this case had been driving when their children were killed—that situation was so much worse than mine. I had been helpful to them at the time, and now they were marvelous to me.

If you know the accidental killer well, the possibility for healing is great. A woman whose mother also had been involved in a fatal accident says, "Just knowing my mom had been there and back helped me to get through it."

Helping to Heal Yourself

If pain is any indicator of growth, the lessons of accidental killing are valuable indeed. But you can do a lot to help yourself heal. Give yourself room to grieve. You need it. As an accidental killer, you have been robbed of something very valuable—your innocence. You can see this as a permanent injury or as something that will heal with time. Grief in U.S. society is acceptable primarily as a response to death. Yet grief follows the loss of anything significant in a person's life. You have your own unique grieving process that must be completed before you can reenter life in a healthy emotional condition. One researcher writes:

> A person may progress quickly through one stage and linger in another, jump from one stage to another, skip one stage and return to it later, or even regress to stages that had apparently been completed. When a person appears to have completed a stage of grief and later returns to it, all the emotions associated with that stage have not been completely processed and resolved. Skipping around and experiencing grief states in different sequences occurs simply because each person experiences grief uniquely.[26]

Try not to let others' need for comfort stifle your grief process. You have a right to regain your health. If you should get stuck in a particular stage for more than six months, you may need professional help. You may think, "No one cares. No one understands. No one has ever grieved as I am grieving." This is true, for no one has experienced grief in exactly the same way. Grief reactions are deeply personal. Just getting through each day may be exhausting. This feeling of isolation is normal, but there are people who care.[27]

For a while, the overwhelming tragedy of an accidental death is likely to overshadow your grief for yourself. The first step in working through your emotions, including anger, is to recognize their legitimacy. Anger against the accident itself, the victim, yourself, society at large, or even others whose lives have not been disrupted is natural. Knowing this can free you to express anger, work through it, and find the power to take steps that will diminish the chances of a future accident.

Probably one of the most empowering things you can do is to start a support group, perhaps using the Twelve-Step model that has proven so effective in helping incest survivors and adult children of alcoholics. One caution for such groups is to keep a positive tone and to emphasize how its members have succeeded in overcoming the effects of their tragedies.

Many accidental killers are enthusiastic about the prospect of sharing experiences with others. One says, "It is my hope that this book will provide a communication network for us to get together and share similar experiences and develop a little bit of kinship. There is no one I feel really shares the depth of my anguish. I need to know that where I've come since this accident has a reality that is shared by others."

To start a support group, you can take out a classified ad, distribute fliers, or contact a local health care organization. See who comes and structure the meetings so they are beneficial to you and others.*

Practical Tactics

Coping with Depression

The most direct approach an accidental killer can take to overcome depression is to dispel the guilt that underlies it. Author George Weinberg suggests treating depression as if it were an illusion and offers these specific actions:

- Impose order on your life. Live punctually. Eat and sleep reasonably.
- Work on your appearance.
- Don't give up a project while you are down.
- Don't suppress any strong emotions—especially anger.
- Study and learn something new each day.

*For workshop information, contact the Center for Self-Renewal, Box 2574, Berkeley, California, 94702-0574.

- Meet all the challenges you possibly can. Find as many ambitions as you can.
- Stop talking about your problems for a specific period.
- Act ethically toward others, even about small things.
- Don't hide or avoid old locales.
- Don't compare yourself or your life with others.
- Do something you've always wanted to do but have never done before.
- Spend time with energetic and helpful people.
- Take note of the good moments in your life—especially unexpected ones.
- Snatch all the fleeting moments of intensity as if they were rafts going by.[28]

Dr. Stearns suggests that you schedule meaningful activities for sensitive times. Do some brisk and challenging work. Knowing you are capable of physical exertion helps reestablish your sense of self-worth. See the work as therapy, and do not expect full performance from yourself. Take extra care of yourself, and treat yourself to special things, such as a hot bath or some flowers. Recognize that the work of recovering from the accident will have to take precedence over other activities for a while. If you are managing to take care of yourself, you are doing well. The fact that this may not be easy does not negate your progress.[29]

Rabbi Harold Kushner recommends avoiding questions that focus on the past or the pain, such as "Why did this happen to me?" Instead ask the question that opens the door to the future: "Now that this has happened, what shall I do about it?"[30] Eventually you will realize that laughter and feelings of joy do not betray the person who died in the accident.

Make the accident your bridge to helping others. Living with compassion and courage and without bitterness is a tribute to the dead person. The life that you and others carry on is the only memory of the deceased.[31]

Forgiving Yourself

Therapists differ on the question of self-forgiveness. Some contend that there are things people really should feel guilty about and that negligence leading to an accidental death is one of them. Others say that coming down hard on yourself is not the best way to handle the situation. It would be unhealthy not to feel guilty after causing someone's death by mistake. The only thing you can do is to love yourself despite the error. If you could have acted differently, you would have. At one time or another, everyone has been negligent. Usually it is forgotten because no disaster occurs, but mistakes are part of the human condition.

Is it ever possible to forgive yourself totally for irreversible damage? Some say no, that forgiveness must be sought from the one(s) wronged—the victim or the surviving family. Although many accidental killers are able to forgive themselves in isolation, facing the victim's family allows you to demonstrate how far you are willing to go to express your regret. This willingness is the only thing you have to offer them and yourself. Showing the family your pain gives them an opportunity to release any resentment they may hold toward you. If you are truly sorry, offer to make amends and find out what the family would like those amends to be. Whatever you determine, it will be easier than carrying around a load of guilt.

If the family refuses to see you, make your gesture by mail. Tell them how you feel and offer to meet with them. In the meantime, offer whatever compensation you feel is suitable, acknowledging that nothing can replace what has been taken from them. You have a right to heal, and this painful process is healing for the victim's family, too. Their ability to heal rests partly in your hands, for as long as they blame you, they will not be free to resolve their grief.

Scrutinizing Your Responsibility

It may be hard to look at the boundary between your contribution to the accident and that of the deceased, but if you are to forgive yourself, it is important to determine the weight of the acts to be forgiven. Often accidental killers blame themselves inappropriately for lacking clairvoyance.

There is such a thing as a subintentional, self-destructive death. A subintentional act is a movement toward a goal that one does not recognize consciously and thus may be hard to identify. It can be as subtle as forgetting something or tripping on a curb or as overt as neglecting one's health, taking excessive risk, or attempting suicide. These ways of hastening one's own doom are, according to psychiatric research, part of many accidental deaths.[32] With all respect to the dead, you may need to make a cold analysis of whether the victim's death involved such elements. This may be difficult to do because U.S. society views suicide and self-destructiveness with embarrassment, shame, and revulsion. But it is important to accept the fact that many accidental deaths are not completely outside the victim's control.[33]

Another possibility is that both you and the person who died may have, at the time of the accident, acted in ways not beneficial to your health. You need to sort out who did what in a rational, objective way. Make a flowchart of the choices you made, given the opportunities available, and rate them as to their contribution to the death. Do the same for the person who died. It may help you to assign percentages of responsibility to yourself, the victim, and uncontrollable causes.

Visiting the Victim

If the victim survives the accident, it is a good idea to go and visit him or her. In the three days a victim survived after being struck by one woman's car, he assured her that it was not her fault. She says, "Above all, I am so grateful I went to the hospital to talk with him. No doubt it was hard, but what a healing effect it has had in my life."

Expressing Yourself

If you cannot discuss your feelings with anyone, write them down. This may be helpful even when listeners are available. Another possibility is expressing yourself through public speaking. One accidental killer notes:

> Even though my life is full, there are times my thoughts turn to the agony of accidental death. I have felt no fear about sharing my experience, and the pain has diminished to a normal level, not unlike that of any family member's death.

I have spoken publicly about my accident and the events that followed. Each time I relive the experience, a new feeling comes out—one of assurance, confidence, and patience.

Reexamining Your View of Death

Acknowledge the victim's death and remember the person who died. An accidental killer says:

> I find now, as I did then, that people don't necessarily know how to cope and may not take the time needed for the healing process. Obviously the incident is very traumatic to all. Everyone is sorry at the time, but after a while the sorrow subsides. But the pain for the person who caused the death remains. I did not forget my brother or the incident, but everything must be kept in perspective, and whatever the purpose of my being on Earth is, I am sure that I am not supposed to let [his death] get me down. My suicidal tendencies are gone. I now have an eight-by-ten photo of my brother at home, so I feel I have come out of the dark. Almost thirty-five years was too long to carry such a burden.

You also may need to change the way you look at death. For instance, you may begin to believe that death serves a purpose. J. J. Bachofen writes:

> Death's realm is not that of being but that of becoming and passing away, the eternal alternation of two colors, the white of life and the black of death. Only through the equal mixture of the two is the survival of the natural world assured. Without death no rejuvenation is possible. . . . The positive power cannot for one moment exist without the negative power. Death, then, is not the opposite but the helper of life.[34]

According to author Joseph Campbell, "Life without death in it is a fixture. It's the death of you that makes the life, the burning."[35] Realize that you will be perpetuated only through your connection with the larger forms of human culture. Open your imagination to your postdeath, postself future, when your mind and body have disintegrated and only the essence of what you value most remains.

The experience of dying may not be as horrible as it is often portrayed. Claude Sautet's film *Les Choses de la Vie* (The Things of Life, 1970) evokes the semiconscious thoughts of a dying man, the victim of a car accident:

> The dying man sees himself not at the wheel of the car, but like a drowned or drowning man, without despair, indifferent, plunged into waters that do not seem hostile. They bear him up for a moment, like a protective medium in which he can still float and make a few gestures before finally sinking for good and disappearing.
>
> The waters in which he is about to disappear are irresistibly reminiscent of the primordial ocean of the first days of the world and, at the same time, of the protective fluids of the womb. Death is associated with a return to birth, or origins.[36]

Victims who die instantly are probably spared any pain. Anyone who has experienced a high-impact crash knows that it is not immediately painful. The thalamus, located in the midbrain, is responsible for feelings of pain and pleasure. Any injury to this area means that pain is impossible to experience. One doctor gives this description of many deaths by disease that he has observed:

> It may be stated generally that it is extremely rare for a physician to observe a painful death. The minor ailments of everyday life involve much more suffering than fatal illness produces. . . . [T]he vital forces give terrific battle to the toxin of disease even in certain death, while the conscious ego of man is soaring in unknown realms, oblivious to the struggles of the flesh.[37]

No one who is alive can know what it feels like to die suddenly. One can, however, look at what people who die and come back say. This is a controversial area. About half the people who are pronounced clinically dead and are then revived have what is called a near death experience (NDE). During this experience, which occurs at the point of greatest physical distress, they hear themselves pronounced dead, feel themselves moving rapidly through a long tunnel, and find themselves outside their physical bodies but are able to see their bodies from a distance. They are often greeted by spirits of departed relatives and friends and see a bright light. They also may view a panoramic playback of the main events in their lives. At some point, they realize that they must go back to Earth but do not want to, being enveloped by feelings of joy and peace. Later they have trouble putting their profound experience into words.[38]

Some researchers take a skeptical view of NDEs. One writes, "Even if everybody who returned from such an extreme experience had the same story to tell, this would not prove that dying is pleasure and death a state of bliss. We would still have a resounding 'no comment' from those who stayed dead. The close call or the temporary death may be quite distinct from the one-way passage."[39]

But if NDEs are to be believed, they teach that besides a sense of peace and well-being, people are aware that they feel no pain or any other bodily sensation. Many people in this situation report no pain until they regain consciousness. Dr. Kenneth Ring writes:

> With few exceptions, accidents of near death or clinical death experiences have shown striking commonalities in stressing the great peace and beauty and all pervading sense of love that characterized their near brush with death. Indeed, the word "pleasant" is far too mild; "ecstatic" would be chosen by many survivors of this experience. No words are truly adequate to describe the sense of ultimate perfection that appears to characterize the entry into death.[40]

The author of two popular books who writes under the name Emmanuel gives his views of why people die and what they experience when they do:

> The process of dying is this: A soul's intent in a human lifetime has been fulfilled and the soul considers whether it wants to remain and begin something else or not. It does not matter how old or young a person is chronologically—this is the process.
>
> The soul ultimately decides, "I've done all I can with this particular circumstance. From here on in it will be unfruitful in some manner and that will not serve Perfect Love. So I choose to come Home."
>
> Well, the decision to come Home is the start of what has been termed "mysterious terminal illness," "accidental death," or whatever it may be. It can even be murder. But once the soul has made that choice, then the body and the life comply.
>
> To the soul, [sudden death] is bliss. You are driving along in a car doing battle with your life as usual, when all of a sudden you are not. You find yourself unexpectedly light, and you wonder what miracle has taken place. Have you become enlightened that you are no longer immersed in the issues of your day? You look around to realize that

the car, which was so important, is now just a heap of rubble and you really don't care at all. Then you see a physical body which looks familiar to you, something you have worn for some years. Yet you are glad to be out of it. You are free.

Violent death is violent only to those who remain behind to view it. To the one who dies, it is simply a wondrous flight Home.[41]

Exploring the Concept of Fate

Nearly all myths, philosophies, and religions include some concept of fate. For example, *moira,* the Greek teaching of divine destiny, is personified in the Fates. Not even Zeus could defy these beings. According to scholar Joseph Campbell,

> The enigma of fate is philosophically impossible to resolve, unless by some such formula as that of Schopenhauer, according to which, when viewed from outside, logically and scientifically, the world's events can be recognized as governed to such a degree by the laws of cause and effect as to be inexorably determined; whereas, when explained from within, from the standpoint of the actual living subject, living yields an experience of choice. The Christian view of fate . . . is not surrender to the invincible force of an outside determinant, but the sense of an inward potentiality in the process of becoming, with however, an approaching inevitable end.[42]

Whether accidents are fated or not, to expect more than is humanly possible is unrealistic. This was well understood among primitive peoples who considered it a grave offense to create any piece of art perfectly because the spirits alone were considered perfect. Into each piece, therefore, was woven, or molded, or painted a flaw so as not to offend the spirits.[43]

Marking the Accident's Anniversary

View the first anniversary of the accident as a significant point of passage. You have survived a full year now. Take a personal inventory. How have you and your family reacted? Do children and adults speak naturally and comfortably about the accident yet? Are you in good health? Are you satisfied with your grief process? What changes have come into your life? What is the hardest thing you have had to do? What has been most helpful to you?[44]

Honor the dead person annually, possibly by performing a ritual on the anniversary of the accident. It should be something life affirming, preferably something that takes into account the cycles of life and death. For example, plant a tree and pay it homage on that day every year.

Trying to Prevent Accidents

Avoiding accidents takes more than just not looking for trouble. It requires forethought, hypothetical contingency plans, and staying alert to danger. It also is important to avoid stress, as people who are stressed have more accidents than those who are not.

One area that deserves special attention is the prevention of accidents among children. Accidents are the biggest cause of death among children in the United States.[45] Part of the problem is that infants sometimes undergo spurts in development, crawling one day and climbing the next. Or they are able to climb before they can walk. Adults sometimes underestimate a child's capabilities. In addition, some parents are careful about harmful substances at home but forget to check for these substances when visiting other houses.

To guard against fatalities in cars and trucks, safety expert Leslie Lieberman strongly recommends the use of seat belts and air bags. She explains:

> Seatbelts reduce your chances of fatal injury about 57 percent. For young children, car seats are proven even more effective than seatbelts. The problem is that if children are not in the car seat, generally they are being carried in their parent's arms. If there is a collision even at a slow speed, the mother's body can crush the child. She can be protected from the blow because of the baby's body. The technology is available to prevent that type of injury from ever having to happen.[46]

Do what you can to maintain a safe environment, but realize that an accident may happen anyway. A lifeguard's description of accidental death points up this fact: "You dread a drowning. People don't understand it can happen like the snap of a finger. Even in a pool, you sometimes can't prevent it. You can turn your head, and some kid can go under. Turn back a second later, and you see nothing. There's no such thing as full coverage."

Planning Your Own Funeral

During the time when you are dealing so directly with death, you may want to take the opportunity to express your wishes in case anything should happen to you. Discuss the issues with your family, then write them down and let your family know where you put them. Polly Doyle's book *Grief Counseling and Sudden Death: A Manual and Guide* provides some guidelines for planning your own funeral or memorial service.[47]

Reexamining Your View of Life

Killing someone accidentally is an object lesson in life's tenuousness. It forces you to recognize that life can end in a flash. But this lesson can open you up to your life as it will be becoming. It may be difficult to see, but the process of groping through recovery brings profound transformation. This is loss's gift. For accidental killers, as for many others, life demands a purpose. Something in the experience of trauma heightens the intensity of this demand. Those who consciously seek this purpose can find significant ways to contribute to the spiritual experiment that is the future being born.

Accidental killing leaves only the morally essential core of every act, the sole basis for living without regret—regardless of the consequences:

>These are the risks worth taking:
>to exult in the being of others
>to give freely
>to hope with abandon
>to love with audacity.[48]

Notes

Introduction

1. E. Becker, *The Denial of Death* (New York: Free Press, 1973).
2. P. Aries, *The Hour of Our Death* (New York: Knopf, 1981).
3. U.S. Bureau of the Census, *Statistical Abstract of the United States: 1990* (Washington, D.C.: U.S. Government Printing Office, 1990), 85.
4. T. Nagel, *Mortal Questions* (Cambridge, Mass.: Cambridge University Press, 1979), 27–32.
5. A. Iskrant and P. Joliet, *Accidents and Homicides*, (Cambridge, Mass.: Harvard University Press, 1968), 16.
6. For a pilot study, ten accidental killers were selected from individuals responding to several short radio and newspaper descriptions of the proposed research. Through extensive interviews these ten accidental killers provided information about questions such as the following: What happens to individuals who accidentally kill someone? What feelings and reactions do they have? How do they handle these feelings and reactions? What resources affect handling of these feelings? How do family, friends, and/or professionals help these individuals cope with the stress caused by accidentally killing another? How does life before the accident affect life after the accident? What variables seem to play an important role in coping and adapting to the stress caused by accidentally killing another?

    The research participants were also asked to rate the accidental killing compared to all the other crises they had ever experienced. All described the accident in which they felt responsible for the death of another as one of the most stressful crises in their lives, if not the worst. Other crises ranked as stressful as accidentally killing a person included the death of a child, a marriage partner, or a parent, alcoholism, divorce, and institutionalization because of a nervous breakdown. An article was published in *Family Relations* describing this pilot study (B. Chesser, "Coping with Accidentally Killing Another Person: A Case Study Approach," *Family Relations*, July 1981/Vol 30: 463–473).

    The pilot study verified the need for more extensive research of the impact of accidentally killing someone else and how to cope with this trauma. A summary of the findings and conclusions from this pilot study appeared in *Psychology Today* along with the request for volunteers for expanded research on accidental killing (G. Gilliam, "The Anguish of Accidental Killers," *Psychology Today,* Sept. 1980/Vol. 14, no. 4: 22–23). From the pilot study interviews, a questionnaire entitled "The Effects of Being Involved in an Accident Resulting in the Death of Someone: Implications for Helping People Cope/Adjust" was developed and used to collect additional information. Other questions for gathering appropriate information were adapted from family crisis, stress, and coping studies as well as death and bereavement research and literature. Professionals in family studies, medicine, social work, and counseling critiqued the questions and provided helpful suggestions. Data were collected through mailed questionnaires, personal interviews, telephone interviews, tape recordings, personal letters, or, in some cases, a combination of these techniques.

7. Iskrant and Joliet, *Accidents and Homicides,* 44.
8. In 1975 alone, 4,651,738.5 years of life were lost violently [P. Holinger, "Violent Deaths among the Young: Recent Trends in Suicide, Homicide, and Accidents," *American Journal of Psychiatry* 136 (September 1979)].
9. U.S. Department of Commerce, *Statistical Abstract of the United States, 1988* (Washington, D.C.: U.S. Government Printing Office, 1988).
10. J. Arena and M. Bachar, *Child Safety Is No Accident: A Parent's Handbook of Emergencies* (Durham, N.C.: Duke University Press, 1978).
11. J. Garbarino, in press.
12. "A much greater threat than any intrinsic in the struggle of man against nature lies in the expansion of that intellectual activity which has led man to create new dangers much more formidable and deadly than those caused by nature or by the animal species, forgotten by evolution. The pressure now comes from our own biologic success" (Iskrant and Joliet, *Accidents and Homicides,* 1).
13. C. Dickens, *David Copperfield,* in John Bartlett (ed.), *Familiar Quotations* (Boston: Little, Brown & Co., 1968), 671.
14. "Observe that ambiguous events . . . are often immensely distracting. Little offstage sounds can draw acute attention to themselves as if they had physically overridden legitimate foci of attention. The reason, of course, is that these ambiguities have to be resolved, lest the individual be forced to remain in doubt about the entire nature of the happenings around him" [E. Goffman, *Frame Analysis: An Essay on the Perception of Experience* (Cambridge, Mass.: Harvard University Press, 1974), 45].
15. Driver success in beating trains at grade crossings encourages fatal risks (H. Leibowitz, "A Behavioral and Perceptual Analysis of Grade Crossing Accidents," in *Proceedings of the 1982 Operation Lifesaver National Symposium,* National Safety Council, Chicago, 12–15).
16. One study found that under equal stress, given equivalent amounts of support, "sensitive" college students would get sick but "coping" ones would not [L. LaGrand, "Loss Reactions of College Students: A Descriptive Analysis," *Death Education* 5 (Fall 1981): 235–248].

Chapter 1

1. P. Levine, personal communication, 24 March 1990.
2. E. Kretschmer, *Hysteria, Reflex, and Instinct* (London: Peter Owen, 1961).
3. E. Jackson, *Coping with the Crises in Your life* (New York: Jason Aronson, 1980).
4. R. Lifton and E. Olson, *Living and Dying* (New York: Praeger, 1974).
5. E. Kübler-Ross, *On Death and Dying* (New York: Macmillan, 1969).
6. M. Horowitz, *Stress Response Syndromes* (New York: Jason Aronson, 1976), 24, 25.
7. "One must wonder what prevented prior knowledge from being of protective value. It appears that repeated performance of a dangerous occupation dulls the capacity for anticipation, fearful or otherwise, of disaster. . . . When injury does occur, the victim is unprepared to cope with the resultant alterations in the self" [R. Leopold and H. Dillon, "Psychoanatomy of a Disaster," *American Journal of Psychiatry* 119, no. 10 [April 1963]: 918).
8. C. Frederick, "Current Thinking About Crisis, or Psychological Intervention in United States Disasters, *Mass Emergencies* 2 (1977): 43–50.
9. H. Moore, "Toward a Theory of Disaster," *American Sociological Review* 21, no. 6 (December 1956): 733–37.
10. C. Fritz and H. Williams, "The Human Being in Disaster," *The Annals* 309 (1957): 42–51.
11. Frederick, "Current Thinking About Crisis."
12. C. Fogleman and V. Parenton, "Disaster and Aftermath: Selected Aspects of Individual and Group Behavior in a Critical Situation," *Social Forces* 38, no. 2 (December 1959): 129–135.
13. Sometimes the fainting response inhibits the attacker's desire for the chase. If the animal is only wounded and then dragged someplace to be eaten, it affords the animal another chance to escape (P. Levine, *The Substitute Tiger,* in press).
14. Karl Menninger, quoted in Horowitz, *Stress Response Syndromes,* 21.
15. P. Friedman and L. Linn, "Some Psychiatric Insights on the *Andrea Doria* Disaster," *American Journal of Psychiatry* 114, no. 5 (November 1959): 426–432.
16. Gerald Glazer, personal communication, 30 January 1983.
17. M. Horowitz, personal communication, 12 July 1985.

Chapter 2

1. Q. Horace, Odes, II, Ode iii, in J. Bartlett (ed.), *Familiar Quotations* (Boston: Little, Brown & Co., 1968), 121.
2. R. Cohen and F. Ahearn, *Handbook for Mental Health Care of Disaster Victims* (Baltimore: Johns Hopkins University Press, 1980).
3. M. Geller, personal communication, 22 January 1986.

4. A. Kliman, *Crisis: Psychological First Aid for Recovery and Growth* (New York: Holt, Rinehart & Winston, 1978).
5. Cohen and Ahearn, *Mental Health Care of Disaster Victims.*
6. E. Jackson, *Coping with the Crises in Your Life.*
7. A. Kardiner, "The Traumatic Neurosis of War," *Psychosomatic Medicine Monograph* (New York: Paul B. Hoeber, 1941), 11–111.
8. M. Horowitz, *Stress Response Syndromes.*
9. S. Freud, "Remembering, Repeating, Working Through," in *The Standard Edition of the Complete Psychological Works of Sigmund Freud,* vol. 12 (London: Hogarth Press, 1953), 145–150.
10. J. Breuer and S. Freud, "Studies on Hysteria," in *The Standard Edition of the Complete Psychological Works of Sigmund Freud,* vol. 2 (London: Hogarth Press, 1955).
11. M. Schur, *The Id and Regulatory Processes of the Ego* (New York: International Universities Press, 1966).
12. Horowitz, *Stress Response Syndromes.*
13. M. Wolfenstein, *Disaster: A Psychological Essay* (Glencoe, Ill.: Free Press, 1957), ix–xvi.
14. R. Lifton, *History and Human Survival* (New York: Vantage Books, 1967).
15. L. Keiser, *The Traumatic Neurosis* (Philadelphia: Lippincott, 1968).
16. M. Horowitz, "Psychic Trauma," *Archives of General Psychiatry* 20, no. 5 (May 1969): 552–59.
17. M. Foeckler, F. Hutcheson Gerrand, C. Chinnis Williams, A. Thomas, and T. Jones, "Vehicle Drivers of Fatal Accidents," *Suicidal and Life-Threatening Behavior* 8, no. 3 (Fall 1978): 174.
18. G. Weinberg, *Self-Creation* (New York: St. Martin's Press, 1978).
19. S. Freud, "Selected Papers on Hysteria, Nervous and Mental Diseases," *Monograph Series* No. 4, 1920.
20. J. Breuer and S. Freud, "Studies on Hysteria."
21. K. Erikson, *Everything in Its Path: Destruction of a Community in the Buffalo Creek Flood* (New York: Simon & Schuster, 1976), 169.
22. Horowitz, "Psychic Trauma."
23. Cohen and Ahearn, *Mental Health Care of Disaster Victims.*
24. I. Janis, *Stress and Frustration* (New York: Harcourt Brace Jovanovich, 1971).
25. H. Ellison, *The Fantasies of Harlan Ellison* (Boston: Gregg Press, 1979), 100.
26. R. Janoff-Bulman and I. Hanson-Frieze, "A Theoretical Perspective for Understanding Reactions of Victimization," *Journal of Social Issues* 39, no. 2 (Summer 1983): 1–17.

Chapter 3

1. G. Hall, "A Study of Anger," *American Journal of Psychology* 10 (1899): 516–591.
2. L. Seneca, "On Anger," in *Moral Essays,* translated by J. W. Basore (Cambridge, Mass.: Harvard University Press, 1963).

3. C. Tavris, *Anger: The Misunderstood Emotion* (New York: Simon & Schuster, 1982), 229–230.
4. A. Kliman, *Crisis: Psychological First Aid for Recovery and Growth.* (New York: Holt, Reinhart, and Winston, 1978).
5. A. Canedo, personal communication, 8 November 1985.
6. Horowitz, *Stress Response Syndromes.*
7. P. Nyce, "Grieving People," *Journal of Pastoral Care* xxxvi, no. 1 (March 1982): 45.
8. E. Higgins, personal communication, 14 April 1983.
9. One researcher goes so far as to theorize that all violent deaths among those under forty years of age, be they accidental or otherwise, may represent suicidal tendencies (Holinger, "Violent Deaths Among the Young").

Chapter 4

1. A. Ross, *On Guilt, Responsibility, and Punishment* (Berkeley and Los Angeles: University of California Press, 1975), 117.
2. Ibid., 118.
3. Ibid., 118–120.
4. S. Rustin, personal communication, 12 December 1985.
5. Sophocles, "Oedipus Rex," in *The Complete Greek Drama,* edited by M. Oates and E. O'Neill (New York: Random House, 1938), 409.
6. A. Hailey, *Airport* (Garden City, N.Y.: Doubleday, 1968).
7. S. Rustin, personal communication, 12 December 1985.
8. A. Kobler, "Police Homicide in Democracy," *Journal of Social Issues* 31, no. 1 (Winter 1975): 163.
9. S. Law and S. Polan, *Pain and Profit: The Politics of Malpractice* (New York: Harper & Row, 1978).
10. W. Goodwin, "The Emotional Reaction of Dentists to Malpractice Suits," *Dental Clinics of North America,* 26, no. 2 (April 1982).
11. J. Mallory, personal communication, 3 April 1981.
12. Iskrant and Joliet, *Accidents and Homicide.*
13. National Safety Council, *Accident Facts.*
14. R. McFarland, et al., *Human Variables in Motor Vehicle Accidents: A Review of the Literature* (Boston: Harvard School of Public Health, 1955); W. Tillman and G. Hobbs, "The Accident-Prone Automobile Driver," *The American Journal of Psychiatry* 6 (November 1949): 321–331; R. Schlensky, "Psychiatric Standards in Driver Licensing," *American Journal of Public Health* 235 (May 1976): 18.
15. Goffman, *Frame Analysis,* 30–34.
16. M. Lerner, *The Belief in a Just World: A Fundamental Delusion* (New York: Plenum Press, 1980).
17. J. Nicolosi, personal communication, 25 February 1983.

Appendix 4

1. P. McGrath, personal communication, 21 March 1985.
2. W. Rorabaugh, *The Alcoholic Republic* (New York: Oxford University Press, 1979), 302.
3. E. Nadlemann, quoted in N. Chomsky, "The Tasks Ahead. III: Problems of Population Control," *Zeta*, November 1989.
4. J. Gusfield, *The Culture of Public Problems: Drinking-Driving and the Symbolic Order* (Chicago: University of Chicago Press, 1981).
5. H. Barry, "Motivational and Cognitive Effects of Alcohol," *Journal of Safety Research*, 5 (1973): 200–221.
6. A. Russell, personal communication, 2 April 1985.
7. Gusfield, *The Culture of Public Problems*, 102.
8. R. Severo and L. Milford, *The Wages of War: When America's Soldiers Came Home—From Valley Forge to Viet Nam* (New York: Simon & Schuster, 1989), 347.
9. C. Welch, "The Post-Traumatic Stress Disorder Syndrome for Vietnam Veterans: The Politics of Etiology," *Emotional First Aid* 1, no. 3 (1984): 30.

Chapter 5

1. G. Weinberg, *Self-Creation* (New York: St. Martin's Press, 1978).
2. A. Schmale, "The Adaptive Role of Depression in Health and Disease," in *Separation and Depression: Clinical and Research Aspects*, edited by J. Scott and E. Senay (Baltimore: Association for the Advancement of Social Science, 1973).
3. M. Foeckler, et al., "Vehicle Drivers of Fatal Accidents."
4. M. Mendleson, *Psychoanalytic Concepts of Depression* (Flushing, N.Y.: Spectrum Publications, 1974).
5. A. Beck, *Depressions: Clinical, Experimental, and Theoretical Aspects* (New York: Harper & Row, 1967).
6. P. McGrath, personal communication, 21 March 1985.
7. E. Levitt, B. Lubin, and J. Brooks, *Depression: Concepts, Controversies, and Some New Facts* (Hillsdale, N.J.: Lawrence Erlbaum Associates, 1983).
8. Horowitz, *Stress Response Syndromes*, 28.
9. I. Starson, "Empirical Findings and Theoretical Problems in the Use of Anxiety Scales," *Psychological Bulletin* 59, no. 5 (September 1960): 403–415.
10. E. Berne, *What Do You Say After You Say Hello?: The Psychology of Human Destiny* (New York: Grove Press, 1972).
11. Kardiner, "The Traumatic Neurosis of War." See also M. Trimble, *Post Traumatic Neurosis* (New York: John Wiley & Sons, 1981).
12. Horowitz, *Stress Response Syndromes*.
13. E. Backett and A. Johnston, "Social Patterns of Road Accidents to Children: Some Characteristics of Vulnerable Families," *British Medical Journal* (February 1959): 409–413.

14. Aggressiveness and conflict with authority originating in an insecure home background and continuing in a history of frequent conflict with community standards differentiates those who have high auto accident rates from those with few accidents [Tillman and Hobbs, "The Accident-Prone Automobile Driver"].

The accident-prone personality has been described as being unconventional, self-oriented, and dissatisfied with everyday life; lacking clearly defined goals; unable to control hostility; tending toward acting-out behavior either verbally or physically; showing poor judgment; lacking contact with reality, especially in social relationships, with a psychopathological tendency toward hostility, withdrawal, or excessive immaturity; being unable to adjust to stress; and feeling insecure [J. Conger, "Psychological and Psychophysiological Factors in Motor Vehicle Accidents," *Journal of the American Medical Association* 169, no. 14 (April 1959): 158–187].

15. P. McGrath, personal communication, 11 March 1985.
16. Iskrant and Joliet, *Accidents and Homicides*.
17. J. Greenstone, "Crisis at Christmas," *Emotional First Aid* (1984): 53.
18. L. Lieberman, personal communication, 15 January 1990.
19. P. McGrath, personal communication, 11 March 1985.
20. M. Horowitz, *States of Mind* (New York: Plenum Press, 1979).
21. Schmale, "The Adaptive Role of Depression."
22. B. Schwartz, "Does Helplessness Cause Depression, or Do Only Depressed People Become Helpless?" *Journal of Experimental Psychiatry: General* 100 (September 1981): 429–435.
23. L. Perloff, "Perceptions of Vulnerability to Victimization," *Journal of Social Issues* 39, no. 1 (Summer 1983): 41–61.
24. Janoff-Bulman and Hanson-Frieze, "Understanding Reactions to Victimization."
25. E. Higgins, personal communication, 14 April 1983.
26. Ibid.
27. I. Gotlib, "Perceptions and Recall of Interpersonal Feedback: Negative Bias in Depression," *Cognitive Therapy and Research* 7 (5 October 1983): 399–412.
28. G. Brown and T. Harris, *Social Origins of Depression* (Riverside, N.J.: Free Press, 1978).
29. P. McGrath, personal communication, 11 March 1985.
30. Ibid.

Chapter 6

1. P. Aries, *The Hour of Our Death*.
2. M. Lerner, *The Belief in a Just World: A Fundamental Delusion* (New York: Plenum Press, 1980).
3. S. Rustin, personal communication, 17 December 1984.
4. Horowitz, *Stress Response Syndromes*.

5. See K. Vonnegut, *Dead Eye Dick* (New York: DeLacorte/Seymour Lawrence, 1982), 90.
6. E. Grollman, personal communication, 3 March 1983.
7. A. Stearns, *Living through Personal Crisis* (New York: Ballantine Books, 1985).

Chapter 7

1. V. Satir, *Peoplemaking* (Palo Alto, Calif.: Science and Behavior Books, 1972).
2. R. Umana, F. Gross, J. Steven, and M. McConville, *Crisis in the Family: Three Approaches* (New York: Garden Press, 1980).
3. M. Bowen, "Family Systems Theory in Society," in *Georgetown Family Symposia,* vol. 2, edited by J. Loris and L. McClenathan (Washington, D.C.: Georgetown Family Center, 1977).
4. F. Kaslow and L. Schwartz, "Vulnerability and Invulnerability to the Cults: An Assessment of Family Dynamics, Functioning, and Values," in *Marital and Family Therapy: New Perspective in Theory Research and Practice,* edited by D. Baragozzi, A. Jurich, and R. Jackson (New York: Human Sciences Press, 1983).
5. Federal Emergency Management Agency, *Behavior and Attitudes under Crisis Conditions: Selected Issues and Findings* (Washington, D.C.: U.S. Government Printing Office, 1984).
6. H. Parad and G. Caplan, "Framework for Studying Families in Crisis," *Social Work* 5 (1960): 5–15.
7. M. Kerr, "Family Systems Theory and Therapy," in *Handbook of Family Therapy,* edited by A. Gurman and D. Kniskern (New York: Brunner/Mazel, 1981).
8. J. Fraser, "Strategic Rapid Intervention Approach," in *Treating Stress in Families,* edited by C. Figley (New York: Brunner/Mazel, 1989).
9. R. Becker, R. Heimberg, and A. Bellack, *Social Skills Training Treatment for Depression* (New York: Pergamon Press, 1987).
10. I. Gotlib and C. Colby, *Treatment of Depression: An Interpersonal Systems Approach* (New York: Pergamon Press, 1987).
11. J. Lemmon, *Family Mediation Practice* (New York: Free Press, 1985).
12. I. Gottesfeld, personal communication, 19 November 1985.
13. M. Eisenberg, "Private Ordering through Negotiations: Dispute Settlement and Rulemaking," *Harvard Law Review* 89, no. 4 (February 1976): 637–681.
14. I. Gottesfeld, personal communication, 19 November 1985.
15. J. Nicolosi, personal communication, 22 January 1984.
16. G. Orr, *New and Selected Poems* (Middletown, Conn.: Wesleyan University Press, 1988), 38.
17. I. Gottesfeld, personal communication, 19 November 1985.

Chapter 8

1. J. de la Fontaine, *Fables,* in J. Bartlett (ed.), *Familiar Quotations* (Boston: Little, Brown & Co., 1968), 359.
2. Janoff-Bulman and Hanson-Frieze, "Understanding Reactions to Victimization."
3. J. Groen, "The Measurement of Emotion and Arousal in the Clinical Physiological Laboratory and in Medical Practice," in *Emotions: Their Parameters and Measurement,* edited by L. Levi (New York: Raven Press, 1975).
4. A. Moulyn, *The Meaning of Suffering: An Interpretation of Human Existence from the Viewpoint of Time* (Westport, Conn.: Greenwood Press, 1982).
5. L. Buscaglia, *Living, Loving, and Learning* (New York: Fawcett Columbine, 1982).
6. T. Wilder, *The Bridge of San Luis Rey* (New York: Harper & Row, 1967), 235.
7. E. Lindemann, "Symptomology and Management of Acute Grief," *American Journal of Psychiatry* 101, no. 2 (September 1944): 141–148.
8. Bob Johns, personal communication, 2 December 1988.
9. Ibid.
10. W. Shakespeare, "King Henry V," in J. Bartlett (ed.), *Familiar Quotations,* 215.
11. W. Frey, personal communication, 29 July 1990.
12. Horowitz, *Stress Response Syndromes,* 17.
13. Levine, *The Substitute Tiger.*
14. M. Horowitz, "Psychoanalytic Therapy," in Kutsch, I., and Schlesinger, L. et al. (eds.), *Handbook on Stress and Anxiety: Contemporary Knowledge, Theory and Treatment.* (San Francisco: Jossey-Bass: 1980), 364.
15. R. Woodworth, *Adjustment and Mastery: Problems in Psychology* (Baltimore: Williams & Wilkins, 1933).
16. S. Rustin, personal communication, 17 December 1984.
17. Ibid.
18. E. Jackson, *Coping with the Crises in Your Life,* 80.
19. S. Rustin, personal communication, 17 December 1984.
20. J. Nicolosi, personal communication, 25 February 1983.
21. S. Rustin, personal communication, 17 December 1984.
22. J. Nicolosi, personal communication, 25 February 1983.
23. Ibid.
24. S. Taylor, J. Wood, and R. Lichtman, "It Could Be Worse: Selective Evaluation as a Response of Victimization," *Journal of Social Issues* 39 (1983): 19.
25. W. James, *Pragmatism, A New Name for Some Old Ways of Thinking Together with Four Related Essays Selected from the Meaning of Truth* (New York: Longmans, 1948).
26. E. Grollman, personal communication, 3 March 1983.
27. S. Rustin, personal communication, 17 December 1984.

Chapter 9

1. J. Martin, *Adlai Stevenson of Illinois* (Garden City, N.Y.: Doubleday, 1976), 41–42.
2. Ibid., p. 43.
3. Ibid, p. 44.
4. Ibid, p. 45.
5. *Burroughs,* documentary film, 1983.
6. Ibid.
7. Ibid.
8. Leopold and Dillon, "Psychoanatomy of a Disaster," 913.
9. Wolfenstein, *Disaster: A Psychological Essay,* 151, 153.
10. E. Grollman, personal communication, 23 January 1983.
11. E. Kübler-Ross, *Death: The Final Stage of Growth* (Englewood Cliffs, N.J.: Prentice-Hall, 1976).
12. R. Shulz, *The Psychology of Death, Dying, and Bereavement* (Reading, Mass.: Addison-Wesley, 1978).
13. J. Cassidy, personal communication, 2 March 1984.
14. S. Rustin, personal communication, 23 November 1985.
15. S. Bellow, *Humbolt's Gift* (New York: Viking Press, 1975).

Chapter 10

1. Foeckler, et al., "Vehicle Drivers of Fatal Accidents," 174.
2. E. Grollman, personal communication, 16 February 1983.
3. Stearns, *Living through Personal Crisis.*
4. R. Kavanaugh, *Facing Death* (Los Angeles: Nash Publishing, 1972), 162.
5. H. Colton, *The Gift of Touch* (New York: Seaview & Putnam, 1983), 119.
6. J. Nicolosi, personal communication, 16 February 1983.
7. E. Grollman, personal communication, 16 February 1983.
8. L. Cottrell, "The Analysis of Situational Fields in Social Psychology," *American Sociological Review* (June 1942): 375–376.
9. J. Donne, "Meditation XVII," *Oxford Dictionary of Quotes,* 3d ed. (Oxford, England: Oxford University Press, 1979), 190.
10. S. Rustin, personal communication, 12 December 1985.
11. R. Korn, "The Self as Agent and the Self as Object: Development, Application, and Demonstration of Transactional Theory of Incompetence and Its Treatment," unpublished dissertation, New York University, 1967, 149–150.
12. S. Jourard, *The Transparent Self* (New York: D. Van Nostrand & Co., 1964), 5.
13. Korn, "The Self as Agent."
14. R. Korn, personal communication, 15 July 1989.

15. J. Nicolosi, personal communication, 25 February 1983.
16. Levine, *The Substitute Tiger.*
17. M. Harmon, personal communication, 3 March 1990.
18. W. Shakespeare, "Much Ado About Nothing," *The Comedies of Shakespeare* (New York: Modern Library, 1943), 71–72.
19. Stearns, *Living through Personal Crisis.*
20. P. Doyle, *Grief Counseling and Sudden Death: A Manual and Guide* (Springfield, Ill.: Thomas, 1980).
21. J. Fraser, "Strategic Rapid Intervention Approach."
22. Doyle, *Grief Counseling.*
23. Stearns, *Living through Personal Crisis,* 71–72.
24. Ibid. Also see A. Stearns, *Coming Back* (New York: Ballantine Books, 1988).
25. Stearns, *Living through Personal Crisis.*
26. S. Ruple, "Grief: The Hidden Crisis," *Emotional First Aid* 2, no. 3 (1985):13.
27. Ibid.
28. G. Weinberg, *Self-Creation.*
29. Stearns, *Living through Personal Crisis.*
30. H. Kushner, *When Bad Things Happen to Good People* (New York: Schoken Books, 1981), 137.
31. Stearns, *Living through Personal Crisis.*
32. E. Schneidman, "Psychiatric Emergencies," *Comprehensive Textbook of Psychiatry,* vol. 2, 2d ed. (Baltimore: Williams & Wilkins, 1975).
33. P. Holinger, *Violent Deaths in the United States: An Epidemiologic Study of Suicide, Homicide, and Accidents* (New York: Guilford Press, 1987).
34. J. Bachofen, *Myth, Religion, and Mother Right* (Princeton, N.J.: Princeton University Press, 1967), 33–34.
35. J. Campbell, *The Masks of God* (Public Broadcasting Service Lecture Series, 1989).
36. P. Aries, *Images of Man and Death* (Cambridge, Mass.: Harvard University Press, 1985), 268.
37. R. Harbin, *Paradoxical Pain* (Boston: Sherman, French & Co., 1916), 183.
38. R. Moody, *Life after Life* (Atlanta, Ga.: Mockingbird Books, 1975), 14.
39. R. Kastenbaum, *Death, Society, and Human Experience* (St. Louis: C.V. Mosby Company, 1981), 23.
40. K. Ring, *Heading Toward Omega: In Search of the Meaning of the Near-Death Experience* (New York: William Morrow & Co., 1984), 19, 136.
41. P. Rodegast and J. Stanton (eds.), *Emmanuel's Book II: The Choice for Love* (New York: Bantam Books, 1989), 134, 138.
42. J. Campbell, *The Masks of God: Creative Mythology* (New York: Penguin Books, 1968), 139.
43. M. Yapko, *When Living Hurts: Directives for Treating Depression* (New York: Brunner/Mazel, 1988).
44. Doyle, *Grief Counseling.*
45. Arena and Bachar, *Child Safety Is No Accident.*

46. L. Lieberman, personal communication, 15 January 1990.
47. Doyle, *Grief Counseling.*
48. T. Blunk in T. Blunk and R. Levasseur (eds.), *Hauling Up the Morning: Writings and Art by Political Prisoners and Prisoners of War in the U.S.* (Trenton, N.J.: Red Sea Press, 1990), 278.

Index

About the
Authors

Gwendolyn Gilliam was graduated magna cum laude from the University of Nebraska at Omaha, where she was named Outstanding Journalism Student of 1978. She has written for *Pacific News Service, Alternative Media, Human Behavior, Psychology Today, The East Village Eye,* and the *San Francisco Bay Guardian.* In 1980, Lexington Books published her first book, *Understanding Abusive Families,* co-authored with James Garbarino, currently in its eleventh printing. That same year, she co-founded, with Pakka Kavan and Sora Kim, *beef* tabloid in Omaha, Nebraska, later writing for its San Francisco-based successor, *versus.* She covered Nicaragua's first free elections in November 1984. In 1987, she became the only print journalist to gain entry to the Lexington Control Unit, a sensory-deprivation prison wing that held women political prisoners of the United States. The unit was subsequently closed under worldwide condemnation. In September 1988, she covered international protests in Berlin organized by the European Autonomen against the convening of the World Bank.

Barbara Russell Chesser graduated summa cum laude as an undergraduate then took her master's degree from Mills College in Family Studies and her doctorate from Texas Woman's University in Human Development and the Family. She has received awards for her teaching at several universities including Texas Woman's University and the University of Nebraska. Her work with families and individuals has taken her to the African countries of Nigeria, Swaziland, Tanzania, and Morocco, and to the Philippines and Greece. Dr. Chesser's research has been published in *Family Perspective, Home Economics Research Journal,* and *The Journal of Religion and Health.* Her articles include "Coping with Accidentally Killing Another

Person: A Case Study Approach," which appeared in *Family Relations*. Co-author of *Marriage: Creating a Partnership*, she has also co-edited with John DeFrain and Nick Stinnett *Building Family Strengths*. A contributor to *Reader's Digest*, Dr. Chesser has also written *Because You Care: Practical Ideas for Helping Those Who Grieve* (1987) and *Twenty-one Myths That Can Wreck Your Marriage* (1990).